From the "Troubles" to Trumpism

From the "Troubles" to Trumpism

Ireland and America, 1960–2023

Stephen Watt

ANTHEM PRESS

Anthem Press
An imprint of Wimbledon Publishing Company
www.anthempress.com

This edition first published in UK and USA 2024
by ANTHEM PRESS
75–76 Blackfriars Road, London SE1 8HA, UK
or PO Box 9779, London SW19 7ZG, UK
and
244 Madison Ave #116, New York, NY 10016, USA

© Stephen Watt 2024

The author asserts the moral right to be identified as the author of this work.

All rights reserved. Without limiting the rights under copyright reserved above, no part of this publication may be reproduced, stored or introduced into a retrieval system, or transmitted, in any form or by any means (electronic, mechanical, photocopying, recording or otherwise), without the prior written permission of both the copyright owner and the above publisher of this book.

British Library Cataloguing-in-Publication Data
A catalogue record for this book is available from the British Library.

Library of Congress Cataloging-in-Publication Data
A catalog record for this book has been requested.
2024936740

ISBN-13: 978-1-83999-264-3 (Hbk)
ISBN-10: 1-83999-264-6 (Hbk)

Cover Credit: Mural at EPIC: The Irish Emigration Museum, Dublin.
Courtesy of Alamy

This title is also available as an e-book.

So, you could say there's always been a little green
behind the red, white and blue.

—Barack Obama, "Remarks by the President at Irish Celebration"
Dublin, Ireland
May 23, 2011

CONTENTS

Acknowledgments		ix
Preface: Dreams, Books and Overdetermination		xi
Chapter 1:	"No Irish Need Apply": From the Tenement to the White House	1
Provocation 1:	Trumpism and Troubles: Climatic Censorship, Authoritarian Populism and the Religious Right	31
Chapter 2:	The Long Road to Good Friday, I: From JFK to Jimmy Carter	47
Provocation 2:	A "Careening Circus of Pratfall Embarrassments": Donald Trump in Ireland	83
Chapter 3:	The Long Road to Good Friday, II: From Reagan to Clinton	91
Provocation 3:	Imagined Communities and Historical Memory, Troubles Time and "Trump Time"	125
Chapter 4:	Reading Our Troubles: Seamus Heaney and the Biden Presidency	133
Provocation 4:	Dangerous Demagogues, Fictional and Otherwise	161
Conclusion:	Victims and Martyrs, Troubles and Civil Wars	175
References		191
Index		215

ACKNOWLEDGMENTS

Seamus Heaney once emphasized how early-in-life experience was "central" to his poetry and how, at times, the work of representation is not "so much trying to describe it as trying to locate it." Excavating the memory of these experiences, he said, is "like putting your hand into a nest and finding something beginning to hatch out in your head." While he was doubtless thinking of the origins of his poems, I think the same metaphor describes the process of historical and critical writing as well, although the eggs in the memorial nest are more often not experiential but critical or analytical.

Such is the case with this book, and writing it meant that, when I reached into my nest, or archive, often more than one idea began to hatch. Some were indeed memories of past experiences. On these occasions, I sought out family, friends and colleagues to help me contextualize past events more precisely in particular times and places. My memories of recent and temporally remote events alike—the passing of Northern Irish political leader John Hume in 2020, or the protests on college campuses over the expansion of the Vietnam war in the spring of 1970—were greatly refined by conversations with my cousin John Watt, my twin brother Rob, and sister Sally. Such wonderful colleagues in Irish Studies as Nelson Ritschel, Marilynn Richtarik, Paige Reynolds and Richard Rankin Russell aided my thinking about this book on other occasions when I dipped my hand into the nest and found only shells, as whatever fledgling ideas that once resided there had taken flight. Charlotte Zietlow made suggestions about the book's argument that were especially helpful. My friends in the Indiana University English department—particularly Ray and Kathy Smith, Edward Dallis-Comentale and Brando Skyhorse—were always great sources of encouragement and advice.

Special thanks are owed to Bob White at Indiana University-Purdue University Indianapolis (IUPUI) who provided me with access to the *Irish People* Collection housed there, suggested illustrations for the book and generously allowed me to reproduce two photographs from his private collection. Thanks to Denise Rayman of the Ruth Lilly Special Collections and Archives for assistance with illustrations in this book, one of the several librarians and archivists who have been an enormous help to me. These include Andrew Payne, Head of Communication and Information at Aras an Uachtaráin; Herbert Ragan at the William J. Clinton Presidential Library; Michael Pinckney at the Ronald Regan Presidential Library and James Hill at the John F. Kennedy Presidential Library. I also want to thank the fine professionals at Alamy for their help with several of the photos in this book and, of course, the great editorial staff at Anthem. Special thanks to Mario Rosair for his patience and Jebaslin Hephzibah for his guidance in navigating the publication process, which from my perspective was entirely smooth and always collegial.

Perhaps the most important librarian who aided me in this project is my wife Nonie, who was kind enough to live with me and this book for several years. Her love and that of my children Caitlin and Brendan have always meant the world to me, even if they, like fledgling ideas, flew the nest some time ago. Their returns to that nest for holidays have always been the happiest days of the year. This book is dedicated to them.

Bloomington, Indiana
April, 2024

PREFACE: DREAMS, BOOKS AND OVERDETERMINATION

> The writing of history and, above all, literary criticism can, and must, always be understood as an attempt to find in the past aspects of human experience that can shed light on the meaning of our own times.
> —Jan Kott, *Shakespeare Our Contemporary* (1964)

The seeds of books germinate in both well-lit and shadowy imaginative spaces. In this way, books exhibit an affinity with the dreams Sigmund Freud studied in *The Interpretation of Dreams* (1900), where he learned that identifying the "background thoughts" from which dream symbols emerge, particularly those intricate or bizarre images resistant to quick explanation, was hardly a simple task. The search for their origins led him to *free association*, a process in which a patient focuses on specific images, not on a complete dream narrative, and to the conclusion that "interpretation *en detail* and not *en masse*" better enables an investigator to uncover the *overdetermined* nature of dream images—their provenance in several sources, not just one. Like dreams, books often arise from an untidy jumble of places: an archive of prior cultural texts (scrivened, visual, aural); major social, scientific and historical developments; and the imprints of individual experiences, large and small, etched on a writer's memory. Some of these are transformative or, in the worst of cases, traumatic—a stunning success or mortifying failure, a once-in-a-century pandemic and a pitched medical battle to vanquish it—while others are tethered to the banalities of everyday life that, surprisingly, demand expression. Such is the case with *From the "Troubles" to Trumpism*.

As a student of Irish history and culture for over forty years, I have enjoyed numerous opportunities to visit Ireland and Northern Ireland, and written about both, most often discussing literature, drama and theatrical production. This engagement constitutes one source of the pages that follow but, again, there are others. One in particular motivates the political bristle of this book: recent socio-political discord in America, particularly that associated with the presidential election of 2020, the insurrection at the Capitol on January 6, 2021 and the shocking state of affairs (and indictments) prefatory to the 2024 elections. The unprecedented nature of the insurrection—let's call it what it was—along with partisan obstruction to the formation of a Congressional committee to examine it undermined my confidence in America more than any other event in my lifetime. This includes the assassinations of John F. Kennedy, his brother Robert and Martin Luther King, Jr. in the 1960s, the expansion of America's involvement in Vietnam in the spring of 1970 (my first year in college), Watergate, the attacks on 9/11 and others. Oddly, the siege of the Capitol seemed vaguely familiar, returning me to things I had both studied *and* lived: the Troubles in Northern Ireland, on the one hand, and social unrest in 1960s and 70s America on the other. How might this dual history help us understand an American tribalism made more legible by the ascendance of Trumpism? Taking a longer view, how might the relationship between Ireland and America over the past six decades or so prove useful in forecasting the consequences of our polarization? To borrow a trope from Barack Obama, how would meditating upon the green behind the red, white, and blue illuminate our American "Troubles," or what many have predicted as an impending civil war? This last question reappears in the pages that follow, and in the book's conclusion I hope to put pressure on the terms "Troubles" and "Civil War," which in my view are not entirely synonymous.

Before outlining what lies ahead, I want to say a bit more about overdetermination and the origins of this book. As scholars often emphasize, although overdetermination rose to prominence in Freud's thought in relation to dreaming, the concept informed such earlier essays as "The Aetiology of Hysteria" (1896), where he distinguishes between an event or object's mere *suitability* as the cause of a symptom and its *traumatic force*, the psychical energy that compels us to relive an episode from the past. While Freud conceded that some wellsprings of hysteria fulfill both requirements—suitability and force—others do not, necessitating a parsing of seemingly unimportant events, objects and the feelings they incite. In my case, such minutiae grew more pressing during my travel through the American Midwest and South in the spring of 2021. By then, the COVID-19 pandemic seemed to be under control (of course, it wasn't); and, after a prolonged dormancy, optimism began to bloom, much like the dogwoods in southern Indiana where my wife and I live. A winter of fear and discontent was thawing as vaccines reached the most remote corners of America, even if some of the residents there had been persuaded not to take them.

In mid-May, we drove to Easley, South Carolina, to help our daughter move into a new apartment, and on our return home we enjoyed a brief holiday in the Smokey Mountains near Asheville, North Carolina. The mountains are, as advertised, stunning. But as we traveled to Cherokee through Maggie Valley, politics sullied the natural beauty too brashly to ignore. For just off the two-lane road not long after we began our nearly 2500-foot ascent, three flags danced on poles in front of a dilapidated general store that sells guns, ammunition and other goods, or so its sun-bleached sign advertised. This triad included a yellow Gadsden banner from 1775 with its coiled snake and "Don't Tread on Me" motto, a Confederate battle flag and one of more recent vintage: "Trump 2024—Keep America Great." More so than the "Trump Pence 2020" signs decorating yards in rural towns across the Midwest months after the disputed election was over, these flags recalled for me the chaos at the Capitol on January 6.

Their display reveals the complex temporality of the present moment, rippled as it is with an American history too often shorn of context and appropriated to justify the unjustifiable. The Gadsden flag, for example, introduced in 1775 to symbolize independence from English rule and later adopted by libertarians, now represents a politics antipathetic to the most fundamental values of democracy and shared civic responsibility, the mitigation of epidemics for instance. Deploying the familiar political strategy Paul M. Renfro mocked in *Time* (April 15, 2020) of "declaring 'war' on any conceivable enemy," President Trump, who initially labelled COVID a "Chinese flu," called for a national response to the pandemic that would rival the country's mobilization during World War II. But the call to action quickly foundered when his army, like their leader, proved unwilling to countenance such inconveniences as wearing a mask in battling the enemy. By the winter of 2021–22, Trump had changed his stance and was loudly booed for admitting in an interview with Bill O'Reilly that he had been vaccinated and "boosted," many anti-maskers also being anti-vaxxers. So much for patriotic mobilizations. Yet, like the waving of decontextualized flags and banners, this disingenuous political strategy accomplished its mission by casting the president as a strong wartime leader in the mold of FDR, Harry Truman and Winston Churchill.

As Congress assembled on January 6 to certify the presidential election, other banners joined the Gadsden and Confederate flags outside the Capitol: the "Come and Take It" standard, for instance, waved by several rioters. Commemorating the Battle of Gonzalez in 1835, a chapter in the Texas republic's fight for independence from Mexico, the new "Come and Take It" flag sports the image of an assault rifle in its upper half. And the "An Appeal to Heaven" or "Pine Tree" flag displayed by insurrectionists at the Capitol connotes divine, specifically Christian, approbation of the enterprise. Taken *en masse*, on January 6 such images announced the arrival of a motley gang of conspiracy theorists, white supremacists and circular logicians similar to those Northern Irish loyalists who at times during the Troubles fought British soldiers to remain British subjects. Befuddled by a similar illogic, and too easily swayed by Trump's allegation that the 2020 election was stolen, Americans attacked democracy in the name of democracy—and in the name of a Christian God— using refashioned or repurposed artifacts to defend their actions.

Flags, mottos and outdated campaign signs serving as lawn ornaments are suitable determinants of the essays that comprise this book. But "suitable" does not mean unimportant. By their very nature, flags and other political paraphernalia invariably accompany and, at times, ignite civil unrest. In her Man Booker Prize-winning novel, *Milkman* (2018), Belfast writer Anna Burns's protagonist aptly observes that flags were invented to be "instinctive and emotional—often pathologically, narcissistically emotional" (25). Dominic Bryan makes a similar point in *Orange Parades: The Politics of Ritual, Tradition and Control* (2000), a study of Northern Irish Protestant marches, by noting that, in the annual July ritual of Orangemen parading through Catholic neighborhoods, banners emblazoned with the founding details of an Orange lodge are unfurled, affixed to poles and carried during marches. As such, they form a supplement to the parades which, more than "any other aspect of politics in Ireland," symbolize stasis, an "uninterrupted tradition" of domination (3,7). Some of them depict King William of Orange mounted on his white stallion at the Battle of the Boyne in 1690, thereby endowing obduracy in the present with a martial precedent from the past. By design, the future plays little part in these spectacles, a temporality that will receive further attention in the pages that follow.

Political iconography in twenty-first-century America functions in much the same performative way. Consider the widely circulated photographs of Donald Trump hugging an American flag at the annual meeting of the Conservative Political Action Conference (CPAC) in March 2019 (available for purchase on Amazon.com and elsewhere), an embrace he repeated in 2024. Appalled by the earlier image, political commentator S.E. Cupp compared the president's embrace of the Stars and Stripes to the "smothering and unwanted advances of an unstable lech" and the clumsy groping of an oversexed high schooler. Cupp's unstable lech might be juxtaposed to what Nick Bryant in *When America Stopped Being Great: A History of the Present* (2021) defined as Trump's comic public persona. Spending a day with him in 2014, Bryant detected in his public appearances a "deliberately cartoonish schtick" he revived later at CPAC (4). In this context, Trump's embrace of Old Glory and fatuous grin were more buffoonish than libidinous, elements of his impersonation of a nineteenth-century stage comedian or hammy vaudevillian.

Such schtick also tended to distract his followers and critics from the more serious failings of his presidency: his rebukes of NATO and the World Health Organization, his intimidation of witnesses subpoenaed by Congress during his second impeachment *even as they were testifying*, his enlistment of dotty confederates oozing hair dye to pressure state officials to overturn the 2020 election, his theft of classified documents—the list is encyclopedic. But as outrageous as these actions were, as suitable as they were in motivating my project, it was Fintan O'Toole's editorial in the *Irish Times* (April 29, 2020), "Donald Trump Has Destroyed the Country He Promised to Make Great Again," that pushed me to the word processor. A respected public intellectual, O'Toole is also much admired in the smaller orbit of Irish Studies, especially by those of us who write about drama and theatre. His theatre criticism has been influential enough to merit the publication of a collection of his reviews—*Critical Moments: Fintan O'Toole on Modern Irish Theatre*—in 2003. In the volume's introduction one of its editors, Julia Furay, lauds his critical disposition, noting that he avoids verbal savagery and is seldom "cruelly dismissive," choosing instead to identify a production's failures with intelligence and moderation (4). She's right.

In such works as *Ship of Fools: How Stupidity and Corruption Sank the Celtic Tiger* (2009), however, O'Toole exposes with considerably more invective the excesses of greedy bankers, corrupt politicians and the *nouveaux riches* during the rise and fall of Ireland's economic boom prior to the 2008 recession. His evisceration of Trump's "outlandish idiocy," "malignant" narcissism and "death-wish defiance of reason" in his *Irish Times* editorial is equally ferocious. But it was neither O'Toole's exposition of Trump's ineptitude nor his prediction that "this will get worse before it gets better" that gave me pause. Nor was it his disdain for Trump's bloated, increasingly unhinged performances and those of an attention-starved cast of bit players—in many cases cowering politicians clinging to his fraying presidential coattails. Rather, it was his implication that the centuries-old relationship between Ireland and America has been irreparably damaged. This notion is hardly unique. In July 2023, Eoghan Smith and Simon Workman echoed O'Toole when introducing a special issue of the *Irish Studies Review*. Recalling Ireland's legalization of Civil Partnerships in 2010 and the election of the first gay man as Taoiseach in 2017, they identified a more tolerant phase in Irish society that runs counter to the myriad intolerances of Trumpism:

> This phase also coincided with a turn away from the US-UK sphere of influence towards a strengthening sense of common European identity that was significantly shaped after 2016 by antagonism within Ireland towards the outcome of the Brexit referendum and the election of Donald Trump as President of the United States. (326)

JFK, Bill Clinton, Barack O'Bama (Irish spelling), "Irish Joe" Biden—since Andrew Jackson's parents left Ulster in 1765 for the Waxhaws on the border of North and South Carolina, America and many of its presidents have enjoyed places of privilege in Irish hearts. But "Donal" and his minions have infected this relationship, and all the ivermectin at the farm co-op won't cure it.

One term in O'Toole's editorial grabbed my attention as much as his larger indictment of Trumpism:

> Over more than two centuries, the United States has stirred a very wide range of feelings in the rest of the world: love and hatred, fear and hope, envy and contempt, awe and anger. But there is one emotion that has never been directed towards the US until now: *pity*. [my emphasis]

In support of this assertion, he later asks, "How many people in Düsseldorf or Dublin are wishing they lived in Detroit or Dallas?" In a few paragraphs, O'Toole reverses the trajectory of the *urtext* of Ireland and America's long history: the emigration of men and women *from* Ireland *to* America who very much wished to live in Boston or New York, Detroit or Dallas. Statistics, however inexact, tell the story. In *Ireland and Irish America: Culture, Class, and Transatlantic Migration* (2008), historian Kerby Miller estimates that between 1750 and 1844 some 1.5 million Irish arrived in North America, the majority of them Ulster Protestants like Andrew Jackson's parents, and between 1845–55 some 2.1 million more emigrants, the majority of them poor and Catholic, followed. During the entirety of the nineteenth century, according to Leonard Dinnerstein and David M. Reimers in *Ethnic Americans: A History of Immigration* (2009), nearly four million Irish came to America.

Moreover, the difficult lives of those left behind were greatly improved when, after settling in America, Irish émigrés sent money and basic necessities back home. In *The Aran Islands* (1907), what Declan Kiberd in *Irish Classics* (2000) terms a "left-wing pastoral that in later decades would go by other names" like "sociology and anthropology" (421), J.M. Synge hints at America's role in helping poor inhabitants of the islands located off the coast of Galway survive:

> Nearly all the families [on Aranmoor] have relations who have had to cross the Atlantic, and all eat of the flour and bacon that is brought from the United States, so they have a vague fear that 'if anything happened to America', their own island would cease to be habitable. (15)

O'Toole's rhetorical question about Irish emigrants choosing not to travel to America thus marks a thematic rupture in the long story of America and Ireland.

But *pity* America? In the opening of *Angela's Ashes* (1996), Frank McCourt depicts the hardships of childhood, reserving his most profound sympathy for "the miserable Irish Catholic childhood" (11). And Irish pity is just as extreme as its misery. On the Aran Islands, Synge experienced the intensity of Irish pity when hearing local women keening, the traditional lamentation heard at the funeral of a spouse, child or—in this case—an elderly neighbor. Synge came to realize that this expression of grief was more than a "personal complaint for the death of one woman over eighty years." Instead, it seemed "to contain the whole passionate rage that lurks somewhere in every native of the island." That is, implicit in this funereal tradition is self-pity, part of which originates in the realization that young islanders who left for America or Britain—or Dublin or Cork—would likely never return (31). In this way, pity on the Aran Islands is associated not only with loss, but with a future of isolation and loneliness, the latter a psychical reality captured by Synge in *The Playboy of the Western World* (1907) and, more recently, in such plays of Martin McDonagh as *The Beauty Queen of Leenane* (1996) and his film *The Banshees of Inishere* (2022).

For these reasons, the notion of a pitiable America seized my attention as much as O'Toole's recapitulation of the Trump regime's most conspicuous failures. Yet, if Nick Bryant is right that "Disunion has long been as much a feature of American life as union" (12), why did this particular moment seem so pitiable? In large part, like the presence of the Confederate and Gadsden flags at the Capitol on January 6, because it raised the specters of other times, other histories. On Synge's remote Aran Islands, these histories often foreground the exodus of family members and the passing of neighbors; in McDonagh's *Banshees of Inishere*, where the sounds of gunfire from Ireland's west coast are plainly audible as a civil war rages on, we are reminded that disputes between old friends can calcify into a destructive implacability. Like old flags and tattered campaign signs, these hauntings from the past returned me to the Troubles. And to the possibility that the nation Synge's Aran Islanders viewed as crucial to their survival has been transformed, changed utterly. And the transformation is far from over.

***

The essays in this book attempt to follow Jan Kott's counsel in the epigraph with which I began: to employ historical investigation and insights gleaned from literature as means of illuminating the present moment, particularly the present *American* moment. In this regard, the dates 1960 and 1923 in my subtitle are hardly accidental. The book's first three chapters concern the history of America's relationship with Ireland during the administrations of the presidents whose terms spanned the pre-history and history of the Troubles. After a glance backward at American and Irish relations in the nineteenth century, the first chapter focuses on the 1960 election of John F. Kennedy, the first Catholic president in America's history and the first to visit Ireland during his term of office. It also juxtaposes Kennedy's jubilant 1963 trip to Ireland with Ronald Reagan's more complicated homecoming in 1984. The next two chapters examine relationships between Ireland, Northern Ireland and the United States from the time after the Kennedy assassination through the administrations of Richard Nixon, Gerald Ford, Jimmy Carter, Ronald Reagan and Bill Clinton, who in 1995 was the first American president to visit Northern Ireland. The fourth chapter begins by juxtaposing the cultural literacy of presidents like Joe Biden and Michael D. Higgins of Ireland with the aversion to reading of President Biden's predecessor, suggesting the necessity of electing readers as national leaders. This discussion begins with the Democratic party primary before the 2020 election, the implications of Biden's reading of Seamus Heaney and his allusions to Heaney's *The Cure at Troy* during his campaign, and the effects of the president's profound sense of Irish identity on his first term in office.

Between these chapters, I have inserted editorials or "provocations" that adduce parallels between a Northern Irish past and an uncertain American future. I cannot make any claims for the originality of this structural device, commonly called the "interchapter," as both creative and scholarly writers before me have employed it to offer supplements to their larger projects. In his short story collection *Walking the Dog* (1994), for example, Bernard MacLaverty interlaces nine stories with ten vignettes, one as short as four lines. In *Inventing Ireland: The Literature of the Modern Nation* (1995), Declan Kiberd inserts interchapters to add texture to more substantial explications of such writers as Synge, James Joyce, Oscar Wilde and many others, as does Richard Rankin Russell in the second edition of *Modernity, Place, and Community in Brian Friel's Drama* (2022).

Unlike the book's chapters, these provocations are not so much scholarly exercises as "op-eds" inflected by the insights of journalists, novelists, playwrights and poets in the context of Trumpism's endangerment of American democracy. There is, admittedly, a certain peculiarity in this undertaking, as Carlos Lozada observes in *What Were We Thinking: A Brief Intellectual History of the Trump Era* (2021): "One of the ironies of our time is that a man who rarely reads," preferring television news and Twitter instead, has motivated an "onslaught of book-length writing about his presidency" (2). As my title's allusion to "Trumpism," not Trump, is meant to suggest, I am less concerned with prosecuting an *argumentum ad hominem* than with assessing the consequences of his cultivation of societal division discussed in such books as Stephen Marche's *The Next Civil War: Dispatches from the American Future* (2022) and Jonathan Greenblatt's *It Could Happen Here: Why America Is Tipping from Hate to the Unthinkable–And How We Can Stop It* (2022). Yet, at the same time, when juxtaposing threats of violence in contemporary America with those that ravaged Northern Ireland and, while greatly ameliorated, still do, at least one ingredient becomes apparent: in addition to socio-economic inequality, institutionalized voter suppression, racism and misogyny, both civil wars and Troubles require bellicose public figures skilled at fomenting hatred and fear in their followers. Thus, my project pursues a kind of historical *retrofitting* that views an increasingly dangerous moment in contemporary America through the lens of recent history.

Do the pages that follow predict a new civil war or "Troubles" in America's future? In many ways, yes. Recalling Fintan O'Toole's startling assertion, even raising such a question suggests our pitiable descent into national chaos.

Chapter 1

"NO IRISH NEED APPLY": FROM THE TENEMENT TO THE WHITE HOUSE

This Americky is heaven's own spot, ma'am, and there's no denyin' it.
—Augustin Daly, *A Flash of Lightning*

In the New World [...] 'no slum was as fearful as the Irish slum.' Of all the immigrant nationalities in Boston, the Irish fared the least well, beginning at a lower rung and rising more slowly on the economic and social ladder than any other group.
—Doris Kearns Goodwin, *The Fitzgeralds and the Kennedys: An American Saga* (1987)

After the great influx of Irish immigrants [...] the Scotch-Irish insisted upon differentiating between the descendants of earlier immigrants from Ireland and more recent arrivals. Thus, as a portion of the Irish diaspora became known as the 'the Irish', a racial (but not ethnic) line invented in Ireland was recreated as an ethnic (but not racial) line in America.
—Noel Ignatiev, *How the Irish Became White* (1995)

My twin brother and I were born in Springfield, Illinois, the "Land of Lincoln," and celebrated our ninth birthdays three months before John F. Kennedy's election as president in November 1960. But even though we watched the evening news attentively on a fuzzy black-and-white television with our parents—a "mixed marriage" of a Protestant father and Catholic mother—neither of us quite understood why the election seemed to matter so much. A few weeks later on Thanksgiving morning, our view got clearer. The day began with helping our mother and grandmother, a second-generation Irish American, prepare for the traditional feast. Our jobs included tearing a mound of stiff, day-old bread into stuffing for the turkey, polishing silverware and carrying plates and other necessities to the table. This year was different, though, because not long after we started our chores mother and grandmother, cooking at the stove, began laughing and crying softly at the same time. I remember asking, "Mom, what's wrong? Did something bad happen?" With a smile she reassured us, "No, boys. These are tears of joy, because grandmother never thought she would live to see an Irish Catholic president in the White House. Now she will."

The larger story of the Irish in America underlies not only my grandmother's joy but also, nearly four decades later, America's role in brokering the Good Friday Agreement in Northern Ireland. Motifs in this story—assimilation and otherness, poverty and socio-economic mobility, sectarian violence and prejudice—recur in a narrative that spans the years from the arrivals of Irish exiles in eighteenth- and nineteenth-century America, to President Kennedy's election, to the administrations of Presidents Richard Nixon, Jimmy Carter and Ronald Reagan, and to the Bill Clinton administration and the ratification of the Agreement. This chapter, the first of four focused on the shared history of Ireland and America, sketches the earliest of these episodes, from immigration to the trips to Ireland of Presidents Kennedy and Ronald Reagan in, respectively, 1963 and 1984, by which time the relationship between the countries had grown far more complex both politically and economically. The two chapters that follow this one move to the post-Kennedy era and the Carter, Reagan and Clinton administrations' interventions in the Troubles in Northern Ireland; and the last chapter concerns the efforts of America's second Irish Catholic president, Joe Biden, to navigate the turbulence of post-January 6, 2021 as aided by insights from Seamus Heaney's writing.

Some numbers might help establish this chapter's function as a preface or, more theatrically speaking, an induction scene to a nearly three-century drama. Recall Kerby Miller's estimate that between 1750 and 1844 as many as 1.5 million Irish immigrants traveled to North America, with some 2.1 million more arriving during the years of the Famine between 1845 and 1855 (*Ireland*, 13).[1] As a result, the populations of major cities, particularly those on the east coast, experienced explosive growth at mid-century. New York City welcomed 1.8 million immigrants between 1847 and 1851, some 848,000 of whom were Irish (Egan, 134); and Boston, which had been averaging 4,000–5,000 new residents per year, welcomed 37,000 immigrants in 1847 alone, the majority of whom were "pallid and weak," half-starved and Irish. The most fortunate of these found work as unskilled laborers at mills in Lowell and Lawrence, with women finding employment as domestics (O'Connor, 91). And several inferences from these data explain both Catholic America's jubilation over Kennedy's victory and the narrowness of its margin. That is, although he won the Electoral College handily with 303 votes, he defeated Richard Nixon in the popular vote by an "alarmingly narrow" margin of

0.17% (Schlesinger, 76). Echoing a phrase from Washington's *Evening Star*, Richard H. Rovere in *The New Yorker* (November 11, 1960) judged the result as a "victory without a verdict and a majority without a mandate" and wondered aloud if Kennedy had actually received the greater share as some states' absentee ballots remained to be counted. (By comparison, in 2016, Donald Trump won 306 Electoral College votes, but lost the popular vote to Hillary Clinton by over two million votes; in 2020, Joe Biden also received 306 Electoral College votes and won the popular vote by over six million.)

How might the struggles of the Famine Irish—and those of some 400,000 Scots-Irish already in America, the majority, like Andrew Jackson's family, Presbyterians from Ulster—inform our understanding of the election of America's first Irish Catholic president?[2] And how might this history recast what was once merely a polite relationship between Ireland and America into one every bit as "special" as that between America and Britain? The uniqueness of this latter relationship is typically put under pressure at times of tension between Ireland and Britain, as the years of the Troubles and the close, but at times tense, partnership of President Reagan and Prime Minister Margaret Thatcher demonstrate. In our own time, the ramifications of Brexit have led both British Tories and Northern loyalists to question the sincerity of America's historically "special" relationship with Britain.

Moments of crystal ball gazing in this book—predictions about where the trajectory of today's American tribalism might end—will be improved, I hope, by their contextualization with the history of the Irish in America, particularly the 115 years or so between the Famine and the Kennedy administration, in part because this history so uncannily anticipates many of the barriers to meaningful dialogue in our own political discourse. This examination is undertaken in the service of a single assertion: that Ireland and America's long relationship, one strained by the Trump presidency as Fintan O'Toole has so persuasively argued, has been not only culturally vital to both countries but crucial to the survival of the American republic. As President Kennedy, the first American president to address the Irish Parliament, phrased it on June 28, 1963: "My presence and your welcome, however, only symbolize the many and the enduring links which have bound the Irish and the Americans since the earliest days." This chapter will examine some of these links.

A Brief Prehistory of Camelot

The epigraphs above both epitomize the struggles of nineteenth-century immigrants and complicate connotations of "Irishness" in the American lexicon. The first, from Irish-American playwright Augustin Daly's melodrama

A Flash of Lightning (1868), captures the sentiment of thousands of Famine exiles who, after weeks (in the worst cases, two months or more) of privation aboard filthy, disease-ridden "coffin" ships bound for North America, viewed "Americky" as "heaven's own spot." But this heaven often proved to be a mirage. In the second epigraph from Doris Kearns Goodwin's chronicle of the Fitzgerald and Kennedy families in Boston—a chronicle that begins with the second wave of emigrants between 1848 and 1855 that included the Fitzgeralds—the image of a paradisical America obscured the miseries of poverty and the torpid pace at which they would be ameliorated. In 1857, Thomas Fitzgerald, Rose Fitzgerald Kennedy's grandfather, acquired both a peddler's license and a wife, selling codfish and haddock he procured at the docks and starting a family. Although some politicians urged immigrants to pursue opportunities in the west—and newspapers like the Boston *Pilot*, appalled by the city's disease-ravaged immigrant tenements, warned that "It's not safe here! Go West!" (Thompson, 68)—Thomas ignored their call. One element of his decision was personal—the chance to work with his brother James—but another may have originated in the reluctance of the famine-era Irish to abandon their communities in which the Catholic Church occupied the center and offered a comforting sense of familiarity.

As Colm Tóibín depicts in *Brooklyn* (2009), a century later many of these conditions persisted. In an early 1950s Catholic parish hall in the novel, dozens of "leftover Irishmen" who had built New York's bridges, tunnels, and highways—now indigent and worn down—gather at Christmas time to enjoy fellowship and a holiday menu of "Irish" food: turkey, "proper stuffing" and "Brussels sprouts boiled to death" (88, 89). For them, the parishioners' generosity and the tradition of Irish hospitality it recalled made their lives a little more bearable. Many of these men, as Tóibín's Father Flood explains, had lived in the city for fifty years or more, and most had "lost touch with everyone" back "home." So, when he attempted on their behalf to contact Irish relatives, his letters typically received no reply (88). Perhaps, like many of the arrivals to Boston, Goodwin describes, these navvies stayed in the city because they associated the west with the desolation Synge experienced on the Aran Islands. For some, the "ample space" of the prairie may have seemed too lawless or simply "too ample, creating an emptiness that seemed more troubling than the overcrowding of the slum" (Goodwin, 15).[3] Better to stay put.

Patrick Kennedy, JFK's great-grandfather, made the same decision when he arrived in Boston in 1848. There, in his mid-twenties, he married Bridget Murphy, with whom he had four children before succumbing to cholera in 1858 at age 35, leaving his family in difficult straits. A skilled cooper, a trade he learned in New Ross before emigrating, Patrick earned a living wage for his young family, but it didn't allow for much savings. A resourceful woman, Bridget had preceded Patrick from County Wexford to East Boston by way of Liverpool, not so much to flee the horrors of the Famine but, as Neal Thompson phrases it in *The First Kennedys: The Humble Roots of an American Dynasty* (2022), in response to a "different kind of hunger, a craving to leave the safety of habit and family and fling herself among strangers toward a strange new land." Like Stephen Dedalus in Joyce's *A Portrait of An Artist as a Young Man* (1916), who decides to "fly" past the "nets" of nationality, language and religion, Bridget was "no emaciated shell of a person in rags" but a vital young woman eager to escape the jurisdiction of a "foreign oppressor" and the gender-based constraints of local culture (Thompson, 7). The city to which she moved, however, was ruled by different oppressors: cholera, consumption and prejudice (39). Children were especially vulnerable to these and, as Thompson documents, Bridget was forced to make a harrowing trip twice from East Boston to a Catholic cemetery in Cambridge, first to bury her infant son and three years later to bury her husband. In those days, even the burial of the dead was affected by religious difference.

Working at and then buying a small shop after her husband's death, Bridget kept the family going until her teenage son P.J. left school, took a job on the docks and purchased a small tavern with his savings. By the time he reached his mid-twenties, he had acquired two more and, before he turned thirty, embarked upon a career in business, forming P. J. Kennedy and Company, a successful liquor-importing company. The opportunity his mother and father sought in making the arduous journey to a new country was beginning to be realized.

But it wasn't easy. To make their projects of assimilation and economic security more daunting, Famine-era immigrants became ensnared in the discourses of nativism, religion and race in antebellum America. Race, of course, was foregrounded in the rhetoric of abolitionists and informed the secession of the Confederate States of America in 1861. Ireland and Irish America hardly spoke in a single voice on this issue, with many nationalists advocating the end of slavery and many Scots-Irish in the South espousing an opposite position. By mid-century, race had insinuated itself into a number of cultural formations and registers, scientific discourse for example. In *The Colors of Zion: Blacks, Jews, and Irish from 1845 to 1945* (2011), George Bornstein outlines the "rise of the polygenists," writers who "tipped the balance toward the racialists and racists" until the "watershed of World War II" (29).

One of these was Scots scientist Robert Knox, whose study *The Races of Man* (1850) indexed Africans and Jews among the darker races, a view that informed his opposition to racial mixing, which could only result in an unnatural hybridity. Knox evinced a "special phobia" for the "Celtic Race of Ireland," whom he regarded as the "most to be dreaded" and "the source of all evil" (qtd. in Bornstein, 29–30). In addition, he alleged that the Irish were predisposed to "idleness, disorder, and violence" (30), slurs underlying the simianization and stereotyping of Irish and African Americans justified by the pseudoscience of phrenology. In *Types of Mankind* (1854), American surgeon Josiah Clark Nott revealed biases similar to Knox's, particularly where miscegenation is concerned. In anthropological studies later in the century, the Irish, particularly those who emigrated from rural counties during the Famine, occupied a high place on an "Index of Nigrescence" (32). From such shibboleths, race insinuated itself into nativist prejudice to justify violence against Irish Catholics, and their vestiges resurfaced a century later when an Irish Catholic politician announced his candidacy for the presidency.

Such so-called "scientific" discourse helps explain instances of anti-Irish sentiment in Daly's *A Flash of Lightning*. When the play opened in the summer of 1868 at Wallack's Theatre in New York, Daly (1838–99) was a well-known theatre reviewer and dramatist, in part because his adaptation of the heart-rending *Leah, the Forsaken* (1862) about a young Jewish woman abandoned by her Gentile lover brought him considerable acclaim. Some thirty years after its premiere, Sarah Bernhardt featured a French version of *Leah* in her American tour and, as described in *Ulysses* (1922), it was revived frequently in London and the *fin de siècle* Dublin that Joyce depicts. In 1867, Daly scored another success with his urban melodrama *Under the Gaslight*, which featured the last-second rescue of a character from an oncoming locomotive. By the time of his death in 1899, Daly operated theatres in New York and London, devising systems of ensemble acting and production that made him, as Don B. Wilmeth summarizes in the *Cambridge Guide to American Theatre* (1993), "one of the first directors in the modern sense, and the first American *régisseur*" (138). Later in his career, he was known for his revivals of Shakespeare that, when produced in London, elicited the derision of Bernard Shaw, who accused Daly's 1895 production of *A Midsummer Night's Dream* of "slaughtering" Shakespeare's poetry in a quest for visual "titivation" (*Our Theatres in the Nineties*, 1.179). Whatever his limitations, Daly influenced the advancement of American theatre, and in 1894 he was honored with the University of Notre Dame's Laetare Medal, the most prestigious award an American Catholic layman can receive. President Kennedy received the same honor in 1962.

A Flash of Lightning, although neither so celebrated nor so enduring as *Leah*, is in the present context more relevant.[4] To be sure, the play offered audiences all the excitements of melodrama—plot twists, a thrilling escape, a spectacular rescue—but it also reflected extant social realities. Before the curtain rises and like Irish exiles before her, Mrs. Dowderry arrived in New York with her children.[5] Stranded on the street until Mrs. Fallon invited her into her home, Mrs. Dowderry asks Ann, the Fallons' Irish maid, "An' how long must we be in Americky till we wear th' green off?" Ann's answer is brilliant in its humble way: "That depinds [sic]. Some wear it on a mortal time. Some drop it aisy, aisy like, till ye'd never know" (5). Mrs. Fallon's once poor, now wealthy, husband Garry has already dropped *his* Irishness "aisy like," which is why when his wife greets her guests and asks Ann to fetch a bundle of clothing she has prepared for them, she cautions her to be "careful that he doesn't see you" (6). Mrs. Fallon's apprehension is warranted, for when Mrs. Dowderry later recognizes Fallon as a relative of a miserly Kerry family she knows, he orders her to leave and threatens to buy an Irish-hating dog to keep her out. A commotion ensues drawing the attention of Skiffley, an unscrupulous detective, who snidely asks, "Irish relations rather troublesome, eh?" Disavowing such "relations," Fallon is reminded that he was born there, to which he responds, "That was accidental. My wife's American, my daughters are American, and my dollars are American" (9). The audience also learns that "no man shall have [his] younger daughter Bessie 'till he earned her" (10); as a result, Jack Ryver, unlike JFK's ancestor Thomas Fitzgerald, has headed west to make his fortune with the Pacific Railroad. Closer to home, Skiffley vows to have Bessie and, after she rejects him, he eventually manacles her to a burning steamboat from which Jack, returned from the west, rescues her.

Daly's play achieves more, however, than the creation of engaging stock characters and theatrical sensation; it also draws upon a growing prejudice outside the theatre to immigrants in general and newly arrived Irish in particular. As in Daly's play, anti-Irish sentiments were also voiced by successful Irish Americans who sought to disavow their heritage, as Mrs. Dowderry complains: "The Merrykins axes [sic] us to come over and it's our own that tries to walk over us when we get here" (9). As Noel Ignatiev observes, such inhospitable "othering" resembles what in Ireland was not a "racial" distinction, but an ethnic and religious one between Protestants and Catholics. In *Born Fighting: How the Scots-Irish Shaped America* (2004), James Webb focuses on the first "great wave" of Presbyterian émigrés from Ulster who traveled to America in the eighteenth and early nineteenth centuries before the influx of Famine refugees (16). This first wave did not represent the "poorest layers of Irish society" but included farmers, artisans, tradesmen and professionals, with one 1820 report estimating that only one-quarter of new arrivals were unskilled workers (Ignatiev, 38).[6] At the same time, many *were* poor and settled in the South, as Andrew Jackson's family did in 1765 in "a tiny place tucked away in the Carolinas" called Waxhaw (Meacham, 8).

The demography of immigration changed during the Famine years, and as a result many Scots-Irish Americans "insisted upon differentiating between the descendants of earlier immigrants" and more recent arrivals (Ignatiev, 39).

Before considering broader connotations of "Irishness," it should be noted that characters like Daly's Garry Fallon are based on an often-overlooked fact of nineteenth-century socio-economics. As Tyler Anbinder argues, because an earlier generation of sociologists and historians tended to neglect such sources as banking records, relying instead upon letters and memoirs, many represented immigrant life "from the bottom up," assuming that Famine Irish formed part of an "unemployed, resourceless proletariat" (742). Anbinder challenges this supposition, as did James T. Farrell in the 1930s even as he described his novels of Irish-American life in late nineteenth- and early twentieth-century Chicago as a "bottom dog" literature of the working and lower middle classes living on the city's South Side.[7] Frank McCourt's portrait of his childhood in early 1930s Brooklyn in *Angela's Ashes* is in some ways similar. Although McCourt's early years were difficult, at least his alcoholic father earned a wage and, when he squandered it, his family's neighbors—Irish, Jewish and Italian—offered their help. The account histories of New York's Emigrant's Savings Bank, founded in 1850, confirm that many Famine Irish achieved considerable prosperity, leading Anbinder to advise historians to abandon the "rags-to-riches paradigm [...] and instead reconceptualize how we think about immigrant economic achievement in America" (743). It's understandable, though, how this paradigm evolved, for like *A Flash of Lightning* several popular plays on the mid-century stage featured Irish-born entrepreneurs who rose to prosperity while retaining their humanity, empathy and love of Ireland.[8]

Still, as Goodwin's and Thompson's representations of life in mid-nineteenth-century Boston suggest, many Famine immigrants found only menial and, at times, dangerous jobs, if they could find work at all. Many languished in crowded, unsanitary tenements (a visit to New York's Tenement Museum on the Lower East Side drives this point home forcefully). It is also the case that anti-Irish biases and hazardous working conditions existed well before the second wave of Irish immigrants reached America. Ignatiev recalls one of the latter, the 1831 construction of the New Basin Canal in New Orleans. Aware of the danger of the project, the Canal Corporation hired Irish workers who were either injured, killed on the job or infected by communicable diseases in their squalid living quarters. These victims were later commemorated in song:

> Ten thousand Micks, they swung with their picks,
> To dig the New Canal.
> But the choleray [sic] was stronger 'n they
> An twice it killed them all. (109)

While estimates of the human cost of the Canal's construction vary, there is some consensus that 8,000 immigrant lives were lost.

In *The Irish in Philadelphia* (1973), Dennis Clark recalls similarly dangerous canal projects. There in the 1850s, as a "prelude to the transportation revolution," the Schuylkill Navigation Company decided to build a canal to Reading, another (the Delaware and Raritan Canal) connecting to Northern New Jersey, and the Lehigh Navigation Canal (65). The labor, "arduous beyond belief," was undertaken largely by gangs of Irishmen hired for economic reasons: "So grueling and dangerous was the work that Irishmen, considered less valuable than Negro slaves, were used at times in preference to an investment in black labor" (66). Thus, while some Irish acquired sufficient wealth to open accounts at the Emigrant Savings Bank, it was still the case that most immigrants were not so fortunate.

This disparity between upwardly mobile Irish and the abjectly poor in America appalled two visitors to New York at mid-century: Charles Dickens in 1842 and Thomas Francis Meagher a decade later. Writing for the *City Journal* in 2018, Douglas Muzzio observes that although New York in 1842 was "already the business and commercial center of the United States," it was also a nexus of "poverty, crime, and corruption" as the Five Points neighborhood exemplified. Enjoying his residence at the Carlton Hotel, Dickens experienced both the comfortable side of American life and its stark opposite:

> New York was glamorous, but it was also filthy, and it stank. Drinking the water could be fatal. Cholera, yellow fever, and typhus periodically ravaged the city. A foul miasma rose from the garbage, carcasses of dead animals, and the offal of butchered livestock. The streets were covered with "corporation pies" and "night soil"—the tons of manure produced by New York's horses, cows, sheep, dogs, and pigs. (Muzzio, "When Boz Came")

In *The Immortal Irishman: The Irish Revolutionary Who Became an American Hero* (2016), Timothy Egan describes Meagher's arrival in New York in 1852, his recruitment of the Irish Brigade to fight for the Union and his ascent to the rank of Brigadier General in the Union Army. Like Dickens before him, Meagher visited Five Points and was shocked by the tenements he saw— "wooden gaols that could combust in a poof from an unintended cigar"— and by a built environment unrelieved by even a blade of green grass or tiny canopy of trees (Egan, 132). Again, although many Irish, including Meagher's former Young Irelander colleagues, flourished in America, others languished as part of what Archbishop John Hughes termed "the poorest and most wretched population that can be found in our world" (qtd. in Egan, 134).

Extreme poverty was not the only challenge immigrants faced, as nativist violence against Irish Catholics entered a more hostile phase with some of the most disturbing incidents occurring before the waves of Famine Irish even arrived. Clark describes the Philadelphia riots of 1844 fomented by the preaching of 100 ministers belonging to The American Protestant Association that, two years earlier, served as one of the "inspirations" for the Nativist or "Know-Nothing" party. On May 6 in Kensington, some five and a half miles north of the city, a Protestant meeting provoked a three-day riot (the "Bible Riots") with the result that two Catholic churches in North Philadelphia were burned to the ground and dozens of Catholic homes destroyed. By the end of a riotous summer, at least twenty people had been killed. Attacks on Catholics and their "popish" politics were repeated throughout the summer, leading many Philadelphians to a conclusion akin to that heard during the "Black Lives Matter" protests in 2020: namely, that the "police and civil forces available to quell disorder" were ill-equipped to do so (20). Eleven years later in 1855, the Know-Nothings' feud with Democrats in Louisville incited shootings, looting and the leveling of at least one block of Catholic-owned homes. Irish and German Catholics were the primary targets of this violence, and twenty-two people were killed (some estimates of the fatalities are considerably higher). As a result, hundreds of Irish Catholics fled the city.

In addition to these episodes, a keen competition between Irish and African America for employment was emerging. By 1855, Irish immigrants "made up eighty-seven percent of New York City's 23,300 unskilled workers," while African Americans accounted for only three percent. Ignatiev quotes an 1851 issue of the *African Repository* which complained that "the influx of white laborers has expelled the Negro *en masse* from the exercises of the ordinary branches of labor" (110–11), and Kerby Miller summarizes the dilemma: "Famine Irish usually entered the American workforce at the very bottom, competing only with free Negroes or—in the South—with slave labor for the dirty, backbreaking, poorly paid jobs that white native Americans and emigrants from elsewhere disdained to perform" (*Emigrants and Exiles*, 318). While jobs grew scarce for black men, black women in Philadelphia were able to find work as washerwomen (Ignatiev, 110). By contrast, as Mark Bulik describes in "1854: No Irish Need Apply," a 2015 retrospective for the *New York Times*, Irish Catholic women in New York were openly discriminated against in advertisements such as these:

> **Clean, active girl wanted**—to do the housework of a private family; must be a first-rate washer and ironer, a good plain cook, and kind and obliging to children. Apply at 27 Lamartine-place, 29th-st, between 8th and 9th avs. No Irish need apply.
> **Chambermaid and waiter wanted.** A girl to wait on the table and do chamber work is wanted at No. 63 East 17th-st. She must be a Protestant and with good recommendations.
> **An intelligent and experience Protestant woman wanted**—to take charge of one child and do light chamber work. No one need apply except those having the highest testimonials from their last employers. Inquire at No. 59 Pierropont-st., Brooklyn.

As these notices indicate, in mid-century New York, "No Irish need apply" often meant "*No Catholics need apply.*" Much the same was true in Boston, as one posting for the caretaker of a two-year-old boy emphasized: "*positively no Irish need apply.*"[9]

Such desperate conditions for both Irish immigrants and African Americans seized the attention of two of the most influential figures of America's nineteenth century—Abraham Lincoln and Frederick Douglass. Niall O'Dowd begins *Lincoln and the Irish: The Untold Story of How the Irish Helped Abraham Lincoln Save the Union* (2018) by underscoring Lincoln's disgust with his former party's prejudice against both blacks and Irish Catholics:

> By 1856, the Whig party Lincoln belonged to had destroyed itself over slavery and the violence of the Know-Nothings, an extremist group of nativists with a deep hatred of immigrants and Catholics that existed as an independent force but who were much closer to the Whigs and later the new Republican Party.
>
> Lincoln by then was well steeped in Irish culture, history, and politics. It was one reason he would have no truck with the Nativists and Know-Nothings. (23)

Know-Nothings feared that America was becoming a "haven for the world's rejects"—"mongrel races" and "Papists" who posed a threat of social contamination in a cultural paranoia that still echoes today when political candidates refer to their opponents as "vermin."

Lincoln, as I have suggested, harbored a very different opinion. And he not only loathed stereotyping but also began to doubt England's commitment to democracy given its colonial occupation of Ireland. This skepticism evolved during his Congressional career when he joined colleagues in drafting a statement in 1848 in support of the Hungarian Revolution, as the document's criticism of Britain's colonial rule intimates:

> [...] There is nothing in the past history of the British government, or in its present expressed policy, to encourage the belief that she will aid, in any manner, in the delivery of continental Europe from the yoke of despotism; and that her treatment of Ireland, of [William Smith] O'Brien, [John] Mitchel, and other worthy patriots, forces the conclusion that she will join her efforts to the despots of Europe in suppressing every effort of the people to establish free governments, based upon the principles of true religious and civil liberty.[10]

Examples of Lincoln's championing of the Irish abound. His defense of a wronged Irish colleague, for example, expands into a larger advocacy of Irishness in general, as the man possessed "a large share of sprightliness and generous feeling, which generally characterize Irishmen who have had anything of a fair chance in the world" (O'Dowd, 13). But he reserved his highest praise for the 150,000 soldiers who, as the Irish Brigade, fought for the Union during the Civil War. Formed in the fall of 1861 from New York's Fighting 69th division, the Brigade served for nearly four years motivated, in part, by Meagher's conviction that the secession of southern states was a "calamity." As a result, in speeches he proclaimed it the "duty" of Irish citizens "who aspire to establish a similar form of government in our native land" to fight for the Union (qtd. in O'Dowd, 60).

During the two decades preceding the War, years marred by Know-Nothing violence and rampant discrimination, the Irish became equated with slaves and British colonizers with white slaveholders. More than a century later, Brendan Behan and Tim Pat Coogan in separate indictments advanced a more damning juxtaposition of Britain's role in the Famine, comparing it to the Nazi "final solution" for Jewish prisoners.[11] In *Frederick Douglass: Prophet of Freedom* (2018), David W. Blight restates the allegation in more restrained terms: "No legacy of the famine is more embittered than the role of British policies, and imperial attitudes toward the Irish people in their time of greatest travail" (151). Copious evidence of such imperialist hubris exists, the most outrageous of which emerged in reports of relief initiatives in the London *Times* in 1847 that identified Irish indolence as responsible for the human tragedy, thus making the extraction of labor from victims advisable before any comfort is provided.

To put the sick and starving to work, the British created public works projects, some of them entirely useless, as Eavan Boland dramatizes in her poem

"The Famine Road" (1975). In the opening stanza, Boland ventriloquizes the orders of Sir Charles Trevelyan, manager of England's relief efforts, as rendered in a letter to his assistant, Colonel Jones, and subsequently presented to the Relief Committee:

> Idle as trout in light Colonel Jones,
> these Irish, give them no coins at all; their bones
> need toil, their characters no less.

The result of this soul-improving "toil"? The construction of roads "going nowhere of course" (*New Collected Poems*, 42). Anger over England's exportation of Irish agricultural products needed to be deflected; investigations of the neglect of absentee landlords, averted. Useless work projects provided a means to achieve both ends.

While most abolitionists, Irish and American, cast a critical eye on Britain's role in the catastrophe, some followed its lead by blaming the Irish themselves. On the eve of the Famine, one of the sharpest accusations of Irish indolence was voiced by Dublin printer Richard Webb, a member of the Hibernian Anti-Slavery Society and, for a time, Douglass's host in Dublin:

> We shall have a famine in Ireland in a month or two owing to the Potato Rot [...]. The government appears to be taking every precaution to lessen the suffering—and the Irish people none at all. (qtd. in Chaffin, 155)

In January 1842, however, three members of the Anti-Slavery Society, including Webb, wrote a document urging Irish America to work to abolish slavery and delivered an "Address from the People of Ireland to their Countrymen and Countrywomen in America" signed by 60,000 Irish citizens at a meeting in Boston's Faneuil Hall. The address included this admonition: "What a *spectacle* does America present to the earth! [...] A land of professing Christian republicans, uniting their energies for the oppression of three million of innocent human beings, the children of one common Father" (qtd. in Fenton, 86–87).[12] The address concluded by calling on Irish Americans to "*treat the colored people as your equals, as your brethren. By all your memories of Ireland, continue to love liberty—hate slavery* [...]" (qtd. in Chaffin, 65).

Frederick Douglass was in attendance that night. From the various discourses (scientific, economic, abolitionist) that compared American slaves with colonized Irish, from the competition between Irish immigrants and African Americans for employment, and from his own experience,

Douglass could hardly ignore the struggles of the Irish. When allowed to leave the Talbot County plantation on which he was enslaved in 1826 and move to what he fantasized as a better life in Baltimore, the then eight-year-old Frederick Bailey recalled the proverb that "being hanged in England is preferable to dying a natural death in Ireland" (*Narrative*, 43). He had, it seems, from his earliest years some intuition of Irish misery and deprivation, just as he occasionally felt a twinge of anti-Irish prejudice. But, as Tom Chaffin observes, Douglass had "affinities for the Emerald Isle. By happenstance, in at least two instances, Ireland had figured in his decision, years earlier, to flee from bondage to freedom" (15). The better known of these two instances occurred in 1830 when Douglass wandered onto a wharf in Baltimore where he helped two Irish navvies unload stones from a scow. After they finished, one of them asked Douglass if he was a "slave for life." When he acknowledged that he was, the "good Irishman" replied that "so fine a little fellow" as he should be free, and both men advised him to flee to the north where he could find both friendship and freedom (*Narrative*, 55). He followed their advice, and years later in August 1845, buoyed by the success of his *Narrative of the Life of Frederick Douglass* published earlier that year, Douglass embarked upon a speaking tour of Ireland and Britain, where he remained until the spring of 1847.

As scholars have emphasized—and as biographers of John F. Kennedy and Ronald Reagan have similarly recognized in their own subjects—Douglass's time in Ireland was transformative. He wrote to Garrison in the fall of 1845 that Irish people "know nothing of the republican negro hate prevalent in our glorious land [...]. Whatever may be said of the aristocracies here, there is none based on the color of a man's skin" (qtd. in Chaffin, 37). As David Blight adds, Douglass "traveled on all conveyances and 'was not treated as a color, but as a man'" (143). And he was an attractive man, drawing large crowds to his lectures and relishing "the adoration from young women" who "turned out in droves to see and hear him" in Cork and other cities (144). For a time, however, Douglass "aggressively thwarted" the "Irish Analogy," the notion that "the oppression and poverty of the Irish was equivalent to American slavery" (149). Nevertheless, the suffering of the Irish peasantry affected him deeply: "Too many self-styled 'philanthropists'," Douglass wrote, "care no more about Irishmen [...] than they care about the whipped, gagged, and thumb-screwed slave. They would as willingly sell on the auction block an Irishman, if it were popular to do so, as an African" (152). And, just as Thomas Meagher had worked to rally three all-Irish regiments into an Irish Brigade, after President Lincoln's reading of the Emancipation Proclamation Douglass barnstormed for the cause of black enlistment in the Union army. At this historic moment, the parallel causes of enslaved black Americans and

Irish subjugated by British rule, the so-called Irish Analogy that once gave Douglass pause, seemed more persuasive.

Five years after Lincoln declared that "all persons held as slaves [...] henceforward shall be free," the emancipation of slaves and Ireland's fight for independence continued to be paired on the New York and other stages. Daly exploits this conjunction in a curtain-lowering tableau in Act III of *A Flash of Lightning* after immigrants save a girl in distress in an underground shelter. As the scene ends, refrains from a song about an Irish soldier returning home after the civil war emphasize these twin struggles for freedom:

> But not alone he sails for home, and anchors in the tide—
> The soldiers of the Union are, a'standing by his side;
> Bold lads that in America had set the bondmen free,
> Now draw the swords for Ireland, 'gainst British tyranny! (52)

At a moment of high dramatic tension, Mrs. Dowderry's son Terry praises the courage of Irish soldiers fighting for the abolition of slavery and acknowledges—as Frederick Douglass had after witnessing the suffering of the Irish peasantry in the early months of the Famine—that freedom for Ireland and for African America were common causes. While speaking in Ireland a century later, an American president invoked this same historical moment and analogy.

Two Presidents in Ireland: Divided by Distance, United by History

> The 13th day of September, 1862, will be a day long remembered in American history. At Fredericksburg, Maryland, thousands of men fought and died on one of the bloodiest battlefields of the American Civil War. One of the most brilliant stories of that day was written by a band of 1200 men who went into battle wearing a green sprig in their hats. They bore a proud heritage and a special courage [...]. I am referring, of course, to the Irish Brigade.
>
> —John F. Kennedy, "Remarks of the President to a Joint Session of the Dáil, and Seanad Eireann," Leinster House, Dublin, Ireland (1963)

After thanking the Speaker of the House (Patrick Hogan), the Taoiseach (Seán Lemass) and members of the Parliament for inviting him to address the Oireachtas Éireann on June 28, 1963, John F. Kennedy began his remarks with this account of the courage of the Irish Brigade at Fredericksburg in a battle that only 258 of 1,200 troops survived. As the president recalled, even Confederate General Robert E. Lee could not contain his admiration of the Brigade: "Never were men so brave. They ennobled their race by their splendid gallantry on that desperate occasion. Their brilliant though hopeless assaults on our lines excited the hearty applause of our officers and soldiers." This episode of Union soldiers advancing in a battle they could never win while their opponents applauded their doomed efforts might have enlivened a playscript in the Theatre of the Absurd of the 1950s and 1960s. Yet, their sacrifice was all too real, the Brigade's persistence more than a Beckettian experiment in the postwar theatre. Instead, their bravery forged one of the "enduring links" that "have bound the Irish and the Americans since the earliest days." To honor their memory, the president presented his hosts with a framed copy of the Brigade's regimental flag because the original had been "torn to shreds by bullets." Like its antecedent, the flag bore the motto, "The Union, our country, and Ireland forever."

In his address, President Kennedy expanded upon this rallying cry, emphasizing both nations' commitment to and stewardship of freedom. Many of the president's examples, like the battle at Fredericksburg, returned his listeners to eighteenth- and nineteenth-century history: from Benjamin Franklin's appearance to the same body in 1772 and Lord Mountjoy's lament before Parliament in 1784 that England has "lost America through the Irish," to John Barry's service as the "Father of the Navy" and Charles Stewart Parnell's extended trip to America in the later nineteenth century. With Ireland in the throes of a second Famine, Parnell, often heralded as Ireland's uncrowned king, spoke before the U.S. House of Representatives on February 2, 1880 outlining the new emergency and its implications for Home Rule. While some congressmen grumbled ungenerously after his speech, Parnell remembered his stay in America fondly, and Kennedy cited his words when praising the encouragement and good will of his own hosts: "'I have seen since I have been in this country,' [Parnell] said, 'so many tokens of good wishes of the American people toward Ireland.' And today [...] I have seen in this country so many tokens of good wishes of the Irish people towards America." Thus, President Kennedy summarized, "our two nations, divided by distance, have been united by history."

Similarly united was the Kennedy family. The president had confessed to a crowd at New Ross in County Wexford the day before that it had taken some 115 years for a Kennedy to return to the home of his great-grandfather. But, as Ryan Tubridy notes in his account of the trip, this admission is slightly inaccurate, as in 1947, JFK accompanied his sister Kathleen to Ireland and driven through Wexford; and, on the eve of his inauguration, he sent a telegram to the people of New Ross expressing his hope to visit there (Tubridy, 110). His hopes were realized, and he began his address there by recalling

Patrick Kennedy's emigration in 1848 and arrival in Boston. Emphasizing that his great-grandfather possessed only a "strong religious faith" and a desire "for liberty," President Kennedy concluded by inviting members of his audience to stop at the White House if they ever visited the United States. This heartfelt gesture may have originated in a sentiment he related the next day: Ireland is a "free country and that is why any American feels at home" there. And it may be why his old friend and Special Assistant Dave Powers described JFK's visit to Ireland as perhaps the "happiest four days of his life."

The unprecedented success of his trip contributed to the president's exuberance. As Tubridy recounts, after landing in Dublin, Kennedy entered the city in an open convertible accompanied by Irish President Éamon de Valera; as the motorcade progressed, "enormous and excited" crowds greeted him. On O'Connell Street, between 60,000 and 80,000 people gave him a rousing reception: "Kitchen staff in white caps, waitresses in aprons and civil servants leaned out windows and cheered from rooftops as thousands threw ticker tape [...]" (102). As President de Valera told an interviewer three years later, "no other visitor, to my knowledge anyhow, has ever received" such a welcome. Not surprisingly given this reception, on June 29 as Kennedy prepared to board Air Force One at Shannon Airport for his return to Washington, he expressed his pride in his "Irish descent" and vowed to return in the spring to "see old Shannon's face again." "Everywhere he went," de Valera recalled, "more and more people got to like him, got an affection for him, and the result was that they were very, very, very sorry when he was leaving" (de Valera, "Recorded Interview," 3). Consistent with Dave Powers's memory, the subtitle of Tubridy's *JFK in Ireland: Four Days that Changed a President* (2010) advances the same thesis: JFK rediscovered his Irishness during his stay and he cherished it.

Twenty-one years later on June 4, 1984, a second American president addressed the Irish Parliament, Ronald Reagan (Richard Nixon visited Ireland in October 1970, but did not speak to the body). In an emotional aside, President Reagan alluded to President Kennedy's vow to return in the spring, a promise that, sadly, he could not keep. The very mention of this unfulfilled pledge induced a reverential silence in his audience, a display of respect that was breached numerous times during Reagan's visit (and before his arrival as well). That is to say, while President Kennedy was universally greeted with affection—as were Barack and Michelle Obama in May 2011, when an enormous crowd at Dublin's College Green applauded such remarks by the president as "Irish signatures are on our founding documents. Irish blood was spilled on our battlefields. Irish sweat built our great cities" (Lee, "President Obama in Dublin")—the reception President Reagan received was marked by loud expressions of disapprobation. Weeks before he arrived, several groups announced their plans to protest his visit. Some 500 protestors met Reagan's plane at Shannon on June 2, and seventy-five Jesuit priests organized nonviolent demonstrations against American policy in Central America. Five days later, 1000 Dubliners "chanted anti-American slogans" and marched through the streets carrying a coffin representing the bodies of three nuns murdered in El Salvador ("Dublin Protest Over Reagan Visit").

In addition, prior to his landing, sixteen members of Parliament announced their decision to boycott Reagan's appearance, and as he began his address on June 4, three members noisily walked out. Outside, protesters burned American flags and demanded that the United States leave El Salvador; others voiced their opposition to American nuclear policy. Two days earlier, public censure of his administration had disrupted his stop in Galway to receive an honorary degree (one of twenty conferred upon him by Notre Dame, Georgetown and other institutions). The news of the conferral on June 2 was well-publicized, leading some graduates to threaten to burn their degrees if University College Galway (since 1997, National University of Ireland-Galway) bestowed the award. Covering the event for the *New York Times*, R. W. Apple, Jr. characterized the mood in Galway as "subdued" and "strangely un-Irish" as the president's parade elicited only "polite applause and a flutter of plastic Irish and American flags rather than full-throated cheering." At some stops along the route, there were more policemen than spectators. Depicting a more lively scene in UPI releases, Cathy Booth noted that 1,000 protesters marched in the rain to the university, at one point releasing 2,500 black balloons, and three previous honorary degree recipients returned to "de-confer" their degrees. Ironically, Marian Robinson, Nancy Reagan's second cousin, was a visiting professor of English at the College. Anticipating Mary Trump's rebukes of her uncle decades later, Robinson voiced her strenuous opposition to Reagan's presidency: "As an American, I feel great shame that he represents my country. It would be nice if he was embarrassed by this protest, but he is so cushioned from any kind of public opinion I doubt he'll hear about it" (qtd. in Booth, "More Than 1000").

Events the next day at Ballyporeen in County Tipperary progressed more smoothly. There, Reagan told a gathering that he had only recently learned "from whence his ancestors came" and that he was very pleased to be at that place (Figure 1). Although as Robert Dallek puts it, Kennedy's family was eager to "replace their 'Irishness' with an American identity" (7), the president nevertheless possessed a "rudimentary" knowledge of his distant relatives (6). By contrast, as President Reagan explained in Ballyporeen, because his father was orphaned before he turned six and thus knew little about his family's background, neither did he, which is why he required the help of genealogists to find what one official there

Figure 1. President Reagan Receiving a Beer during a Visit to O'Farrell's Pub in Ballyporeen, Ireland, June 3, 1984. Ronald Reagan Presidential Library.

identified as his "ancestral home." After receiving several gifts, the president conveyed his thanks for the "wonderful homecoming" and for welcoming him home "after a long journey." The occasion proved so transformative that after his death, the Ronald Reagan Presidential Library and Museum memorialized it by purchasing the pub the president enjoyed so much. Its owners, the O'Farrell family, had already renamed a section of their seating area the "Ronald Reagan Salon" in his honor and, after a century of operation, closed the establishment in 2004. The Library purchased its beer and ale taps, fixtures and furnishings, had them shipped to California, and reassembled them in the museum.

Seemingly undisturbed by opposition to his visit—or, as Marian Robinson hypothesized, "insulated" from it—President Reagan, like President Kennedy, repeated the word "home" in his remarks to several Irish audiences. And like JFK and Frederick Douglass, he was deeply moved by his discoveries there. By this time in America, he had become known as a "Friend of Ireland," particularly after his huge electoral victory in 1984 (he received 525 electoral votes compared to Walter Mondale's 13 and won almost 59% of the popular vote). But the impact of his trip was more significant than a newly acquired knowledge of his roots; it reaffirmed his commitment to bipartisan support of Ireland and helped focus his attention on the violence in Northern Ireland.

This was not always the case. During his 1980 campaign, as a headline from a 2004 issue of *Independent.ie* recalled, "Reagan Feared his Irish Roots Would Damage his Career." As a result, candidate Reagan on occasion "played down" his Irishness and gave the impression that he was a "pedigree WASP." He adopted this tactic, some speculated, to please Republican voters. In supporting this claim, the *Independet.ie* described a conversation between Reagan and former Irish ambassador Seán Donlon before the 1980 election:

Donlon: You must be Irish, what part of Ireland do you come from?
Reagan: No, no, I am not Irish. I have an English background.

After his resounding victory over Jimmy Carter and independent candidate John Anderson, Reagan is alleged to have then said to the ambassador, "Now, I will be happy to embrace my Irishness. I will come to the embassy on St. Patrick's Day." And he did—more than once.

Some contend that Reagan's belated Irishness was the result of an earlier calculation that to cultivate support from Democratic leaders in Congress, he needed what Chris Matthews terms the "reinvention" of an Irish identity. That is, in *Tip and The Gipper* (2013), Matthews notes that at times President Reagan courted "disaffected Democrats—the Irish and Italians and Polish-Americans [...] who just didn't 'get' Jimmy Carter" (4). On these occasions, much as Kennedy recognized the importance of America's melting pot of immigrants, Reagan "morphed into if not quite an Irishman's Irishman then certainly a recognizable fellow ethnic" (5). This identity became more comfortable to inhabit after his victory in 1980 and his trip to Ireland.

Two weeks after his first election, Reagan visited Speaker of the House of Representatives Tip O'Neill in his office. Matthews recalls the Speaker's description of the pair as "two Irish-American pols" whose conversation that day was enlivened by stories of Notre Dame football and Reagan's role in *Knute Rockne, All American*. Recalling the conversation fondly, O'Neill added that despite their inevitable disagreements, "we were always friends after six o'clock and on weekends" (qtd. in Matthews 36, 37). In underscoring this growing friendship, both Matthews and Richard Aldous in *Reagan & Thatcher: The Difficult Relationship* (2012) describe in somewhat different ways one of the Reagans' first private dinners at the White House after his inauguration in 1981. Matthews identifies the guests as O'Neill and his wife, Millie; Jim Baker, Reagan's Chief of Staff, and his wife Susan; and Max Friedersdorf, Assistant to the President for Legislative Affairs, and his wife, Priscilla. Demonstrating his considerable skills as a raconteur, O'Neill related "colorful tales" that left his listeners "spellbound"; for his part, Reagan was "well stocked" with anecdotes and jokes that "enhanced the sense of camaraderie as he kept the group well entertained" (45). Aldous, by contrast, paints a more intimate portrait of two men who disagreed with each other in public but, while Nancy Reagan led Mrs. O'Neill on a tour of the White House, enjoyed whiskey, "aul Irish stories" and good-natured "craic" (53). In either case, an important relationship was beginning to evolve.

The first year of Reagan's presidency, March in particular, proved difficult, as I will describe in more detail in the next chapter. The month began with Bobby Sands's refusal of food at Long Kesh prison southwest of Belfast, sparking a hunger strike that claimed ten republicans' lives, and ended with John Hinckley, Jr.'s attempted assassination of the president, seriously wounding Reagan and three others including Press Secretary James Brady and Secret Service agent Tim McCarthy. Thanks to the quick actions of Special Agent Jerry Parr, and after several weeks of recovery, the president returned to work—and skirmishes with his sparring partner. The president described his interactions with the Speaker far better than I have when, five years later in the spring of 1986, he spoke at a dinner organized by Boston College honoring O'Neill. There, Reagan playfully characterized the relationship between these "two not-so-shy and not-so-retiring Irishmen" in a way he might not have expressed in 1980: "Imagine one Irishman trying to corner another Irishman in the Oval Office." At times, however, this friendship was tested as political tensions in America regarding Northern Ireland grew, and Reagan's alliance with Prime Minister Thatcher complicated matters. He also had to contend with the "Four Horsemen"—O'Neill, Democratic Senators Edward Kennedy and Daniel Patrick Moynihan, and New York Governor Hugh Carey—who lobbied for Ireland and Irish America on a host of issues with which Reagan could not always agree. Still, as Niall O'Dowd wrote in 2009 recalling the 1980s and the impact of Senator Kennedy's death on Irish-American relations, "It helped that another Irishman Ronald Reagan, also partial to the old sod, was in the White House." In portraying the Irish Reagan, O'Dowd referenced a "famous cartoon of the period" showing "Tip O'Neill and Reagan as two old Irish fishwives haggling over costs" ("A Staggering Blow"). And, no doubt, enjoying every minute of the dispute.

A More Complicated Irishness, "God Damn It"

> Fitzgerald, Earl of Kildare, poet, soldier [...] was summoned to Rome to explain his conduct in burning the Cathedral. The Pope asked why he had committed this enormous sacrilege. His lordship replied: 'I declare to Jesus, your holiness, I would have never have done it but I thought the archbishop was inside.'
> —Brendan Behan to JFK relating an anecdote about the fifteenth-century head of the president's "maternal clan," July 15, 1961

If Ronald Reagan embraced his Irishness after winning the 1980 election and visiting Ireland, the consensus is that JFK did as well after his trip to the "old sod" in 1963. Yet, as I have mentioned, while growing up Kennedy was encouraged to distance himself from his family's heritage, an estrangement Robert Dallek outlines in *An Unfinished Life: John F. Kennedy 1917–1963* (2003). In fact, Dallek begins his biography with an anecdote about Joseph P. Kennedy that echoes Garry Fallon's anti-Irish polemic in Augustin Daly's *A Flash of Lightning*:

> 'Goddamn it!' [Kennedy's father] once sputtered after a Boston newspaper identified him [as Irish]. 'I was born in this country! My children were born in this country! What the hell does someone have to do to become an American?' (3)

Inevitably, his antipathy affected his children, including young Jack whose friends regarded him as "more English than Irish" (3). This characterization, albeit expressed in more muted tones, persisted even as Kennedy's sense of Irish identity deepened after his 1963 trip, if not gradually and unevenly before (for example, he joined the Ancient Order of Hibernians in 1947). As Arthur Schlesinger, Jr., recalls, Kennedy's arrival in Dublin on June 26—earlier in the day, he had addressed a raucous crowd in West Berlin estimated at 450,000—initiated a "blissful interlude of homecoming, at once sentimental and ironic." Like Dave Powers, Schlesinger quickly sensed a change in the president: "I imagine that he was *never* easier, happier, more involved and detached, *more complexly himself*, than in the next few days" (885, my emphasis).

The disparity between this setting and that of Cold War Germany intensified his elation. Hours before his arrival in Ireland, Kennedy contemplated what had just taken place, "shocked and appalled" by the scene at the Berlin Wall where a "seething" horde in Rudolf Wilde Platz had "compressed itself into a single, excited, impassioned mass" (Schlesinger, 884). As if he were channeling Gustave Le Bon's *The Crowd: A Study of the Popular Mind* (1895), Schlesinger portrays an irrational mob that "roared like an animal" at Kennedy's remarks, and after the president uttered the famous "*Ich bin ein Berliner*" an "hysteria spread almost visibly through the square." Kennedy was "first exhilarated, then disturbed," Schlesinger recalled; "he felt [...] that if he had said 'March to the wall—tear it down,' his listeners would have marched" (885). The contrast between this frenzy and the warm homecomings he received in Wexford, Cork and Dublin was palpable; and in Limerick Kennedy reaffirmed his Irishness, stressing that while Ireland was not the land of his birth, "it is the land for which I hold the greatest affection."

As the years have passed, this idyllic account of President Kennedy's Irish trip has seldom been sullied by the revelation of an awkward encounter or embarrassing contretemps. But some *do* exist. One concerns his allusions to Irish literature in his remarks to the Parliament. To be fair, these errors seem—no, *are*—exquisitely petty, not "such stuff as dreams are made on" but rather the "stuff" with which pedants afflict their students. But they also afford glimpses into both his sentimentalism and his larger, forward-looking political goals.

While both Kennedy's and Reagan's speeches featured excerpts from Irish writing and political oratory, Kennedy's was the more literary. This is hardly surprising, for while both men were avid readers (contrary to snarky aspersions of Reagan by Margaret Thatcher's advisors and other critics), JFK was particularly interested in histories, biographies and modern literature.[13] And his tastes were eclectic. For example, when Kennedy first met Norman Mailer, Schlesinger imagined that the novelist must have answered scores more questions about his much-acclaimed *The Naked and the Dead* than about *The Deer Park*, which Kennedy discussed with him. Similarly, when meeting James Michener, the president revealed his fondness for *Fires of Spring*, not "the inevitable *Tales of the South Pacific*" (63). Indeed, his list of ten favorite books, first published in *Life* in 1961, spans a range of titles from works on John Quincy Adams, Abraham Lincoln and Lord Byron to Stendhal's *The Red and the Black* and Ian Fleming's *From Russia with Love*, although Schlesinger confides that the president's "supposed addiction to James Bond was partly a publicity gag" (105).

Missing from this list are any titles by Irish authors, although he must have enjoyed the irreverent humor in a note he received from Brendan Behan, who arrived in New York for the September 20, 1960, Broadway premiere of his play *The Hostage* and almost immediately became "ardently pro John F. Kennedy."[14] It may be the case, however, that the president didn't know the work of James Joyce and Bernard Shaw well, as he misquoted both in his address in Dublin. Alternatively, if, as Mark K. Updegrove remarks in *Incomparable Grace: JFK in the Presidency* (2022), Kennedy's speechwriters had failed him in Berlin—"This is terrible," Major General James Polk complained after reading a draft of his speech (243–44)—perhaps they did so again in Ireland. One error was identified by Joyce scholar Robert Nicholson, who wrote to the *Irish Times* (June 6, 2009) about Kennedy's misquotation of *Ulysses*. In his address, the president referred to Joyce's metaphorization of the Atlantic Ocean as a "bowl of bitter tears" but, as Nicholson points out, in the first episode of *Ulysses* Dublin Bay, not the Atlantic Ocean, is described as a "bowl of bitter *waters*." The president "or his speech-writer," Nicholson speculates, "probably guessed that none of his audience knew *Ulysses* well enough to catch him out" when recasting Joyce, the "proud and willful exile," as "yet another sentimental Irishman grieving over the Diaspora." Nicholson's correction illuminates a well-worn stereotype of American Irishness that hardly connotes Joycean pride or willfulness. Instead, the image of the Atlantic Ocean as a tureen of "bitter tears" evokes a sorrow that misrepresents the ambitions of émigrés like JFK's great-grandparents Patrick and Bridget eager to find greater opportunity in a new home.

Kennedy's reference to Shaw's *Back to Methuselah* (1922), subtitled "A Metabiological Pentateuch" or "A Play Cycle in Five Parts," is more complicated and significant. He introduced the oft-quoted passage very simply: "George Bernard Shaw, speaking as an Irishman, summed up an approach to life." But in the lines the president (mis)quotes, Shaw was *not* speaking as an Irishman; in fact, he wasn't speaking at all. Rather, this line, commonly associated with Robert Kennedy and printed on posters that adorned college dormitory rooms in the 1970s, was spoken to Eve in the play's opening act by the Serpent in the Garden of Eden. Here is the version the president read:

"Other peoples," he said, "see things and say:
'Why?' [...] But I dream things that never were—
And I say: 'Why not?'"

In Part One of *Back to Methuselah*, however, the passage is rendered very differently as the Serpent addresses Eve:

THE SERPENT: When you and Adam talk, I hear you say 'Why?' Always 'Why?' You see things; and you say 'Why?' But I dream things that never were; and I say 'Why not?' (Shaw, *CPP* 2: 7).

The Serpent attributes Adam's obsession with causality—Why did something happen? Why are things as they are?—to his privileging of the past over *her* hopeful vision of the future (Shaw feminizes the snake). Which will Eve find more attractive, his past or her future? His fear or her hope? As Adam makes clear, "Fear is stronger in me than hope. I must have certainty"; as such, he regards hope as "wicked" while certainty is "blessed" (*CPP* 2: 17). Conversely, with her eyes cast straight ahead, the Serpent claims, "I fear certainty as you fear uncertainty [...]. If I bind the future I bind my will. If I bind my will I strangle creation." Eve sides with the Snake: "Creation must not be strangled. I tell you I will create [...]" (*CPP* 2: 18).

A similar tension distinguishes Kennedy's Irishness—an amalgam of nostalgic sentiment and progressive, forward-looking hope—from that of

President Reagan, whose Irish identity transported him back to a genealogy of which he was largely unaware. This ignorance may have been something of an asset, as nostalgia would have clashed with his staff's promotion of Reagan and Margaret Thatcher as forward-thinking, "like-minded leaders" with their "sleeves rolled up" and a shared disposition of "sobriety with optimism" (Aldous, 35). At the same time, his newly discovered Irishness helped him develop a rapport with powerful Democratic congressmen, and both Ireland and America were the better for it. At the same time, Reagan's Irishness had little to do with Catholicism, while for Kennedy Irishness and Catholicism were so tightly braided as to be inseparable. Or so it seemed in moments when both religion and ethnic origin posed obstacles to his political success. As the 1960 election neared, however, his Catholicism proved to be the greater concern.

Little Boy Blue, "That Old Asshole" and the Pope

> Contrary to common newspaper usage, I am not the Catholic candidate for President. I am the Democratic Party's candidate for President who happens also to be Catholic.
> —John F. Kennedy, September 12, 1960

> I denounce you as the anti-Christ.
> —Ian Paisley to Pope John Paul II, 12 October 1988

In his "Address to the Greater Houston Ministerial Association" less than two months before the 1960 election, Kennedy attempted to allay his audience's anxiety that the Pope controls Catholics' every decision. Nearly thirty years later in 1988, anti-Catholic prejudice continued to inflect politics, in this instance international politics. For as he began to address the European Parliament, Pope John Paul II was interrupted, much as Ronald Reagan had been in Dublin speaking to the Irish Parliament, by shouts from the back of the assembly. The heckler was the Reverend Ian Paisley, leader of Northern Ireland's Democratic Unionist Party (DUP), who outrageously denounced the pope as the "anti-Christ" and gave voice to the same superstitions that lingered in the atmosphere of 1960s America. Three years after JFK's assassination, Éamon de Valera remembered his earlier concerns in 1960 that, in the privacy of the voting booth, Americans might succumb to the same biases:

> We followed [Kennedy's] candidature fairly closely. We were wondering whether the prejudice which operated so severely against Al Smith would still be strong enough to defeat him. ("Recorded Interview")

Here, de Valera is referring to Smith's 1928 nomination for president, the first Catholic to win a major political party's endorsement. His fears were well-founded, for just three years before Smith's candidacy 1,000 members of the Ku Klux Klan marched in Washington to protest the possibility of any Roman Catholic's election to an office in the federal government.

Historians tend to agree that, of Kennedy's several liabilities as a candidate, his Catholicism was potentially the most serious. But there were others, his youth for example. Mark Updegrove describes Kennedy's cool amicability with Dwight D. Eisenhower in the transition meetings before his inauguration. In fact, after the election Kennedy and his team met twice with Eisenhower's staff, even though the outgoing president was "stung" by the young senator's attacks on his record and regarded his election victory as a "repudiation of his administration" (11). Behind the scenes, their aides on occasion used the humorous, if unflattering, sobriquets their bosses had invented for the other man: to Eisenhower, Kennedy was "Little Boy Blue"; for Kennedy, his predecessor was "that old asshole," a "military term reserved by junior officers for the top brass" (Updegrove, 10). Dallek observes that the "two men did not have high regard for each other" and that Kennedy tended to view his elder as a "fuddy-duddy, a sort of seventy-year-old fossil." For his part, Eisenhower's "Little Boy Blue" was also a "young whippersnapper," more "a celebrity than a public servant" (Dallek, 302). Since then, with the elections of a movie actor (Reagan), a jazz saxophonist wannabe (Clinton) and a reality television star (Trump), this last charge constitutes more of a comment on the ascendant power of celebrity in an age of mass and social media than a substantial criticism. After all, by December 6, 1960, the date of their first meeting, Kennedy had served in the House and Senate since 1947, refuting Eisenhower's deprecation of the Kennedys as "arrivistes" (Dallek, 302). Like the issue of age (Little Boy Blue was 43 in 1960), questions about his health persisted: he suffered from colitis, Addison's disease and chronic back pain made worse after his PT boat was rammed by a Japanese destroyer on August 2, 1943, near the Solomon Islands. As George Smathers (D-FL) portrayed him in 1947 when he and Kennedy began their Congressional careers, Kennedy "didn't look well. He was not well, he was in pain most of the time."

As I have mentioned, Kennedy's ethnicity presented another potential problem that was slowly transmuted into an asset. His mother and sisters hosted popular teas attended by Irish American women, many of whom then worked on his campaign. And his candidacy was supported by a number of ethnic Americans: Italians, Jews, Poles, Slovaks, Greeks and others (Dallek, 175). For Torby Macdonald, a Massachusetts congressman and former roommate of Kennedy at Harvard, such endorsements augured a major advance for the ongoing project of American multiculturalism. He shared this intuition with his friend:

> I think that you represent the best of the new generation. Not generation in age but minorities, really. The newer arrived people [...]. I think there are more of the newly arrived people than there are of the old-line Yankees. (qtd. in Dallek, 175)

There is, to be sure, an irony in this observation for at that time, Dallek alleges, Kennedy's interest in the burgeoning civil rights movement was "more political than moral." To his detractors, both Kennedy's and Lyndon Johnson's commitment to the civil rights of minority Americans seemed little more than a "strategy," the "best way to advance their presidential ambitions" (215). Of course, the civil rights movement would evolve into much more than a political stratagem in both America and Northern Ireland.

Yet however transactional his political strategies or accurate Andrew Young's criticism that Kennedy knew "almost nothing" about race (qtd. in Updegrove, 85), he played an indispensable role in the creation of a more inclusive and diverse society. And however dubious the thesis that a wealthy, white Ivy Leaguer could represent "newly arrived" immigrants and ethnic minorities, this argument gained traction in the 1960 presidential election. Four years earlier in 1956, his father had encouraged Jack with a prediction that anticipated Macdonald's on this very issue: "There's a whole new generation out there and it's filled with the sons and daughters of immigrants from all over the world and those people are going to be mighty proud that one of their own was running for President." Besides, the elder Kennedy added, "this country is not a private preserve for Protestants" anymore (qtd. in Dallek, 211).

In the months preceding the election, his son, like my grandmother and President de Valera, was not so sure: "Most discouraging to Jack was the persistence of the country's irrational anti-Catholicism. Fourteen years had passed since he entered politics, and still Jack was being asked the same offensive questions" (Dallek, 246). In April 1960, the results of primary voting in Wisconsin brought this prejudice more sharply into focus, for even though he won some 60% of the state's convention delegates, he lost to Hubert Humphrey in Protestant-dominated western and rural areas. "When Jack heard the returns," Dallek observed, "he jumped from his seat and paced the room, muttering, 'Damn religious thing'" (251). And, as is well known, that "religious thing" reemerged on the night of the presidential election, particularly in Illinois where, late in the evening (actually, early in the morning of the next day), a huge vote for Kennedy in Chicago initially appeared not to "offset the overwhelmingly heavy Nixon vote" downstate. As Doris Kearns Goodwin so beautifully describes, "Downstate Illinois was as Protestant and Republican as Cook County was Democratic and Catholic: their alien ways of life fixed in suspicious confrontation across the borders of Cook County" (805). Much like the border at Newry between Northern Ireland and the Republic, that between the "Second City" and the Illinois heartland marked much more than differences in architectures, religion or lifestyles. It still does.[15]

Historians like Dallek and Updegrove adduce other reasons for Kennedy's wariness of America's anti-Catholic bias. Updegrove recalls the scuffles he and his brothers fought as schoolboys, and the obstacles their mother confronted in her "attempts to climb the social ranks in New York," all originating in their religion (34). Years later, after coming close to making the 1956 Democratic ticket as its vice-presidential candidate, Kennedy told his father that he "had fun" in the attempt and didn't "make a fool" of himself. Updegrove revises this sentiment in more positive ways: "Far from that, he had shined elegantly in the national spotlight, proving that he could be a viable national candidate despite his Catholicism" (44).

To bolster this viability four years later, two months before the 1960 election, Kennedy appeared before 300 ministers in Houston hoping to revise their misconceptions about Catholicism and ease their anxieties about him. There, he outlined priorities that he believed had been "obscured" by questions about his faith: the spread of communist influence in the west, the "humiliating treatment" of the president by foreign leaders who no longer respected America, and the plights of hungry children in West Virginia and older citizens who could no longer pay their doctors' bills. Of equal importance, he then moved to what today is one of Trumpism's most dangerous advocacies: Christian nationalism. In Kennedy's vision of America, because "no Catholic prelate or Protestant minister" dictates or interferes with an administration's decision-making, presidents are not torn by any "divided loyalty." With admirable tenacity, he observed that while he fought in the Pacific and his older brother Joe died in Europe defending America, no one accused them of belonging to a "disloyal group" ("Address to the Greater Houston Ministerial Association"). Why should this insinuation seem creditable now?

This question led him to the *raison d'être* of his appearance and anticipates Ian Paisley's character assassination of the Pope two decades later: the suspicion that a Catholic president or world leader would serve as a puppet of the Church and therefore could not act in the people's best interest. Although Kennedy mentioned the Pope only once, his comments returned his audience to his principled resistance to the putative manipulations of "Catholic prelates" and "Church leaders."

If elected, he vowed not to serve as the "instrument of any religious group"; thus, the "pamphlets and publications [...] that carefully select quotations out of context from the statements of Catholic Church leaders, usually in other countries, frequently in other centuries" are guilty of intentionally misleading their readership and fomenting unfounded conspiracy theories ("Address to the Greater Houston").

Kennedy was eventually able to overcome such prejudice; further, in his capacity as a cultural and political analyst that night in Houston, some of his predictions were uncannily accurate, none more so than the first issue on his list of challenges obscured by anti-Catholic prejudice: the expanding influence of communism ninety miles off the American shore. This premonition of the Cuban missile crisis was preceded by an equally astute conclusion about Ireland that Kennedy, working as a journalist fifteen years earlier, reached in noting that "the problem of partition seems very far from being solved" ("Eamon de Valera Seeks to Unite all Ireland"). The two chapters that follow examine this problem and America's evolving commitment to help Ireland address partitioning and its consequences. That is to say, and numerous scholars and historians have said it, while Kennedy may have been "transformed" personally by his experiences in Ireland, U.S. foreign policy concerning Ireland remained largely unchanged during his term of office. It would take the work of later presidents from both parties, even ones not always warmly embraced in Ireland, to help effect this change as aided by often unheralded diplomats, aides and their counterparts in England, Ireland and Northern Ireland. This challenge is the subject of the next two chapters.

Notes

1 The precise number of exiles who left Ireland during the Famine is almost impossible to calculate. In *Ethnic Americans: A History of Immigration* (5th edition, 2009), Leonard Dinnerstein and David M. Reimers set the number slightly lower than Miller, at 1.7 million Irish entering America between 1840 and 1860. That Miller includes Canada in his data may account for the difference.
2 In *Born Fighting*, James Webb estimates that, in the first of three great migrations between 1717 and the Revolutionary War, some 250,000–400,000 people, the majority Scots-Irish Presbyterians from Ulster, settled in America.
3 Returning to New York from his trip west in *A Flash of Lightning*, Jack Ryver exclaims, "The West—you know out west, where I've been, on the borders of the world [...]. No homes, no love, no women! [...] Men are no more than brutes. Cheating, swindling, murder!" (34).
4 There is room for disagreement with my claim about the importance of *A Flash of Lightning*. The subtitle of Jonathan M. Hess's *Deborah and Her Sisters: How One Nineteenth-Century Melodrama and Host of Celebrity Actresses Put Judaism on the World Stage* (Philadelphia: University of Pennsylvania Press, 2017), for example, tracks the influence of *Leah*. That Daly would dramatize the struggles of both Jewish and Irish characters isn't surprising.

As Doris Kearns Goodwin implies by quoting twice from Irving Howe's *World of Our Fathers*, the struggles of Irish and Jewish immigrants were in many ways similar (See Goodwin 6, 13).

5   This estimate comes from Timothy Egan, *The Immortal Irishman*, 134.
6   In *The First Kennedys*, Neal Thompson emphasizes that, upon arriving in America in 1847, Kennedy's great-grandmother Bridget Murphy described her occupation by giving "the answer most women on board did" : she "declared herself a *servant*" (22).
7   See Charles Fanning's introduction to James T. Farrell's *A World I Never Made*, x-xiv, which discusses Farrell's objections to the stereotyping and predictable forms of proletarian literature. Farrell borrowed the term "bottom dog" from the title of a 1930 Edward Dahlberg novel.
8   Fallon is identified as hailing from County Kerry, not from Ulster, and Anbinder notes that "five times as many natives of impoverished County Kerry" patronized New York's Emigrant Savings Bank "as did immigrants from more prosperous County Antrim" (748). Although Goodwin, Ignatiev, Clark and others are right to stress the hardships of Irish immigrants, not all new arrivals from counties hard hit by the Famine were doomed to poverty.
9   See Thompson, 47–55, for this advertisement and other disparagements of Irish "biddies."
10 Quoted in O'Dowd, 13. Lincoln's regard of Young Ireland anticipates that of James Joyce, who valued the movement's literary contributions as highly as Lincoln did its thirst for freedom. See Joyce's essay "James Clarence Mangan," in *James Joyce: The Critical Writings*, 175–86.
11 For a discussion of this homology, see my *"Something Dreadful and Grand,"* 179–89.
12 Fenton renders the title of this "Address" slightly differently. I have used both the title as specified by Tom Chaffin in *Giant's Causeway* and his punctuation of its conclusion.
13 Before Mrs. Thatcher met with Reagan in February 1981, she had been warned by advisors that he "did not appear 'to suffer from an excess of reading or any marked thirst for the more complicated sorts of information'" (qtd. in Aldous, 37). Such aspersions led some to view Reagan as lacking the intellectual wherewithal to be president, a criticism rebutted by the fact that he was a "keen and constant bookworm" and by the assessments of such White House staffers as David Gergen, who believed "most people underestimated the president's 'steel-trap mind'" (qtd. in Aldous, 27).
14 Rae Jeffs describes Behan as "ardently pro John Kennedy" (140). For this reason, as he describes in *Brendan Behan's New York*, Behan felt "privileged to receive" an invitation to Kennedy's inauguration (28), an invitation he was forced to decline because of his health. Ironically, Behan completed the book on November 22, 1963, but the exhilaration of doing so was quickly displaced by news of the president's assassination. In Dublin at the time helping Behan finish the book, Jeffs was immediately worried about how he would react to the tragedy (238). A diabetic and heart patient, he sought consolation from an old demon, alcohol, and its effects killed him some four months later.
15 The rift between Chicago and downstate Illinois continues. In 2019, some GOP legislators sought to force Chicago to secede from the state and become the 51st state; in 2022, 20 downstate counties introduced referendums to separate themselves from Cook County. See Whitney Lloyd and James Nevereau.

Provocation 1

TRUMPISM AND TROUBLES: CLIMATIC CENSORSHIP, AUTHORITARIAN POPULISM AND THE RELIGIOUS RIGHT

Trumpism (Trump-izm) *n.* **1.** Beliefs held by supporters of Donald Trump, also known as the MAGA movement, rendering many incapable of "reasonable argumentation," one way in which Trumpism is "adjacent to fascism" (Kristol). **2.** A politics supported by evangelical Christians, many of whom advocate for a Christian nationalism. **3.** A cult of personality predisposed to misogynistic, homophobic, xenophobic and racist rhetoric; to the abuse of such terms as "patriot," "political prisoner" and "traitor"; and to the dissemination of conspiracy theories. **4.** A nationalist zealotry that promotes American exceptionalism and devalues historical alliances. **5.** A politics committed to the acquisition and maintenance of power through such means as voter suppression, gerrymandering, and vilification. **6.** An authoritarian populism similar to Thatcherism in 1980s Britain in which a deregulated capitalism akin to that championed by neoliberalism and lower taxes for the wealthy are promoted as beneficial to all social classes. **7.** A grift or con. **8.** A worldview that disparages expertise as elitism and attacks educational and governmental institutions. **9.** A "progressive disease" (Taylor).

On June 17, 2022, Donald Trump addressed the "Road to Majority" conference in Nashville, Tennessee, organized by the Faith and Freedom Coalition. In addition to the former president, other featured speakers included former Secretary of State Mike Pompeo and Press Secretary Kayleigh McEnany, then GOP Chair Ronna McDaniel, televangelist and senior pastor at the First Baptist Church in Dallas Dr. Robert Jeffress, and radio show host Michael Medved. With the exception of Medved, whom a 2016 *Politico* article dubbed the only "vehemently anti-Donald Trump" host at Salem Media

(Gold, "Michael Medved"), the roster of keynote speakers confirmed the pro-Trump tone of the meeting as reported on the Coalition's website: "Evangelical activists reinforce[d] Trump's dominance of the GOP" and gave the former president a "warm reception" (June 21, 2022). In his remarks, Trump attacked the Select Committee on January 6, particularly its finding that he pressured Vice President Mike Pence either to return electors' votes to the states or declare the 2020 presidential election invalid. As the Committee's hearings continued into the fall of 2022 and a flurry of indictments followed in 2023, other revelations caused defendant Trump—and much of the nation—even greater consternation.

But not most evangelicals. As a headline in the *Washington Post* emphasized on January 16, 2024, reporting on the Iowa caucuses, "Trump's biggest Iowa gains are in evangelical areas, smallest wins in cities" (Keating et al.). And, as Tim Alberta reminds readers in *The Kingdom, the Power, and the Glory: American Evangelicals in an Age of Extremism* (2023), this same "lecherous, impenitent scoundrel" received 81% of the evangelical vote in 2016 (1). Eight years later, after ninety-one indictments and verdicts of civil liability for sexual assault, defamation and corporate fraud, white evangelicals still support a man who, through his demonization of immigrants and penchant for lying about opponents, would "have made Barabbas blush" (Alberta, 77).

Over the same June weekend of 2022, the Republican Party of Texas gathered in Houston to debate a platform of defining "planks." These included the allegation that Joe Biden's 2020 presidential victory was not legitimate, a condemnation of homosexuality as an "abnormal lifestyle choice," the mandate that school children study the "humanity of the pre-born child" and the recommendation that Texas should secede from the Union. As *The Texas Tribune* (June 18, 2022) reported, these proposals "capped a convention that highlighted how adamantly opposed the party's most active and vocal members are to compromising with Democrats or moderating on social positions, even as the state has grown more diverse and Republican margins in statewide elections have shrunk [...]" (Chan and Neugeboren, "Texas Republican Convention"). The meeting also provided opportunities for attendees to malign politicians whose positions were deemed insufficiently Trumpian. Some loudly booed Senator John Cornyn, for example, the lead Republican in bipartisan discussions of gun safety in the Senate. And his efforts to appease his detractors by boasting that he had "kept President Biden's gun grabbing wish list off the table" and prevented assault rifles from being banned were wildly ineffective.

Representative Dan Crenshaw was greeted in an even more unsettling way. At one moment, he and his aides were assaulted, and the Congressman was disparaged as a "globalist RINO," a pejorative Trump applied in 2023 to Cornyn, Rupert Murdoch and Representative Tom Emmer (R-MN) after he was nominated to replace Kevin McCarthy as Speaker of the House. At another moment, Crenshaw was taunted as "eyepatch McCain." The former slur stems from his endorsement of the World Economic Forum's support of Ukraine, which was opposed by several "almost pro-Russian" Republicans, or so he countered. He was also branded a "traitor" by one attendee at the meeting, who recommended that he be hanged. As for the "eyepatch McCain" slur, Crenshaw, a former Navy SEAL wounded in an explosion in Afghanistan, *does* resemble John McCain: both men were highly decorated for their military service, Crenshaw receiving a Purple Heart and two Bronze Stars. Trumpism sneers at military bravery and selflessness, perverting the language traditionally descriptive of heroism and love of country. In this lexicon, the mob that attacked Capitol police with baseball bats and hockey sticks on January 6 were "patriots"; a soldier partially blinded in battle is a "traitor"—or a "loser."

Shortly after the "Road to Majority" conference ended, MAGA Republicans confirmed one of the more insidious of the overdetermined origins of Trumpism, one contrary to the reassurances John F. Kennedy offered an audience of ministers in 1960: namely, that religion would never dictate his governance and that his administration would insist on the separation of Church and State. But this tenet is under siege by Trump supporters. Speaking at the Cornerstone Christian Center in Basalt, Colorado a week after the Nashville conference, self-described "ultra MAGA" supporter Representative Lauren Boebert (R-CO) defiantly told the congregation that "The church is supposed to direct the government." She added: "I'm tired of this separation of church and state junk that's not in the Constitution. It was in a stinking letter [by Thomas Jefferson], and it means nothing like what they say it does" (Suliman and Bella, "GOP Rep. Boebert"). This inchoate rant apparently resonated with the organizers of CPAC 2023, where Boebert was a featured speaker. As JFK warned, the separation of Church and State is essential to democracy's survival, and Trumpism imperils democracy by endorsing the notion of a Christian nationalism (Figure 2).

MAGA doctrine is rooted in more secular ideology as well, in its opposition to globalism, for example, its selective disregard of globalization and its legitimation of violence. In addition to its abuse of insufficiently Trumpian republicans, MAGA loyalists exhibit a total indifference to Donald Trump's former reliance upon desperately poor Chinese workers to manufacture silk ties bearing his name—ties, as Marissa Miller reported in 2016, made in Shengzhou under "horrific, sweatshop-like conditions"—and the fact that the items in his daughter Ivanka's now defunct fashion line were

Figure 2. Donald Trump Embracing the American Flag in 2019, as displayed at the 2024 Conservative Political Action Conference (CPAC). Courtesy of Alamy.

manufactured outside the United States. MAGA's deployment of such terms as "globalist RINO," in other words, threatens more than fragile supply chains. It conceals the identities and hypocrisy of the real exploiters of globalized labor.

Like a virus, MAGA's legitimation of violence directed at "others" has not been confined to America. In Ireland, as Patrick Freyne and Ula Mullaly reported in the *Irish Times*, 2022 was the "most violent year" for LGBTQ+ people in Europe in the past decade. In 2023, the resurgence of hostility between Israel and Hamas sparked anti-immigrant riots in Dublin's City Centre. On the evening of November 23, as Garda Commissioner Drew Harris described, a "lunatic faction driven by far-right ideology" responded to a knife attack supposedly perpetrated by a "foreigner" by igniting firebombs and looting stores, a riot that took 400 police officers to quell. On October 31, 2023, FBI Director Christopher Wray, testifying in front of Congress on rising antisemitism, calculated that "a group that makes up 2.4%, roughly, of the American public" are the victims of "something like 60% of all religious-based hate crimes." Attacks on Palestinians and anti-Muslim incidents are on the rise in America, paralleling candidate Trump's threat to implement ideological "screening" of immigrants. "If you don't like our religion—which a lot of them don't," he said, "then we don't want you in our country [...]" (qtd. in Bump, "Trump pledges"). This incivility shows no signs of subsiding without both a principled dialogue between opposing political parties *and*, as I shall explain, the freedom to object to the policies or actions of their own tribe without fear of reprisal or ostracism, an issue John Hume foregrounded in the years preceding the violence of the Troubles.

Climatic Censorship, Inclusion and Consent

Some six months after President Kennedy's assassination, John Hume (1937–2020) published a seminal two-part article in the *Irish Times* (May 18 and 19, 1964). Then just twenty-seven and a teacher in Derry where he was born, Hume went on to cofound the Social Democratic and Labour Party (SDLP) in 1970; and, along with Ulster Unionist David Trimble, was awarded the Nobel Peace Prize in 1998 for playing pivotal roles in brokering the Belfast (Good Friday) Agreement. Years later Senator George Mitchell, who presided over the negotiations, called Hume the "primary architect" of the Agreement and, as such, a "Founding Father" of the new Northern Ireland (Fitzpatrick, "John Hume," ix, x). While there is more to be said about both Nobel honorees, for now I want to juxtapose the thesis of Hume's 1964 essay with the current politico-ideological moment in America. For, as I mentioned in the previous chapter, much like President Kennedy, who in a 1947 article regarded the creation of Northern Ireland (a.k.a. "the partition") as an almost insuperable obstacle to Irish unification and peace, Hume in 1964 foresaw the ramifications of an obdurate and calcifying sectarianism. Sixty years later, many of the symptoms he diagnosed define Trumpism in America.

In the early 1960s, Hume sensed the beginning of Troubles in the emergence of the civil rights movement and responses to the marches that followed culminating in the January 4, 1969, ambush at the Burntollet Bridge outside Derry. Novels and plays set in the period often foreground the subjective histories that parallel these violent confrontations, forming a chronicle of psychical injury and the changed feeling of daily life. In Louise Kennedy's *Trespasses* (2022), for example, the novel's protagonist Cushla Lavery "lived in a garrison town, although it had not felt like one until 1969, when the [British] troops were sent in [...]" (8). As the violence raged, collective anxiety grew, even for the children Cushla taught:

> Booby trap. Incendiary device. Gelignite. Nitroglycerine. Petrol bomb. Rubber bullets Saracen. Internment. The Special Powers Act. Vanguard. The vocabulary of a seven-year-old child now. (18)

Troubles, like Trumpism, invade consciousness itself; vocabularies expand and feeling is altered by such terms as "wokeness" and "internment," "vermin" and "petrol bomb."

Hume was hardly the only observer who anticipated violence on the Ulster horizon. Former Sinn Féin president Gerry Adams, who as a teenager in 1965 worked as a barman at a public house in a Protestant neighborhood, felt much the same sense of foreboding. Then, he noted, patrons of the pub "felt under no threat and they presented no threat," but just a year later, the social fabric had grown threadbare, and "peaceful polarization was fraying at the edges" (Adams, 41, 42). One of Hume's suggestions to counter this social unraveling is equally relevant today: foster inclusion *across* faiths. Only then, he argued, can religion begin "to make its exit from politics." Otherwise, discrimination against Northern Catholics would continue to restrict their franchise and foreclose the possibility of equal opportunities in housing, education and employment. Because these inequities also led to a rising tide of emigration, Hume underscored the urgency of the crisis: "In the waiting the fear is that frustrations may force one to leave the North. It is little wonder that many do." Although Trumpism has not yet sparked such an exodus—the ramifications of the Supreme Court's 2022 repeal of *Roe v. Wade* may eventually necessitate a revision of this sentence—Hume's point is nonetheless applicable to a twenty-first-century America riven by division and mistrust. Because his argument also cautioned that "weak opposition leads to corrupt government," opponents of Trumpism need both to acknowledge their prior failures in responding to it and redouble their efforts in exposing its danger.

Hume's 1964 essay was reissued by the *Irish Times* in a "Special Tribute Supplement" on August 8, 2020, to commemorate his passing on August 3 and was accompanied by articles lauding his many accomplishments. Several of these reference the widening political chasm in contemporary America, one catalyst of which originates in what Hume termed *climatic censorship* that contributed to the near absence of meaningful debate. He employed the term in referring to a self-censorship discernible in the reluctance of many Catholics "to speak their minds for fear of recrimination" from other Catholics. In contemporary America, a similar phenomenon explains the ill-treatment of John Cornyn and Dan Crenshaw at the 2022 meeting of Texas Republicans, and MAGA condemnation of Representatives Liz Cheney and Adam Kinzinger for participating in the January 6 Congressional hearings. As a result, Hume saw that "little freedom of thought or expression" existed in Belfast or Derry in the 1960s, which in turn complicated efforts at problem-solving and suppressing hostile impulses (Figure 3). Climatic censorship also contributed to harmful stereotyping: "A man [who] wishes

Figure 3. John Hume Investigating Disturbance in Derry, 1996. Courtesy of Robert W. White.

Northern Ireland to remain part of the United Kingdom" is not necessarily "a bigot or a discriminator," Hume maintained, and the "dangerous equation of nationalism and Catholicism has [...] contributed to the postponement of the emergence of normal politics," making "the task of the unionist ascendancy simpler."

How can a "normal" politics be restored if citizens are afraid to speak, or if they are punished by their own political side for doing so? Although much of the blame for the absence of meaningful dialogue might be ascribed to the Unionist government, Hume did not re-narrativize sectarian division as a melodrama with Protestant villains and Catholic heroes, nor did he absolve nationalists of responsibility for the country's ills, particularly insofar as their negativism is concerned: "Nationalists in opposition have been in no way constructive. They have quite rightly been loud in their demands for rights, but they have remained silent and inactive about their duties." One of these duties is to make it possible for members of both communities to achieve a measure of social and economic success: "Who can conceive a prosperous North attached to either London or Dublin," he asked, "without the Northern Protestant?" (7). The answer relies neither upon "magical thinking" nor a vision of the dissolution of Northern Ireland;

rather, it is rooted in Hume's insistence that the mode of change should be "gradualist, participatory, and inclusive" (Fitzpatrick, 3).

But, like political compromise in twenty-first-century America, inclusiveness and meaningful dialogue between disputants in 1960s Northern Ireland seemed unrealistic, even utopian. Aware of this, as Fionnuala O'Connor recounts, Hume was determined to ensure "that the voice of anti-violence nationalism be heard over the noise of war," a pacifism difficult to cultivate in a city like Derry "subdued by gerrymandering and discrimination." There, the Catholic majority "was crammed into one ward with eight seats on Derry Corporation," while the "much smaller Protestant community spread over two wards had twelve" (6). This also meant, among other things, that while overcrowding and the spread of disease plagued Catholic neighborhoods, they couldn't find housing anywhere else, in part because their relocation might impact the gerrymander instituted to dilute the strength of their vote.

Similar tactics are much in evidence in contemporary America. As MSNBC journalist Ari Melber reported on *The Beat* (and in a tweet on January 20, 2023), although Michigan Democrats won more votes in four recent elections (2012, 2014, 2018, 2020), Republicans nonetheless retained control of the statehouse, losing it only in 2022 when the vaunted "Red Wave" midterm elections turned out to be a harmless trickle. In Texas, as Elvia Limón reported in *The Texas Tribune* on October 25, 2021, "In a bid to hold the political turf, Republicans zeroed in on some communities with high shares of potential voters—who are more likely to support Democrats—and grafted them onto massive districts dominated by white voters." Troubles and their attendant violence are inevitable when the vote is manipulated in these ways. How different, finally, are the results of this tactic from those produced by the British occupation of Derry in the early 1970s when a courageous Hume shouted at soldiers patrolling Catholic streets, "You may govern us, but you do not have our consent!" (Mallon, 3). Without *consent*, particularly the consent of a majority, peace and democracy have little chance of flourishing.

Does this condition accurately describe contemporary America? Are we careening toward thirty years or more of unrelenting tribal violence? Historians generally agree that the most violent year of the Troubles was 1972 when, in Derry on January 30, British paratroopers killed thirteen civilians, seven of whom were teenagers. An inquiry into the events of "Bloody Sunday" led by Lord John Widgery largely absolved the soldiers of culpability, even though the Inquiry concluded that "None of the deceased or wounded is proved to have been shot whilst handling a firearm or bomb" (Widgery, 99). The Tribunal defended its findings, in part, by insisting that "There would have been no deaths in Londonderry on 30 January if those who organized the illegal march had not thereby created a highly dangerous situation" (97). It also introduced as exculpatory evidence a "Yellow Card" delineating the military's rules of engagement that every British paratrooper in Derry that day was required to carry. One of its rules describes what happened: "When hostile firing is taking place the soldiers of 1 Para will fire on a person who appears to be using a firearm against them without always waiting until they can positively identify the weapon" (91). Although the Tribunal deemed the rule to be "satisfactory," it also determined that some Paras' conduct "bordered on the reckless" (99). Fortunately, none of the teenagers killed that day had AR-15s, high capacity magazines or body armor—an American "Bloody Sunday" would claim many more lives.

The entire year of 1972 was marked by horrific violence, as Fionnuala O'Connor calculated: "497 killed, almost 5,000 injured, about 2,000 explosions, an average of about 30 shootings per day." But raw, decontextualized data scarcely capture the scale of the horror. In the early 1970s, Northern Ireland had a population of approximately 1.5 million people, roughly the size of present-day San Diego, San Antonio or metro Philadelphia. Over the Memorial Day weekend of 2022, there were an estimated forty shootings in Philadelphia between Friday afternoon and Monday night, leading to the ABC News headline "Cities Across US rocked by Memorial Day weekend shootings" (Hutchinson, May 31, 2022). Forty shootings over four days, or ten per day—*not thirty a day*, as in 1972 during the Troubles. The city of Chicago's population is nearly twice that of Northern Ireland in the 1970s, and its metro area is five times larger. According to reports from various media outlets, over the Labor Day weekend of 2023 Philadelphia, Atlanta, Washington and Chicago had a combined total of eighty-nine shootings with twenty-four fatalities. Imagine reading headlines like this *every* weekend, then add accounts of bombings that maimed innocent civilians and stories of the disappearances of neighbors never to be seen again.

During the Troubles, cars, bus stations, trains and business districts were routinely subject to bombings. In January 1972, a car bomb attack began in Belfast's City Centre, in one instance shattering the windows of a department store and propelling "glass bullets" that injured sixty-three shoppers. Another explosion on March 4 was caused by a device left under a table in the back of a coffee shop. A young man seated nearby eventually lost both of his legs; and, after shopping for wedding dresses and enjoying a cup of tea, two sisters were preparing to pay their bill when the device was detonated. Some months later at the wedding, both the bride, then twenty-two, and her sister, a bridesmaid, traveled up the aisle in wheelchairs. Over two years later, the young man injured at the coffee shop was also married, walking on prosthetic legs at the ceremony. But, in addition to his severe physical injuries, he alluded to an affective wound that is perhaps more damaging: "The terrifying thing is that the explosion could have happened to anyone" (qtd. in Hennessey, 4). Precisely—it could happen to anyone, anywhere, at any time.

The subjective effects of bombings, this daily anxiety and feeling of *dis-ease*, were pervasive. And even though incidents of shootings and explosions declined in the 1980s, the fear of sudden attacks remained. In *Eureka Street* (1996), one of the most sardonic novels ever written about the Troubles, Robert McLiam Wilson's narrator describes this reality:

> Northern Ireland had never dealt in epic murder sites: alleyways, corner shops, betting shops, sandwich shops, mobile shops, crap shops, bad dance halls [...]. (223)

Earlier, he characterized the psychical impact of bombs in particular:

> What were bombs like? They were loud and frightening in your gut like when you were a child and you fell on your head and couldn't understand why it hurt [...]. It wasn't the bombs that were scary. It was the bombed. Public death was a special mortality. (15)

The wit of Wilson's novel hardly diminishes his representation of the terror of daily life in Northern Ireland.

Trumpism and Authoritarian Populism

> When, in a crisis the traditional alignments are disrupted, it is possible, on the very ground of this break, to construct the people into a populist political subject; *with*, not against, the power bloc; in alliance with new political forces in a great national crusade to 'make Britain *Great* once more.'
> —Stuart Hall, "The Great Moving Right Show" (1983)

These sentences introduce *The Politics of Thatcherism* (1983), an anthology of essays that examines Prime Minister Margaret Thatcher's stated goal in the 1980s to "make Britain great once again." The slogan has a familiar ring. Her plans for remodeling were ambitious to say the least: from the weakening of labor unions to the dismantling of the National Health Service; from the promotion of monetarism to the flexing of imperial muscle in responding to Argentina's occupation of the Falkland Islands. Returning to Stuart Hall and his colleagues to better understand Thatcherism's role in the Troubles, I quickly realized that many of the emphases and operations of Trumpism not only recall the Troubles but also bear striking resemblance to the authoritarian populism of Thatcherism. In his contribution to the anthology, for example, economist Michael Bleaney derides Thatcherism as an "ideology run riot so that it no longer responds to reality but pursues its blinkered course regardless of where it culminates" (132). Who could offer a more astute characterization of the riotous Trumpism of our own times? For this and other reasons, Thatcherism's authoritarian populism with its weakening of democratic norms and institutions is included in my definition.

Similarities between the two are numerous. Trumpism, as I have described, focuses on the past—the 2020 presidential election, to be sure, but a more distant past as well—with a preoccupation bordering on obsession. And, like the Thatcherism Bleaney scrutinizes, this backward gaze promotes the mythology of an imaginary country, a trope central to conceptions of nationhood described in a later provocation. This fictive place existed before *Roe v. Wade* in 1973, before the Civil Rights and Voting Rights Acts of the 1960s, and in extreme cases before the passage of the Nineteenth Amendment in 1920. Christian nationalists like Lauren Boebert look back even further when dismissing Thomas Jefferson's insistence on the separation of Church and State. In this place, "wokeness" doesn't exist, people of color can't vote, and a fundamentalist version of Christianity dictates policies on abortion, the rights of gay and lesbian citizens, and more.

Like Thatcherism, Trumpism sustains these fantasies in part by making education a singularly contested "field of struggle" (Hall, 35), as Florida's attack on higher education in February 2023 and my home state of Indiana's similar legislation in 2024 demonstrate. A MAGA-driven bill in Florida exemplifies this struggle:

> A new Florida bill would aid and abet Governor Ron DeSantis's full-on attempt to make Florida higher education serve the right-wing agenda he's trying to implement [...]. House Bill 999 [...] is a sweeping and astoundingly bad bill that would dictate university curricula, ban any funding for diversity, equity, and inclusion (DEI) initiatives at Florida institutions, take the hiring of faculty out of faculty hands, and give governing boards the power to review the tenure status of college faculty anytime they please. (Neitzel, "New Bill")

The Florida bill also bans Gender Studies and general education courses that contain "unproven, theoretical, or exploratory content," whatever these are. Courses that define "American history as contrary to the creation of a new nation based on universal principles stated in the Declaration of Independence" would also be eliminated. This policing of curricula by political loyalists—and such actions as the firing of Patricia Okker, president of Florida's New College, in 2023, and her replacement by a politician appointed by Florida's Governor—will, one supposes, help "Make America Great Again."

The motives for President Okker's ouster at New College are transparent and subtly connected to the evangelical support of Trumpism. As someone who has known Patricia Okker for some thirty years, I regard her removal as an especially egregious assault on higher education. On two separate occasions, I had the pleasure of working with her in her capacity as a department chair at the University of Missouri–Columbia and from afar followed her rise at Missouri to the dean of the College of Arts and Sciences, where she managed some thirty-six departments and programs. She possesses superb scholarly credentials and managerial experience. By contrast, Richard Corcoran, her replacement, is a Florida politician with a law degree from Regent University, whose website trumpets the institution's goal of producing "Christian Leaders." He is *not* a scholar, *not* a teacher, and has little experience as an administrator. He previously worked for Senator Marco Rubio (R-FL), was named the Florida Commissioner of Education in 2018 and was once the Speaker of the Florida House of Representatives—and he will receive a considerably higher salary than his predecessor earned.

No surprise here—Trumpism attacks expertise at every turn, and Christian nationalists despise what they perceive as "woke" culture. After the appointments of six new members to the New College Board of Trustees and the installation of a staunch Christian as its new president, it was announced that the school would receive an additional $15 million from the legislature to help return it to the Florida government's vision of a "classical liberal arts" institution. By August 2023, as reported by *Inside Higher Education*, forty faculty members had left the school, students were unable to find courses in their "area of concentration" (i.e., major), and they were advised to take something else (Alonso, "Chaos at New College"). The transfer process began and will continue as remaining students struggle to enroll in the courses they need.

Thatcherism similarly advocated a return to a mythologized past—a sanitized version of the Victorian era—that would make Britain great again. And, like the redacted American history Florida politicians promote, Thatcher's vision of the Victorian age was shorn of such unseemly realities as poverty and urban blight. Instead, as University of Ulster scholars Frank Gaffikin and Mike Morrissey explain in *Northern Ireland: The Thatcher Years* (1990), Thatcherism alluded to a "Victorian age when a resilient people with resourceful spirit were supposed to have prospered on the virtues of enterprise, thrift, discipline, morality and patriotism" (9). Such virtues parallel "the kind of moral world held dear by Ulster fundamentalists" as well (36). As Raphael Samuel contends in a special issue of the *Proceedings of the British Academy* on Victorian Values, these emphases were not so much repressive—a well-traveled connotation descriptive of "Victorian" prudishness—as traditional and old-fashioned, the opposite of the permissiveness Mrs. Thatcher associated with the welfare state. She also complained that the age of Victoria had been "very badly treated in socialist propaganda" when it was actually the "heyday of free enterprise in Britain," a model for restoring business "to a place of honor in national life" (Samuel, 11, 12). For Mrs. Thatcher, Victorian "self-reliance and thrift" were "gospel truths"; "work ethic," her "favored idiom"; and privatization, her "tonic for energizing the economy" (13). As Hall summarizes, this "moralism was, in many ways, the centerpiece" of Thatcherism. Transformed by such virtues, "Being British" would mean "the restoration of competition and profitability" to the economy: No more "coddling" of feckless "scroungers"; no shirkers, just workers (29).

Yet, like Trumpism's faux utopia, Mrs. Thatcher's Victorian England is hardly an accurate historical representation. Her aversion to socialist dissections of this period, for example, evokes pictures of the wretched slums where workers lived in such works as Friedrich Engels's *The Condition of the Working Class in England* (1845). As Samuel notes, Thatcherism's Victorianism is devoid of the "cruelty, misery, drudgery, squalor and ignorance" of the cityscapes Charles Dickens paints in many of his novels. Like slavery, Jim Crow or the causes of Rosa Parks's civil disobedience that cannot be accommodated by Trumpism, the sooty fog and voluminous mud of Lincoln's Inn Fields in *Bleak House* (1853) and Coketown's purple river reeking of "ill-smelling dye" in *Hard Times* (1854) are glaringly absent from Thatcherism's idyllic depiction of Victorian England.

But there is more. Both Thatcherism and Trumpism engaged in a "struggle for hegemony [...] against both social democracy and the moderate wing of [their] own [parties]"; and both attempted to colonize the press in an effort to redefine the "common sense of the times" (Hall 25, 29). Both also waged unrelenting attacks on collectivism, especially socialism and unionism, which could then be denigrated when compared to the individual freedoms they ostensibly protected. In the case of Trumpism, this means greater latitude for corporate America by the cutting of eight regulations for the drafting of every new one, thus allegedly saving the country millions of dollars and every household an estimated $3,100/year. Or so the October 21, 2019 "Fact Sheet-President Trump's Historic Deregulation Is Benefitting All Americans" claimed. All workers, it underscored, would benefit because the president's deregulation would "unleash the American economy, leading to more than 6 million new jobs, rising wages, and low unemployment." As much a sales pitch as a statement of policy, the sheet communicated as many aspirations—and criticisms of the previous administration—as facts.

To be fair, its several boasts are difficult to prove or verify in the wake of the COVID pandemic during which millions of jobs were lost. But even in more "normal" times, deregulation is a contested concept. Does it produce as many jobs as political puff pieces claim? What about its unintended consequences? Was the train derailment near East Palestine Ohio in February of 2023 and a second derailment a month later the result of deregulation? Perhaps a more modest addition to definitions of Trumpism, then, would be that, like Thatcherites, Trumpists are, in a sense, neoliberals convinced of the virtues of unfettered free market capitalism and resistant to any ideology "built around the social-democratic principles of protection of the weak" (Bleaney, 137). Trump's emphasis on deregulation was also accompanied by strategies similar to those in Mrs. Thatcher's budgetary plan for 1979: a reduced income tax rate for the country's wealthiest citizens, budget cuts, and in Thatcher's case, a controversial increase in the Value Added Taxes (VAT). Although Mrs. Thatcher resisted the increase, she eventually relented after meetings with her advisors (Moore, 263–64). Proposals by some American Republicans calling for abolition of the federal income tax and its replacement by a national sales tax (or "consumption tax," as some advocates phrase it) resemble this gambit, a version of which was rationalized in the Thatcher budget of 1979 by the contention that a lower tax rate would facilitate the "achievements of a comparatively small number of talented and determined people" otherwise known as entrepreneurs (qtd. in Moore, 465). The devastating impact such a policy would have on the poor? That's another matter.

In short, definitions of Trumpism should include a consideration of the social and economic tenets of authoritarian populism. Equally important, as John Hume advised before the Troubles erupted in Northern Ireland, both sides—in America, this means red and blue states—must be involved in formulating responses to them. If Americans choose to remain silent, as Miles Taylor implies in *Blowback: A Warning to Save Democracy from the Next Trump* (2023), like Parkinson's and Multiple Sclerosis, that progressive disease known as Trumpism will continue to weaken the body politic for years to come.

Postscript

In a *New York Times* editorial (February 12, 2022), "Joyce and D.C.—Both Incomprehensible," Maureen Dowd describes hurrying in an Uber to attend a graduate course in modern literature at Columbia. Unfortunately, the car was involved in a minor traffic accident so, anxious not to miss the class, she left the vehicle in a sprint. The year 2022 marked the centenary of the publication of James Joyce's *Ulysses*, so it was hardly surprising that graduate students like Dowd were assigned to read it. Turning to the novel's "Proteus" episode and its challenging, at times arcane, language, she stared vacantly at several pages as if she had been concussed as a result of the traffic mishap. "Ineluctable modality of the visible," "Diaphane," "Morose delectation Aquinas tunbelly calls this, *frate porcospino*" (*U*3: 1, 7–8, 385)—what do these phrases and allusions mean? At first, Dowd found them as indecipherable as Donald Trump's "upside-down utterances," Kevin McCarthy's "demented backtracking" and Marjorie Taylor Greene's "inanity" when accusing former Speaker of the House Nancy Pelosi of "siccing her gazpacho police" on political opponents. Dazed by this readerly collision with Joyce's prose, Dowd returns to the inanity in D.C.: "the only thing that can save President Biden and the Democrats now is Republicans showing how fringy and far out they've gotten [...]."

It should be noted that James Joyce and *Ulysses* bear no responsibility for Republicans' fringy far-outness.

Tim Alberta reaches a similar conclusion in *The Kingdom, the Power, and the Glory*, in this case not about the Joycean text but about the bizarreness of evangelicals' support of Trumpism. Discussing the metamorphosis of Lynchburg Baptist College into present-day Liberty University, for example, Alberta traces Jerry Falwell Sr.'s efforts in the 1970s to rebrand the school through a double use of "liberty": first, through a quotation from Second Corinthians etched on the wall in DeMoss Hall on campus, "[...] where the Spirit of the Lord is, there is Liberty," an inscription Jerry Falwell, Jr., calls a "marketing thing"; and, second, through an appeal "to a sense of patriotism that was big in Christianity at that time" (59). Of greater impact in the school's evolution, however, was not merely the elder Falwell's endorsement of Republican presidential candidate Gerald Ford in 1976, but his mission to "destroy the Democratic nominee," Jimmy Carter. To this end, he seized on Carter's confession in a *Playboy* interview (September 24, 1976) that he had looked on some women "with lust," committing "adultery in [his] heart" (qtd. in Alberta, 61). Falwell deemed the revelation "beneath the dignity" of a president; henceforth, evangelical Christians would "turn Democratic rule into a referendum on American morality" (61). And they would take charge of shaping this message. After Barack Obama was elected in 2008, Liberty refused to recognize the school's College Democratic club and "seized editorial control of the campus newspaper" (76). GOP candidates were invited to speak at Liberty and other Christian schools, as Trump has done and Ronald Reagan did when addressing a crowd at Bob Jones University in January of 1980 before the school's tax exemption fracas strained its ties with the Reagan administration. The Moral Majority, Alberta concludes, "had taken over the Republican Party" (68).

For these and other reasons, Dowd's recommendation that Democrats would be well-advised to expose how "fringy and far out" Republicans have gotten is well worth considering. And, lest there be any confusion about this point, by early 2024, the term "Republican" was replaced by MAGA or Trumpist: Trump won primaries decisively and manipulated the GOP to install his daughter-in-law Lara as the party's cochair. On Valentine's Day, 2024, Ms. Trump promptly announced that "every single penny" donated to the party would go to her father-in-law. He is the party.

Admittedly, this is hardly compelling evidence of fringy behavior, of living at the boundaries of convention, but rather manifestations of autocratic inclination and financial desperation. More fringy is Trump's joining country singer Lee Greenwood during Holy Week of 2024 in hawking a "God Bless the U.S.A" edition of the Bible for $59.99 a copy. Advocates of Christian nationalism like Congresswoman Boebert, weary of Jeffersonian "crap" about the separation of Church and State, were doubtless overjoyed to learn that this edition will include a reprinting of the United State Constitution, the Bill of Rights, and other documents (including the lyrics of Mr. Greenwood's 1984 hit song "God Bless the U.S.A."). Alleging that Christianity is "under siege" and on the eve of his trial for funneling hush money to a porn star, the former president explained that he wanted to help "Make America Pray Again." In the 1970s for Falwell's Moral Majority, simply admitting sexual desire disqualified a presidential candidate; by the 2020s philandering, a dalliance with an adult film star and a court finding of rape does not. Ninety-one felony counts? A witch hunt. A featured role at the CPAC meeting in 2024 that gleefully welcomed the audience to "the end of democracy"? No big deal.

That's how fringy and far out the Republican Party (aka Trumpism) has become.

Chapter 2

THE LONG ROAD TO GOOD FRIDAY, I: FROM JFK TO JIMMY CARTER

> We know the winter earth upon the body of the young
> President, and the early dark falling;
> we know the veins grown quiet in his temples and
> wrists, and his hands and eyes grown quiet;
> we know his name written in the black capitals
> of his death, and the mourners standing in the
> rain, and the leaves falling […].
> —Wendell Berry, "November Twenty Sixth
> Nineteen Sixty Three" (1963/1964)

> President [Lyndon B.] Johnson's attitude to Ireland and the Irish will be warm and friendly […] but of course without [the] usual depth of feeling."
> —Irish Ambassador Thomas J. Kiernan, quoted in Loftus, "The Politics of Cordiality" (2009)

> Goldwater, a libertarian Westerner, doesn't deserve to have his pursuit of the Presidency equated with the weird, conspiracy-minded, race-baiting campaign of Donald J. Trump, the former reality-show performer, real-estate developer, and expert bully, who is about to claim his party's nomination and apparently wants to claim a piece of Goldwater's history as well.
> —Jeffrey Frank, "Extreme Conventions,"
> *The New Yorker* (June 21, 2016)

In the same spring that John Hume's seminal article appeared in the *Irish Times* (May 1964) advocating for nonviolent means of addressing a growing crisis in Northern Ireland, Wendell Berry published his first book of poetry. Accompanied by stunning illustrations, the book was comprised of a single elegy, "November Twenty Six Nineteen Sixty Three," which first appeared the previous December in *The Nation*. At the same time, profound social change was occurring in Ireland, Northern Ireland and America that would redefine the relationships between all three—and between all three and Britain.

In America on October 1, 1962, after the governor of Mississippi defied a Supreme Court order and a riot ensued that required the National Guard to subdue, James Meredith became the first African American to matriculate at the University of Mississippi. Some 250,000 civil rights marchers traveled to Washington the following August, where Martin Luther King Jr.'s "I Have a Dream" speech reverberated through the Lincoln Memorial. In the summer of 1964, the Civil Rights Act was passed, with the Voting Rights Act signed into law a year later. The impact of these events was enormous, and it was not confined to America. As access to television spread, audiences in Ireland and Northern Ireland witnessed the efficacy of nonviolent protest in pursuit of social justice, where once they could only read about it in newspapers or hear about it in broadcasts on the ubiquitous "wireless."

A civil rights *movement* with its connotation of forward progress, however, inevitably confronts a force akin to that defined by Isaac Newton's Third Law of Motion: for every action, there exists an equal and opposite reaction. In the summer of 1964 in America, this axiom was embodied by a phalanx of conservatives poised to wrest control of the Republican party from more moderate "Rockefeller Republicans" at what Rick Perlstein describes as "the ugliest" political convention since 1912. Its fractiousness was foreshadowed when a reporter asked eventual presidential nominee Barry Goldwater about his campaign's objections to a plank in the party platform affirming the constitutionality of the Civil Rights Act. Instead of answering directly, Goldwater disparaged Lyndon Johnson as the "phoniest individual who ever came around," an opportunist who opposed civil rights reforms until it became expedient to reverse his position. The tenor of Goldwater's rejoinder anticipated that of later interactions at the convention between "entrenched moderates" and "conservative insurgents," with the latter group finally winning the day (Perlstein, "How the 1964 Convention").

Before Republicans arrived in Cleveland in 2016, Jeffrey Frank looked back on that 1964 convention, concluding that whatever similarities obtained between Donald Trump's and Barry Goldwater's politics, major differences distinguish them and the two men themselves. Like Perlstein, Frank regarded the 1964 convention as "awful": Nelson Rockefeller was booed by the crowd, and in his acceptance speech, Goldwater defended extremism in the defense of liberty as a virtue. In an aside, Frank recalled that Pennsylvania governor William Scranton, nominated for presidential candidacy at the convention by Milton Eisenhower, derided "Goldwaterism" as a "crazy-quilt collection of absurd and dangerous positions." Yet, however familiar mismatched ideological patchworks have become in our own time, Frank, correctly I think, viewed comparisons of the libertarian from Arizona with the "conspiracy-minded, race-baiting" real estate developer who became America's forty-fifth president as essentially unfair (Frank, "Extreme Conventions"). The times themselves, the differences between the 1960s and our own historical moment, are another matter.

Some similarities between these politicians and their followers, however, are difficult to ignore. Like Trump, Goldwater attracted, in Jeb Stuart Magruder's words, zealots who were "uncontrollable" and "cared nothing about the Republican party" (qtd. in Goldberg, 219). Like Trump's erratic behavior, Goldwater's intemperance motivated psychiatrists to diagnose him as, alternatively, a "dangerous lunatic" or "paranoid schizophrenic" with dark tendencies recalling those of the century's most infamous autocrats (223).[1] These analyses in turn created apprehensions that if Cold War tensions precipitated a nuclear showdown, Goldwater wouldn't flinch at the prospect of pushing a cataclysmic button, which led to the ironic revision of his campaign slogan from "In your heart you know he's right" to "In your heart you know he *might*." This now-familiar slogan has been variously revised and applied to Trump (as in *The Daily Beast*'s headline in 2016, "In your heart you know he's nuts").

Analogies between the two grew more thoughtful—and complicated—during Trump's first year in office with the publication of *The Dangerous Case of Donald Trump: 27 Psychiatrists and Mental Health Experts Assess a President* (2017; an expanded edition appeared two years later). As its editor, Yale psychiatrist Bandy X. Lee, explains, the diagnosis of a public figure from afar has been debated since the American Psychiatric Association drafted the "Goldwater Rule" in 1973. The rule's inception was the result of 12,356 responses in 1964 to a magazine's question, "Do you believe Barry Goldwater is psychologically fit to serve as President of the United States?" The question prompted answers that resembled professional diagnosis more than political opinion: Goldwater was a "paranoid schizophrenic"; he demonstrated a "megalomaniacal, grandiose omnipotence"; he revealed a "psychological makeup" comparable to that of Adolf Hitler. Such observations invariably merged psychiatry with politics, hence the distinction central to the Goldwater rule: "It is unethical for a psychiatrist to offer a *professional* opinion unless he or she has conducted an examination and has been granted authorization for such a statement" (qtd. in Levin; my emphasis). Within months of his election, and in some quarters even earlier, Trump provoked an ethical debate that recalled concerns over Barry Goldwater's fitness for office a half-century earlier.

But the two men's differences are far more significant. Unlike Trump's co-optation of the religious right, Goldwater kept his distance from Christian fundamentalists, particularly on the issues of abortion and gays serving in the military. Nearly thirty years after his failed bid for the presidency on the eve of the 1992 national convention, he warned that a "strict anti-abortion stance" would leave the GOP "in shambles" ("Goldwater Opposes GOP"). Although he had tamed his rhetoric somewhat when running for the Senate in 1980, he renewed his objection to religion intruding into politics the following year when the Moral Majority opposed Ronald Reagan's nomination of Sandra Day O'Connor for the Supreme Court. As Judith Miller reported in the *New York Times*, Goldwater accused the new right of subverting "the basic American principle of separation of church and state" by flexing the "muscle of religion" to achieve political ends. In defending O'Connor's nomination, he also vented his contempt for "political preachers" and encouraged "every good Christian" to kick Jerry Falwell "right in the ass."[2] In a more thoughtful mood when addressing his Senate colleagues, Goldwater laid bare his wariness of theocracy: "The uncompromising position of these groups is a divisive element that could tear apart the very spirit of our representative system if they gain sufficient strength" (qtd. in Miller).

Also unlike Trump, who can neither contain his loathing of political opponents nor suppress his instinct to savage his critics on social media, Goldwater harbored great affection for several of his—and it was returned. In *My Life* (2004), Bill Clinton recalls that on the issue of banning gays from military service, Goldwater, a veteran and "old-fashioned conservative," agreed with him about lifting the ban (484–85). Later in *My Life*, alluding to Goldwater's death on May 29, 1998, Clinton identifies a more personal source of his affection: "I was saddened by his passing. Although we were of different parties and philosophies, Goldwater had been uncommonly kind to Hillary and me. I also respected him for being a genuine patriot [...]" (791). In *Promises to Keep* (2007), Joe Biden recounts Goldwater's close relationship with Hubert Humphrey, one that withstood the latter's "shot across the bow of Goldwaterism" during the 1964 election. By late 1977, when the Minnesota senator's battle with cancer was nearing its end, Goldwater crossed the Senate floor to envelop his frail colleague in a long and moving embrace (135).

And then there is his well-documented friendship with John F. Kennedy, however much they sparred in public over such issues as the Cuban Missile Crisis.[3] Robert Alan Goldberg revisits Goldwater's sorrow over the president's assassination, his cancellation of appearances on television and, fearing that his criticism of Kennedy's New Frontier policies "had provoked a right-wing extremist to act," his temporary suspension of his campaign (179). After returning to the race and making his last appearance in Fredonia, a town near the Grand Canyon to which he often retreated after an exhausting itinerary of speeches and interviews, Goldwater took in the natural beauty he had fought most of his political life to protect. There, he contemplated the spirited rivalry he might have enjoyed with his friend: "If Jack were here, we would have had a good campaign" (qtd. in Goldberg, 232). But it was not to be.

Goldwaterism thus scarcely resembles Trumpism's worldview of grievances, conspiracy theories and unrelenting hostility to political opponents or institutions it seeks to undermine or destroy. Goldwater's commitments to democracy, individual freedoms, and the separation of Church and State clearly distinguish him from Trump and Trumpism.

Similar laws of motion, of action and reaction, emerged in Northern Ireland in the early 1960s before the term "Troubles" entered our vocabulary. In January 1964, Conn and Patricia McCluskey founded the Campaign for Social Justice in Dungannon, County Tyrone, to bring "the light of publicity to bear on the discrimination which exists in our community" against Catholics, who "represent more than one-third of the total population" (qtd. in Collins, 26). Later that May, sixty-seven women led by Patricia McCluskey formed the Homeless Citizens League to protest the construction of 142 new houses in a Unionist ward, while some 300 Catholic families waited to secure even temporary housing.[4] Several mothers threatened to place their babies in welfare homes if at least some Catholics weren't permitted to move into the prefabricated structures Protestants vacated when relocating to the new houses, and seventeen families, denigrated as "squatters," eventually took over the "pre-fabs" (Dooley, 29–31). As Brian Dooley recounts, within a fortnight the seventeen families had doubled to thirty-five, leaving the Dungannon Council little choice but to allow them to stay and making this "first act of civil disobedience by the new civil rights campaigners" a decisive victory (32).

Unfortunately, the victory exerted little effect on the suppression of Catholic votes in cities like Derry, or on the inequity of a "ratepayers" franchise that awarded property owners additional votes. As Glenn Patterson notes in *Backstop Land* (2019), the Northern Ireland Civil Rights Association's demand for "One Man, One Vote" later in the 1960s actually "looked in two directions: giving to those who had none and taking from those who had too many." Patterson also explains that the Stormont government did not mandate property ownership as a prerequisite for enfranchisement; rather, unlike "the rest of the UK" that abolished the requirement for local elections "immediately" after World War II, it had neglected to remove it (9). Other means of constraining the Catholic vote were in force as well. In 1964, a national census was canceled for fear "of throwing 'into relief difficult political questions of redistribution'" in local races (Mulholland, 47). Reporting on the protest in Dungannon, the press depicted Northern Catholics as "white negroes" facing obstacles similar to those African Americans confronted (Dooley, 32). Disenfranchisement was one of these.

Comparisons between Northern Irish Catholics and African Americans grew throughout the 1960s and 1970s emphasizing their similarities, yet often overlooking their differences. As I have already mentioned, Frederick Douglass meditated on the same issue a century earlier after witnessing the devastations of the Great Famine that "deeply affected, even changed" him (Blight, 153). After returning to America, however, as Lauren Onkey outlines in *Blackness and Transatlantic Irish Identity* (2010), Douglass began to distinguish the abjection of slaves from the misery of the Irish, as he did in an 1850 speech in Rochester, New York:

> It is often said, by the opponents of the anti-slavery cause, that the condition of the people of Ireland is more deplorable than that of the American slaves. *Far* be it from me to underrate the sufferings of the Irish people [...]. Yet I must say that there is no analogy between the two cases. The Irishman is poor, but he is *not* a slave. He *may* be in rags, but he is *not* a slave. He is still the master of his own body. (qtd. in Onkey, 16)

A fictional Douglass in Colum McCann's novel *TransAtlantic* (2013) calculates the horrific costs of this lack of mastery: an owner's initials "burned into your skin," an "iron bit in your mouth" and myriad indignities ruthlessly inscribed on captive flesh (51).

A century after the Great Hunger, the analogous struggles of African Americans and Northern Catholics seemed compelling, a thesis facilitated by greater access to television in the North. In 1954, BBC television broadcasts were viewed in some 10,000 Northern Irish households; by 1962, that number grew to 194,000, by which time a second channel, UTV, became available (Dooley, 28). Dooley stresses the impact of coverage of American civil rights marches, sit-ins, and other demonstrations in inspiring such activists as Gerry Adams and Michael Farrell, the latter then a student at Queen's University and a leader of the People's Democracy, founded in 1968. Television, however, was only one medium contributing to the transatlantic argument, as music, fashion and an ascendant youth culture attentive to social injustice not only underscored the hurdles that defined both groups' marginalization but also raised questions about human subjectivity and identity: How, for example, is blackness imbricated in working-class Irish and Northern Catholics' senses of minoritarian identity?

Several novels of the 1970s and 1980s explore this question. Cutting wood on a rare day of gratifying work away from the Protestant estate in which he was constantly bullied, Bernard MacLaverty's teenaged protagonist in *Cal* (1983) chanted a "negro work song"; later, looking into a mirror, he "spoke to his image in a Negro voice" (47, 51). An aspiring guitarist, Cal listens to Muddy Waters and the Rolling Stones, whose early repertory featured songs by Chuck Berry, Willie Dixon and other black artists, much as Belfast's Van Morrison covered blues classics by Sonny Boy Williamson, John Lee Hooker and Bobby Bland. For MacLaverty's alienated teenager, the blues provide a shelter where, as Onkey describes, he can "hide from the only identities he has available": an unemployed Catholic living on the dole and a wary participant in republican violence (164). In Roddy Doyle's *The Commitments* (1987), a young Dubliner who regards the working class as the "blacks" of Europe forms a band to play Al Green's "Take Me to the River" and the soul music of Eddie Floyd, Aretha Franklin and Wilson Pickett, most of which was recorded in the 1960s and 1970s. Soul music, unlike the jazz one of the Commitments reviles, is "about where you're from an' the sort o' people yeh come from" (13). It originates in the rhythms of the community and the working class, not in the loneliness of the blues or the technical virtuosity of jazz.

As these examples suggest, in Ireland, Northern Ireland and America, culture and social life more generally were changing; and in the 1980s, when MacLaverty and Doyle published their novels, blues and soul music were still transforming the dominant culture. At the same time, in what may seem a counterintuitive generalization given Ireland's affection for President Kennedy, and his for Ireland, American and Irish leaders struggled to deepen the countries' "cordial" but not always mutually beneficial association. From the later 1960s onward, American foreign policy toward Ireland conveyed an indifference that as John Dumbrell, among others, argues took years to soften.[5] This project grew more urgent as America, Irish America in particular, grew increasingly alarmed by violence in the North.

A series of articles written in *The Irish People*, a weekly New York City newspaper founded in 1972, reflects this alarm. And in the *New York Times*, accused from time to time of having a pro-British bias, Bernard Weinraub depicted life in the North in startling detail, noting that by mid-October 1972 citizens of Belfast were both inured to violence and exhausted by it:

> After turbulent and violent months Belfast and the province have settled into the rhythm of sporadic sniper fire and explosions, army searches, threats and counterthreats by Roman Catholics and Protestants, and apparently mindless sectarian murders—more than 60 since July, most of them by terror squads on both sides.[6] ("Belfast Soured")

While the British government accused the IRA of fomenting violence and manipulating the "emotions" of Irish America, claiming that by the mid-1970s "three-quarters" of its arsenal was funded, if not directly supplied, by Americans (Dumbrell, "The United States," 109), Weinraub exposed the culpability of British paratroopers in the murder of thirteen civilians in Derry on Bloody Sunday, January 30, 1972. A week later, he reported on the efforts of 5,000 British soldiers, whirring helicopters and twenty roadblocks in managing a march in Newry.[7] One of the protesters was Bernadette Devlin, who by this time was well-known in America. As she explained before the protest began, responsibility for the bloodshed in Derry the week before was clear, as was her fear that it might be repeated:

> "Of course we are worried about what could happen," Bernadette Devlin said this afternoon, walking on the bleak main street of Newry [...]. "We're human beings and we don't want to die at the hands of British soldiers."[8] (Weinraub, "Catholic Protesters")

Such stark accounts stunned American readers, and a "private, grudging admiration" for the nationalist movement in Northern Ireland grew among "self-consciously 'respectable' members of the third or fourth immigrant generation" of Irish Americans (Dumbrell, "The United States," 108). Sadly, as Weinraub reported in the summer of 1976, the number of casualties continued to rise. Since 1969, "more than 1,500 people have died as a result of terrorist activities," he calculated, "and nearly 14,000 have been injured. This year, with more than 200 people dead so far, is expected to be one of the bloodiest since 1972." The victims were not all militants. They included not only the British ambassador to Ireland and British soldiers stationed in the North, but also, as David McKittrick observed in the *Irish Times*, innocent bystanders, as shootouts between rivals in back alleys were replaced by more frequent attacks on "soft targets" like department stores and railway stations (qtd. in Weinraub, "More Than 1,500").

Albeit slowly, these widely reported incidents, combined with such developments as the internment of Northern Catholics in the summer of 1971 and Prime Minister Edward Heath's suspension of the Stormont government in March of 1972, initiated a long overdue reassessment of American foreign policy. Stated another way, however personally transformative President Kennedy's 1963 trip to Ireland might have been—something to which his widow Jacqueline, old friend Dave Powers, and Ryan Tubridy all attest— his failure to address America's noninterventionism has troubled many.[9] P. J. McLoughlin and Alison Meagher argue that while the president was gratified by the adulation he received during his 1963 trip, he was "determined not to raise the issue of Northern Ireland" when visiting London (677). Maurice Fitzgerald is even more acerbic when juxtaposing American policy toward Ireland and Northern Ireland during the Kennedy years with the unrealistic (and unfulfilled) expectations of his Irish admirers:

> During his presidency, as Irish hopes of partition being resolved rose to their zenith, the reality was the complete opposite [...]. Kennedy looked at partition as coldly and with as much detachment as he would any other foreign policy issue. (197)

Quite clearly, for many this "detachment" was more consequential than his misquotation of *Ulysses*. Could his wit and ease, as Irish Ambassador Thomas J. Kiernan theorized, be underpinned by "something that wasn't Irish at all"—a "cold summing-up, the logical follow up" (qtd. in Fitzgerald, 197)? Or is the matter more easily unpacked, as Feargal Cochrane concludes: "Typically when a US president opened their mouth to speak about Northern Ireland, the state department's words came out [...]" (qtd. in McLoughlin and Meagher, 676)?

Like all relationships, that between America and Ireland required attention, an issue politicians on both sides of the Atlantic recognized well before JFK's inauguration. In 1956, although Taoiseach John A. Costello viewed America as "very friendly disposed" toward Ireland, he saw the need for an even closer alliance: "Without subservience and while maintaining our independence," he urged, "we must consolidate that friendship and make it a cardinal point in our policy" (qtd. in Loftus, 154). In the 1960s, however, Ireland and Northern Ireland were hardly "cardinal points" in American policy as more pressing crises emerged: the Cold War, missiles in Cuba and a simmering conflict in Vietnam. "Cordial" might thus be better construed as "minor," for as Ambassador Kiernan observed, Ireland was "much too unimportant for the State Department to waste good men by sending them there" (qtd. in Loftus, 146). Or good women. As a result, the postwar American embassy in Dublin seemed to many observers to be a repository for political cronies or "loose cannons" (Fitzgerald, 188). Some three decades later, after eighty-three-year-old William H.G. FitzGerald was appointed by President George Bush in 1992, *Irish Times* journalist Conor O'Clery similarly portrayed the Ambassador's residence in Phoenix Park as "a rest home for retired political fundraisers" (*Daring Diplomacy*, 43). FitzGerald was a controversial choice, especially after his bumbling remark during his confirmation hearings that he hoped to promote dialogue "between the unionists and the loyalists" in Northern Ireland ("US envoy in early 90s").

These discouraging facts notwithstanding, headway in the relationship between countries was being made as Kennedy's appointment of Grant Stockdale as Envoy to Ireland in 1961 demonstrates. Stockdale, a Miami politician and businessman who during the campaign occasionally signed notes as "Florida Agent #1 for Kennedy for President," was an old and trusted friend. And, as Morris McLemore in the *Miami Daily News* (March 20, 1961) reported, at a large celebration of his imminent confirmation Stockdale "declaimed strongly against printed suggestions" that he lacked "a depth of experience" or "thoughtful study of Ireland." A month earlier on February 10 Stockdale wrote Evelyn Lincoln, the president's secretary, alluding to an avalanche of requests from London newspapers for a summary of his political experience, which in several ways was impressive. As a member of the Florida House of Representatives, he introduced legislation banning the wearing of Ku Klux Klan paraphernalia in public and sponsored the "Woman's Jury Bill" that paved the way for women to serve on Florida juries (see Stockdale Letters, Kennedy Presidential Library). Having neglected to include this information in his official biography, he wanted Lincoln to add it to his file. Still, for some naysayers, these legislative accomplishments and his extensive travel in Europe did not constitute diplomatic expertise; for them, Kennedy had reneged on his pledge to nominate only able diplomats for such appointments. Confirmed on March 28, Stockdale served as Ambassador until the time of his resignation on July 7, 1962.

Although brief, his tenure brought with it significant progress, as Stockdale encouraged Kennedy to finalize a project that had been discussed since the late 1950s: the building of a new embassy. The president agreed. Designed by Harvard Graduate School of Design and New York architect John M. Johansen, the new embassy in Ballsbridge was modeled after a Celtic fortress, its circular shape recalling the Martello towers erected by the British government in the early nineteenth century. When two congressmen in later 1961 questioned this design and asked Kennedy to approve it, he did so, calling its construction "way behind schedule" (Memo to Dean Rusk, August 28, 1961). Three decades later after its opening when Jean Kennedy Smith was confirmed as Ambassador to Ireland, this embassy became her office. By contrast to her octogenarian predecessor, Smith knew Ireland and its history well; and between 1993 and 1998, along with Nixon appointee John Moore, she became America's longest-serving envoy to Ireland since the end of World War II. Like its predecessor, this iconic building, once called "the showpiece of Europe," became too small to accommodate the size and scope of the Irish mission, and the Biden administration announced plans in 2023 for a new $700 million structure to replace it.

Still, "cordiality" in foreign policy of the 1960s, as John D. Hickerson, Director of the Office of European Affairs for President Truman and

Assistant Secretary of State from 1949 until 1953, once explained, connoted more than "unimportant." It meant "non-interventionist":

> It has long been the view of this Department that the subject of the boundary which partitions Ireland and Northern Ireland is one for discussion between the Irish and British governments and one in in which this country should not intrude. (qtd. in Fitzgerald, 195)

At the same time, at the risk of repetition, advances were being made. After World War II, the Eisenhower administration recognized the benefit of improving relations with Ireland, tendering an invitation to the Irish president to visit the White House. Because President Seán T. O'Kelly was recovering from a heart attack in 1956, Taoiseach Costello took his place, carefully avoiding the rhetorical quicksand of the partition. Three years later, a recovered O'Kelly came to America, the first Irish president to make an official visit to Washington, a gesture reciprocated by President Kennedy in the summer of 1963 and repeated in May of 1964 when Éamon de Valera visited America. Northern Ireland's Prime Minister Terence O'Neill had met with President Johnson just two months earlier.

But, as Senator George Mitchell implied when chronicling the frustrations of spearheading the Good Friday Agreement of 1998, more than formal receptions and White House dinners—more than cordiality—were required to achieve something of consequence. In *Making Peace* (1999), he noted that the "dispute in Northern Ireland is not purely or even primarily economic in origin or nature. There are many other strands to this complex conflict" (12). These include, quite obviously, religion and national identity, yet Mitchell quickly returns to the topic with which I will begin my narrative of a friendly but shallow relationship evolving into a more meaningful partnership: "Economic deprivation is a contributing factor in the problems in Northern Ireland," Mitchell writes. "Some estimates suggest that as many as a third of [Catholic] men are born, live out their lives, and die without ever having held a job." For some, he argued, membership in a paramilitary offered a "steady" salary that occasional or "casual" employment could not (13); for unsalaried others like Patrick Magee, who joined the PIRA in the spring of 1972 and later played a central role in an attempt to assassinate Margaret Thatcher, membership provided an opportunity to repay the perpetrators of violence or harassment in kind (Carroll, *Killing Thatcher*, 51). For many young people between eighteen and thirty seeking a secure future, however, emigration seemed the only viable alternative.

In what follows, I reassess the key, occasionally inadvertent, contributions of the Nixon and Carter administrations to America's changing relationships with England, Ireland and Northern Ireland, emphasizing the importance of economic development and recognizing political actors that have been too often overlooked. That is to say, although my focus throughout is trained on leaders—Presidents, Prime Ministers, Taoiseachs and party leaders in Northern Ireland—I also want to acknowledge the contributions of lesser-known officials in building a more proactive foreign policy. This discussion also serves as a preface to the next chapter that begins with America's changing, at times confused, responses to events in Northern Ireland, especially in the 1980s, and continues through the Good Friday Agreement and beyond. The resulting two-chapter narrative features a *dramatis personae* of almost Shakespearean dimension—Bernadette Devlin, John Hume, Ian Paisley, Bobby Sands, Ronald Reagan, Margaret Thatcher, Garret FitzGerald, Gerry Adams, Charles Haughey, Bill Clinton and George Mitchell— but also foregrounds lesser-known players like Ambassadors John Moore and Jean Kennedy Smith, British Cabinet member John Goodall, and the too-often underappreciated actions of Presidents Carter, and after the Good Friday Treaty was signed, George W. Bush. Throughout both chapters, I foreground parallels between the causes of the Troubles and the sources of contemporary America's discontent: tensions between the rural and the metropolitan, the intrusions of fundamentalist religion into politics, the disenfranchisement of minority voters and the infringement of women's freedom. Just as the sons and daughters of Ireland came to America's aid in the Revolutionary and Civil Wars, a century later in the 1960s America's time to reciprocate had arrived. Such progress was at times painfully slow, however, and this chapter traces this dilatory process.

Building a New Economy: From Agriculture to Tourism

> There is indeed a division in the people here. Some call it religion, some call it politics. But the most reliable, the most ubiquitous division is money. Money is the division you can always put your money on.
> —Robert McLiam Wilson, *Eureka Street* (1996)

> Do we give up fighting so the tourists come, or fight the harder so they stay home?
> —Derek Mahon, "An Bonnán Buí," *The Yellow Book* (1998)

The past year was "one of strong expansion in the American economy," as the United States Bureau of Economic Analysis emphasized in its January 1965 report in the *Survey of Current Business*. New records in "production and sales, in employee compensation and profits, in employment and living conditions" were set, as 1964 marked the "fourth successive year of upturn" in a continuing recovery from the recession of 1958. Although several factors account for this success, the Bureau pointed to a reduction in the federal income tax rate that "brought about an increase in disposable income and a sharp rise in consumer spending" as perhaps the most significant (1). The forecast for the near term was equally bullish, as there was "little question that the rise in activity in the first quarter of 1965 would be very substantial." While the nation's economic complexion was not entirely unblemished—growing demand for new cars, for instance, meant that buyers waited "a longer time than average" for the delivery of their purchases (3)—such annoyances hardly mattered to an economy with an expanding GNP, lower taxes and shiny new Buicks.

Such exuberance was seldom heard in postwar Ireland, where unemployment and an enervated economy posed seemingly insuperable challenges. As Enda Delaney explains, between 1951 and 1961 over 400,000 people left independent Ireland, "nearly a sixth of the total population in 1951." The emigrants were "predominantly young people, both men and women," and by 1971 "one in three of these aged 30 years or under had left the country," the majority traveling to England (81). Casual employment—"a few weeks here, a few weeks there" with long periods of inactivity in between (83)—failed to provide a consistent salary and the security that comes with it. It had to be found elsewhere:

> [...] Many young Irish people in the 1950s faced a bleak future. Employment in agriculture was an unattractive choice of livelihood and there was little prospect of large-scale employment in the non-agricultural sectors. Unemployment increased in urban areas—prompting street protests in Dublin—from June 1953, stark evidence of the crisis in the Irish economy at the time. (82)

As the decade progressed, economic insecurity spread. In the 1956 census, every town with fewer than 10,000 residents reported a decline in population, as did central Dublin, although minimal increases were recorded in Dublin County, Meath and Louth (Mary E. Daly, 186). As "involuntary exiles"—Kerby Miller's term for earlier generations of migrants in *Emigrants and Exiles*—fled the country, the term "ghost town" appeared more frequently to describe the stark realities of a changing landscape.

The Irish government was well aware of this exodus and its ramifications. Spearheaded by Seán Lemass, Minister for Industry and Commerce from 1957 to 59, and economist T. K. Whitaker, Secretary of the Department of Finance, the Government devised two programs for economic expansion: the first in 1958 and the second five years later. The Introduction of the former plan, distributed to both houses of the Oireachtas in November, defines one principal motive for its creation and anticipates potential challenges that lie ahead:

> The establishment of a Free Trade Area in Europe will, whether we join or not [...] call for a special effort on our part if output and living standards are not to lag behind those of neighboring countries. Apart from this, the difficulties associated with a restricted home market will become more serious if the population fails to rise [...]. Emigration will not be checked nor will unemployment be permanently reduced until the rate of increase in national output is greatly accelerated. (7)

The program then outlines such topics as the improvement of grasslands, particularly for beef and mutton production; the markets for pigs, poultry and eggs; the improvement of tillage crops; and the need for greater investment in agricultural education. Later (and shorter) sections of the plan discuss such topics as fisheries, forestry and industry, including a handful of paragraphs on tourism and the elimination of restrictive practices.

The introduction of the *Second Programme* in 1963 summarized the "Aims and Achievements" of its predecessor, including the "role of the State in promoting economic development" through both direct investment and the "encouragement of private enterprise by grants, loans, tax incentives, and other means" (7). It also invoked the "deliberately modest" goal of a 2% increase in GNP five years earlier and reported that between 1958 and 1962 the GNP had actually risen by 18.5% (7–8). During 1961–62, emigration's effect on population versus "the rate of natural increase of the population was reversed," albeit "slowly" (8). These achievements—the founding of new enterprises, "increased productive investment," a "more confident, dynamic spirit" and thus "a pronounced change in the national mentality"—were to be celebrated (8). But the report cautioned that the seven-year period of the program from 1964 to 1970 would be "dominated by the urgent need to adapt" (9).

Emigration and an overreliance on agricultural exportation remained challenges, as did the "dismantling [of] the Irish protectionist regime in preparation for European Economic Community (EEC) membership" (Kelly, 'A *Failed Political Entity*, 43–44). The exodus *out* of Ireland, however, was not the only provenance of the emigration dilemma, as *internal* migration from rural communities to larger cities also played a role. In some areas, particularly in the agrarian west, the relocation of young women to cities in search of work led to a gender imbalance that constrained marriage possibilities, as did many men's inability to earn a salary sufficient to support a family (Daly, 43). Theatre-going Americans may be familiar with the latter dilemmas, as both Gar O'Donnell's hope of marriage and his fantasies of the high life could never be realized in the rural Ballybeg of Brian Friel's *Philadelphia, Here I Come!*, which enjoyed a 326-performance run on Broadway in 1966. But more than lonely villages like Ballybeg with disaffected young men like Gar experienced declines in population. "Only two European countries," as Mary E. Daly emphasizes, "experienced a fall in population during the 1950s: Ireland and East Germany" (183).

In independent Ireland, this crisis was not ameliorated by policies rooted in a mythology all too familiar in twenty-first century America. For just as some Americans believe that the real nation is being replaced by non-white races and their "woke" discourses (multiculturalism, critical race theory), in postwar Ireland many feared that a rural, authentic nation was being overtaken by the modernity of cities like Dublin. This authenticity required protection even as its agrarian economy, while crucial to the nation's GNP, was unable to stimulate necessary economic growth. Cattle, for instance, were the "only Irish agricultural commodity that could be exported without a subsidy," but its production created few jobs and little profit for smaller farmers (Daly, 33). John Bradley, Research Professor at Dublin's Economic and Social Research Institute, further argues that the "strong web of dependency between Ireland and the UK" was attenuated in the later 1950s as foreign direct investment increased. The export of Irish commodities to the UK between 1960 and 1995 was cut by more than half and Ireland's importation of British goods also declined (113). What economic stimuli could compensate for this change, and what useful role might America play?

Answers to these questions grew more urgent in a climate of postwar debt. Having been approved in April 1948 for a loan of "ten million dollars for the first three months of the European Recovery Programme under the terms of the Marshall Plan," as Irene Furlong explains, Ireland needed to "increase its dollar-earning capacity." So as the 50s began, the government turned to tourism "because it was the largest single dollar-earning source, offering the greatest possibilities of rapid expansion" ("Tourism," 166). Yet, even though Ireland had benefited from tourism in the past, creating a more professional industry proved to be a challenge: transatlantic air travel had to be improved, as did local roadways; cultural and recreational opportunities had to be created or expanded; marketing strategies were needed; and, most difficult of all, suitable accommodations, well-appointed hotels in particular, had to be built and existing structures renovated. This imperative continued "to bedevil the industry throughout the 1950s," despite "efforts to provide financial aid to the hotel sector" ("Tourism," 167). The hurdles, however, extended beyond questions of subsidy, as hoteliers traveled to America to study the amenities offered by major hotel chains, to identify the needs of distinct types of consumers and to review marketing strategies. Americans had to be encouraged to take their holidays in Ireland, and Ireland needed to make sure they enjoyed their stay.

In 1952, An Bord Fáilte was founded in response to one of six key recommendations made in a *Synthesis of Reports on Tourism 1950–1951* that called for a more professional management of the emergent industry (a new agency would later coordinate tourism efforts in Northern Ireland and the Republic). But the transformation was slow. Travel between England and Ireland was inadequate, and between 1952 and 1957 the number of rooms in hotels and guesthouses actually decreased ("Tourism," 166–67). Nonetheless, Seán Lemass, as Minister for Industry and Commerce during the 50s and as Taoiseach from 1959 to 1966, was committed to the initiative as he assured the Congress of International Hotel Associations in 1960:

> While we are new to, and somewhat inexperienced in, the organized international tourism business, the Irish people have a reputation going back a long way for hospitality, and a flair for hospitality is not a bad foundation on which to build a tourist industry. (qtd. in "Tourism," 178)

Not surprisingly, the tourist industry floundered in the North, not only because of sectarian conflict but, as Bernadette Devlin complained, because of a "medieval mentality" resistant both to making Northern Ireland "worth seeing" and to building even one "top-grade hotel" (*Price*, 49–50). Eventually, tourism evolved into a "model of cooperative success and a source of dialogue," as it had been in the months after the partition (Zuelow, 17). Decades later in 2019, as reported by the Department of Tourism, Culture, Arts, Gaeltacht, Sport, and Media, tourism created over 325,000 jobs and brought some 9.3 billion euros into the Irish economy.

Postwar investment in tourism was facilitated not only by the inception of Bord Fáilte Éireann and the Tourist Traffic Act of 1952 but also by the Tourist Traffic Act of 1959 that provided an annual stipend of £500,000 to award as accommodation development grants and £1 million for resort development. The Tourist Traffic Act, 1963 raised the former amount to £1.5 million, which was increased to £3 million in 1966 and to £5 million by the Tourist Traffic Act, 1968. When Brian Lenihan, Sr., Minister for Transport and Power, addressed the Seanad Éireann on July 30, 1970, he recalled this history while noting that as of March 30, the Bord was owed more than £500,000 and an additional remittance from the government. This increase was the product of numerous studies, including a more granular parsing of the diversity of visitors to the country and their needs. Between 1960 and 1970, bedrooms in hotels and guesthouses increased from 17,800 to nearly 28,000, and the quality of these accommodations also improved ("Tourist Traffic Bill," 1970). In addition, hotels, guesthouses, caravan and camping sites, and cottages (the "Rent-a-Cottage" scheme) were also constructed. Such diversity of accommodation was intended "to match the growth in demand and the standards tourists seek," and continued funding ensured that "accommodation expansion keeps pace with the needs of tourism" ("Tourist Traffic Bill, 1970").

By 1969, Lenihan observed, this pace had slowed, and in Northern Ireland it was expected to decline further "for obvious reasons." Other challenges existed as well, as Irish Tourism had to compete for business on an international basis ("Tourist Traffic Bill, 1970"). For Philip Heneghan, these conditions augured the collapse of the industry (fortunately, by 1974 income from tourism improved by 80%). From a macroeconomic view, between 1962 and 1972 international tourist arrivals *in toto* increased from some 81 million/year to nearly 200 million. In 1973, however, although this number rose internationally, the proportion of tourists arriving in Europe declined by three percent, a shortfall only partially attributable to an energy crisis and the Troubles. Still, the downturn was significant; Irish tourism, Heneghan estimates, was "set back by over twelve years" (226). Technological developments in aviation also affected the industry, and in the early 1960s officials presumed that most visitors would travel from Britain and Northern Ireland. But by the end of the decade, propeller-driven aircraft was beginning to be replaced by the DC10 and Boeing 747, reducing the travel time of transatlantic flights. Accordingly, the arrival of more Americans suggested the need for more American-style hotels.

As the 1970 debate in the Seanad Éireann indicates, this prediction wasn't entirely accurate, as many tourists weren't interested in large Dublin hotels or camping sites. The taxonomy of tourist types was expanding to include "mobile tourists" who traveled from Britain by way of "roll-on/roll-off" ferries that began operating in the later 1960s. These vessels, variations of which were deployed in World War I to transport troops and equipment, conveyed mobile tourists *with* their cars who required differently designed motor hotels, restaurant options and entertainment (Heneghan, 229). Similarly, as Ashleigh Bixby describes, as the Troubles in the North receded at the end of the century, "conflict tourists," a subset of the larger "heritage tourist" category, began to appear in Belfast, Derry and elsewhere to view areas of unrest and artifacts associated with it (wall murals, for example).[10] All of these tourists had unique needs, and Ireland at times struggled to meet them. In the 1970 debate, Lenihan emphasized that, however worrisome the present downturn might be, the £36 million invested in accommodation development since 1959 had reaped appreciable dividends as revenue rose from £39 million to almost £98 million. This larger sum, moreover, did not reflect tourism's benefit as an economic "stimulus" in creating jobs in the West where "prospects of industrial development" remained "limited" ("Tourist Traffic Bill, 1970").

Not surprisingly, some of Lenihan's colleagues balked at appropriating additional funds. One questioned the wisdom of building hotels that replicated those found in New York, Boston or London, labeling it a "grave mistake" to present an "image almost wholly out of character with the traditions of this country." Many visitors expected something "genuine" and "unspoiled," not ersatz versions of the Waldorf Astoria.[11] Another complained that developers' efforts to recover their investments in new construction led to exorbitant pricing for accommodations and other services. Could it be, Lenihan's colleague wondered aloud, that "we are pricing ourselves out of the tourist market"? Another speaker urged greater cooperation with the North, a search for common ground formalized in 2000 with the founding of Irish Tourism, and the facilitation of opportunities for visitors to interact with local communities. He recommended a revised licensure allowing public houses to offer more expansive menus and a renewed focus on traditional, family-friendly evening entertainments. These issues notwithstanding, solicitor and economist Alexis Fitzgerald seemed to speak for the assembly by noting that although the number of visits fell by nearly a third during the previous year, tourism was indispensable to the Irish economy and its importance would grow.

There were, predictably, implications in the development of tourism that many, including Brian Friel, could not countenance. In *The Mundy Scheme* (1969), Friel's satirical lancing of Ireland's predicament, Taoiseach F. X. Ryan heads a country that is failing financially, a nation that "has been manipulated and abused by a huge colonial power for hundreds of years" (157). The opening scene conveys the severity of the crisis as Ryan's private secretary dictates a letter responding to a request for subsidy: "The Taoiseach asks me to inform you that at the moment he cannot support in principle the channeling of any state monies whatever into any new industry" (159). Moments later, Ryan enters followed by Neil Boyle, Minister of Finance, who announces that investors who have previously "shored up" the country now think "we're beyond repair" (173). Only a "flood" of capital investment will reverse rising emigration, create jobs and fund an expanded airstrip—and once reliable sources of investment are no longer available.

New investors from America, however, are a possibility. The U.S. Defense Department hopes to build a communication center in Cork and Galway to support their nuclear submarines, a proposal Boyle endorses. Ryan, though, has already rejected the idea and does so again. Boyle wonders if just one in Galway might be acceptable: "Beggars can't be choosers." But Ryan again disparages the notion:

> A beggar may be destitute but he can still have his honor and his integrity and his independence. Whatever small strength we have is in our absolute neutrality [...] Throw open our doors to the American forces and we become another kept woman. (175–76)

At the same time, he is well aware of Ireland's dire predicament: "The country [is] on the threshold of a great new abyss—the people about to be plunged into a spiritual and economic depression [...]" (179). What is the solution?

Moments later, Michael Moloney, Minister for External Affairs, arrives promoting the "most revolutionary and most rewarding commercial transaction that this country has ever undertaken" (193). It will spur capital investment, stem the tide of emigration, lead to "full employment in depressed areas," fuel a "300 percent leap in tourism" and—most significantly—transform the "whole barren west into the most wealthy and most productive part of the country" (194). "Productive" resonates with irony as Moloney summarizes the Mundy Scheme, named for Homer Mundy, the multimillionaire Texan who conceived it. The Scheme involves the purchase of 5,000 square miles of land in such counties as Mayo, Sligo and Connemara to create a "final resting place" for the Irish diaspora scattered across the world. Cemeteries take up valuable space in cities like New York, Moloney argues, so the concept will be popular in the United States. The opening act ends with his ideas for marketing the Scheme:

> France is the recognized home of good food; America is the acknowledged center of art; Switzerland is the center of Europe's banking. Let's make the west of Ireland the acknowledged [...] eternal resting place. (204)

Add "deceased, permanent visitors" to the ever-expanding roster of tourist types.

Predictable disagreements follow. Once uncertain about the idea, Taoiseach Ryan becomes its most avid proponent after acquiring land that will increase in value once it is adopted. He addresses a national television audience to garner support for it, assuring viewers that John F. Kennedy and the Pope would have endorsed it. Other businesses will also benefit, as "The World Alliance of Morticians" and "The European Florists Association" will schedule conventions in Ireland. In the final scene, as Ryan and his Cabinet toast their victory, a television in the background shows flights of mourners arriving in Dublin and traveling to a cemetery on Achill where their deceased relatives will find eternal rest. There, Mundy addresses the crowd, rebutting the aspersion that "wherever she stretched her tentacles, America spread decadence and death," and confidently predicting that more Americans will "settle here permanently" (305). The west of Ireland, the authentic nation, is saved.

When *The Mundy Scheme* opened in Dublin in June of 1969, serious socio-economic inequities were tearing at the fabric of American, Irish and Northern Irish societies. In America, the early 1960s recovery from the recession had little effect on social inequality. In 1967, while the summer of love was celebrated in San Francisco, Detroit and Newark were on fire where rioting in July claimed, respectively, 43 and 26 lives. Through an executive order, President Johnson established the National Advisory Commission on Civil Disorders, chaired by former Illinois governor Otto Kerner, to investigate the causes of the violence. While its findings emphasized the lack of economic opportunity and ineffective or abusive policing, the Commission attributed much of these disasters to white racism: "*Segregation and poverty have created in the racial ghetto a destructive environment totally unknown to most white Americans [...]. White institutions created it, white institutions maintain it, and white society condones it*" (2). Released in February 1968, the *Report* concluded that curing America's "racial disorders" was the nation's "major unfinished business" (1, 2).

At the same time, Northern Ireland became a more prominent topic in American and international headlines. Less than two weeks after the "Battle of the Bogside" in Derry, a confrontation that produced over 1,000 injuries and moved Taoiseach Jack Lynch to establish field hospitals along the Irish border while also calling for the British government's and United Nations' humanitarian assistance, Bernadette Devlin appeared on NBC's *Meet the Press* on August 24, 1969. Douglas Kiker, one of her four male interlocutors, pressed Devlin for assurances that her fund-raising efforts in America would not benefit the IRA. She countered by reiterating her intention to aid Catholic families fleeing the North; their homes were destroyed, and these refugees were in desperate need of shelter, food and medical attention. Pursuing his inquisition, Kiker reminded her that Protestant homes were also razed, and he seemed disconcerted by Devlin's answer to an earlier question about her possible meeting at the White House, an event that did not occur. In her answer, she outlined her goals for a conversation with Richard Nixon: help for refugees and an end to the exportation of American arms to Britain, who then supplied them to the Royal Ulster Constabulary (RUC) that in turn gave them to the "B Specials," a ruthless, largely Protestant police force. Only twenty-two and a newcomer to public life, Devlin acquitted herself skillfully. On March 25, 1972, after Edward Heath's suspension of the Stormont government, she appeared on *Firing Line*, whose host

William F. Buckley, Jr. alluded to Joan of Arc in introducing her, one of several "fancy labels" for which she held little affection.[12] Like her medieval predecessor, Devlin intruded into a world governed by older men, many of whom evinced little interest in her project.

The more Irish America learned about the human misery Devlin reported, the more concerned it became. But it did not respond in a single voice as her commitment to racial equality, to breaking "the bonds of *economic* slavery," evoked a range of reactions (Devlin, vii). Reporting on a 2010 documentary about her life, journalist Tom Deignan recalled many Irish Americans' expectation that she would relate melodramatic yarns of "dirty Brits" and Protestants oppressing innocent Catholics. On occasion, she did so, but things got more tense when she juxtaposed the struggles of Northern Catholics to those of black Americans (Deignan, "When Northern Irish Activist"). For Matthew J. O'Brien, her 1969 trip taxed Devlin's "seemingly inexhaustible spirit," a fatigue not solely attributable to a hectic two-week schedule (84). Many "contemporary commentators" contrasted her "irrepressible support for the American civil rights movement" with many older Irish Americans' "reticence, or outright hostility" to it. This disagreement flared more controversially when she declined Mayor Richard Daley's invitation to meet in Chicago, choosing instead to tour Jesse Jackson's Operation Breadbasket. Some eighteen months later, she returned to America, speaking in San Francisco on behalf of the imprisoned Angela Davis, emphasizing that she and Davis were engaged in the same class struggle.

As the 1970s began, unrest in Northern Ireland and America coupled with the demands of an emergent global economy required greater cooperation and created new pressures for the administrations of Richard Nixon and Gerald Ford . And, as James Cooper, among others, has argued, the United States' tepid disposition toward the Troubles grew increasingly unsustainable (99). In what follows, I hope to trace evidence of America's more meaningful engagement with Ireland, beginning in particular with revisions in foreign policy effectuated during the Nixon and Carter administrations. Slowly but surely, and necessarily, relationships between America, Ireland and Northern Ireland were changing.

From Cordiality to Commitment

> We are indeed greatly honored to have been invited here during your Bicentennial Year [...]. Mr. President, I am deeply touched by your *warm* welcome, and I am certain that our visit will further strengthen the *warm* bonds of [our] special friendship [...].
> —Liam Cosgrave, Remarks to President Gerald Ford
> (March 17, 1976)

> Almost one new US plant per week has opened in Ireland over the past two years […] and indeed investment by US companies is still growing dramatically.
> —Charles J. Haughey, "Ireland's Corner on US Business," from an address to the Economic Club of New York (May 24, 1982)

Any competition for the most tumultuous year in later twentieth-century America would feature several contenders. The rioting in Detroit and Newark, for instance, would easily qualify 1967 and 1968 for the title—and 1969 wasn't much better. The peace and love of Woodstock in the summer of 1969 were notably absent from December's "Woodstock West" festival at the Altamont Speedway in Livermore, California. For by the time the Rolling Stones finished their set at the end of the night, Marty Balin of Jefferson Airplane had been knocked unconscious, and four people in a crowd of 300,000 lay dead—one from knife wounds and a beating by members of the Hell's Angels motorcycle gang, who had been paid $500 worth of beer to provide security. Their victim was a young black man whom several Angels mugged while another stabbed him. As an eyewitness recalled, attempting to ward off his attackers Meredith Hunter drew a .22 handgun, waving it in the air when a young woman screamed, "Don't shoot anyone." He didn't, the gun was taken from him and he was assaulted again. Hunter was eighteen with a white girlfriend; and in *Just a Shot Away: Peace, Love, and Tragedy with the Rolling Stones at Altamont* (2018), Saul Austerlitz identifies one all-too-evident cause of his murder: he "had gone somewhere white men did not want him to be" (148). While the unrest of 1968 caused by the assassination of Martin Luther King, Jr., in April and police brutality during the Democratic National Convention in Chicago later that August had subsided, violence continued in 1969, including the Stonewall Riot in New York in June.

One source of violence in Northern Ireland paralleled that at Altamont: people going places other people didn't want them to go. Planning the "Selma" of Northern Ireland, members of the People's Democracy and other activists—many of them university students—met in Belfast on New Year's Day, 1969, to begin a civil rights march to Derry.[13] On January 2 Michael Farrell, one of the march's organizers, told a reporter that they had been prevented from passing through certain areas; like their counterparts in the southern United States, they were denied what Farrell called "the basic democratic liberty of free procession." Carrying banners and singing Pete Seeger's "We Shall Overcome," the group grew in number, and outside Derry they were warned that a hostile reception awaited them (Farrell was told that he might even be killed). Organized by a police official influenced by Ian Paisley and armed with rocks, clubs and police batons, 300 counter-demonstrators, many of them "B Specials," were positioned around the Burntollet Bridge. At home in an increasingly tense housing estate, a teenaged Bobby Sands watched these events unfold on television, the attack on the marchers imprinting itself on his mind "like a scar." For the first time in his young life, he took a "real interest in what was going on" (qtd. in O'Hearn, 9). That interest would grow.

So would sectarian conflict. Echoing the slurs of autocrats like Adolf Hitler and anticipating Donald Trump's denigration of his political opponents and immigrants arriving at the country's Southern border during the 2024 American presidential campaign, Paisley alleged that Catholics "breed like rabbits and multiply like *vermin*" (Alexander, "Ian Paisley's Most Caustic Quotes").[14] Seemingly oblivious to the roles of women in the civil rights movement, he also contended that most nationalist protesters were actually IRA *men* in disguise. And, much as the marchers from Selma to Montgomery on Bloody Sunday in 1965 were brutalized by white policemen as they crossed the Edmund Pettus Bridge, those who undertook the trek from Belfast to Derry were ruthlessly attacked. Fueled by the hostile screeds at which Paisley excelled, the events that day led many to conclude, as Bernadette Devlin did during her first tour of America, that the struggle ahead would not only pit Catholic against Protestant, but a younger generation against an older one that too often regarded social change as a parasitic contamination of the social order.

In *The Price of My Soul* (1969), Devlin is shaken by evidence of this hatred as manifested by the "wee" Protestant woman who lived across the road. Despite their religious differences, this neighbor "thought the world" of Devlin's mother and was one of the "most genuine friends" her family had. Yet, when Devlin campaigned for Parliament, this same woman disparaged her in public as "Fenian scum!" Why? "Because of the Reverend Ian Paisley, and civil rights, and unemployment" (48). Here, like the Kerner Commission, Devlin identifies two perennial sources of social unrest: the struggle for equal rights and what Andrew Undershaft in Bernard Shaw's *Major Barbara* (1905) deems the "worst of crimes"—poverty. Importantly, while being insulted, Devlin recognized a third, staple ingredient of "Troubles": a bellicose leader preaching hatred to followers that hang on his every word.

Tensions wrought in the 1960s exploded in the 1970s. The splitting of the republican movement into political (Sinn Féin) and military (Provisional IRA or PIRA) wings, for example, produced enormous consequences. As Thomas Hennessey argues in *The Evolution of the Troubles, 1970–1872* (2007), meetings in January of 1970 not only concretized the PIRA's determination to defend against Loyalist and British Army aggression in the upcoming marching season, but also led to a program of "combined defense and retaliation" and, later, to an "all-out offensive action against the 'British occupation system'" (7).

The British reaction to these developments was excessive, culminating in internment in August 1971. In *Noraid and the Northern Ireland Troubles 1970–1994* (2022), Robert Collins notes that during the first four days of the policy 342 suspects were arrested; and, although loyalist paramilitaries were responsible for twenty-two deaths in 1971 and by the end of 1972 had killed 107 Catholics with "little or no connection" to the PIRA, it was not until 1973 that the first two loyalists were interned. The policy's bias was conspicuous; and by the time internment ended on December 5, 1975, "1,981 people had been interned, of which 1,874 (94.6%) were Nationalist and 107 (5.4%) were Loyalist" (Collins, 38).

Citing David McKittrick and his colleagues' *Lost Lives* (1999), Glenn Patterson also underscores the prejudice inherent to the policy, recalling that of an estimated 3,637 "Troubles-related deaths" the first two murders in 1966 were actually committed by the Ulster Volunteer Force (UVF) and one of the last by loyalist paramilitaries (*Backstop Nation*, 109). "Loyalists," he recalls, "went after unarmed Catholics as a matter of course and with a viciousness that at moments looked gleeful" (114). Driven from their homes and fearing for their safety, more than 5,000 refugees, most from a "nationalist background," fled to the Republic in 1971 (McClements. "Northern Ireland's"), with 10,000 more following the next summer (Barry, "Thousands of Northern Refugees").[15]

In an instance of understatement, Collins mentions that the "one-sided nature" of internment "appeared to have stoked a response in Irish America" (42). Indeed, it did. In August 1971, the Irish Northern Aid Committee (INA or Noraid) picketed the British Consulate on Fifth Avenue, and in September, the American Committee for Ulster Justice (ACUJ) posted a full-page advertisement in the *New York Times* (Collins, 41). Appalled by the suspension of *habeas corpus*, Senators Kennedy, Abraham Ribicoff (D–CT) and others joined the American Congress for Irish Freedom (ACIF) in denouncing the policy. In October 1971, they drafted a resolution—introduced by Kennedy in the Senate, Hugh Carey in the House—calling for the "immediate withdrawal of British troops from Ulster and the establishment of a united Ireland. Without a firm commitment to troop withdrawal and unification, there can be no peace in Northern Ireland." In a now (in)famous analogy, Kennedy added: "Ulster is becoming Britain's Vietnam." The resolution elicited the ire of both Unionist Prime Minister Brian Faulkner in Belfast, who accused Kennedy of "playing American politics with Ulster people's lives," and Prime Minister Heath in London, who dismissed the proposal as an "ignorant outburst" (qtd. in Wilson, 60). Ignorant or not, by the end of the 1970s, Kennedy's indictment became almost irrefutable.

Equally important, the "Kennedy Resolution" initiated a process of revisiting and revising existing policies. For just a year before, as he prepared to visit Ireland, Richard Nixon was reminded by Henry Kissinger that "We have made clear repeatedly that we consider Northern Ireland under British sovereignty"; thus, the president should only "demonstrate tacit support" for Taoiseach Jack Lynch's "moderate and conciliatory" approach (Sanders, *Long Peace*, 42). A year later, Nixon remained unmoved by both the resolution and a letter from Kennedy that reiterated his concern:

> The continuing reign of killing and violence in Ulster is a source of deep concern to millions of citizens in America and peoples throughout the world [...]. I believe that the Administration has a greater responsibility to speak and act than it has shown so far. (qtd. in Sanders, *Long Peace*, 64)

Although Kennedy was assured of Nixon's broaching this issue with the British government, he remained skeptical. In the spring of 1972, he called John Hume and met him in Bonn for the first of many conversations about Northern Ireland. These talks intensified in 1976 when Hume was invited to spend a semester at Harvard.

Internment also contributed to the PIRA's decision to initiate bombing campaigns that not only caused more than 3,600 deaths but to thousands of injuries and the maiming of innocent victims. Such was the case on June 16, 1970, when three bombmakers (and two young children) in Derry became the first PIRA members to be killed by their own bomb (by 1973, forty-four bombmakers were killed in the manufacture of explosive devices).[16] In a 2020 report on the incident, Seamus McKinney outlined the circumstances: "With the outbreak of the Troubles, the three found themselves among the most senior IRA members in Derry" ("New Video"). As a result, they were tasked with assembling a bomb to protest Bernadette Devlin's arrest for participating in the Battle of the Bogside. Regardless of the dangers involved in producing bombs, as urban sociologist Mike Davis argues, their destructive potential proved seductive to paramilitary leaders even if, as Belfast journalist Ed Moloney observed, their use "greatly increased the risk of civilian deaths in careless or bungled operations" (qtd. in Davis, 56). One of the most notorious of these was the failed attempt by the UVF in the early hours of July 31, 1975, to conceal a bomb in a van driven by the popular Miami Showband returning to Dublin from a performance in Banbridge, County Down. Two paramilitaries were killed by the blast and, in an attempt to silence potential witnesses, their remaining colleagues (and a British officer) shot and killed three band members.

For Davis, this proliferation of bombs paralleled the use of explosives in student protests on American college and university campuses.

In particular, Richard Nixon's televised address on April 30, 1970, announcing the expansion of fighting on the Vietnamese-Cambodian border precipitated what Amanda Miller of the University of Washington's Civil Rights and Labor History Consortium terms "one of the largest coordinated sequences of disruptive protests in American history" affecting "more than **883 campuses**" and involving "more than a million students" (emphasis in original). Within hours of the broadcast, protests erupted across the country; within days, four students were killed by National Guardsmen at Kent State on May 4, and fourteen students were shot by police at Jackson State College in the early morning hours of May 15, two fatally.[17]

Rioting on college and university campuses forced many schools to end the 1969–70 academic year early. On several campuses, Reserve Officer Training Corps (ROTC) facilities became targets for firebombing even before the tragedy at Kent State. In February 1970, the ROTC cadet lounge at the University of Illinois at Urbana-Champaign, my alma mater, was bombed, and thirty-five bomb threats were made at the university that year. As reported in the *New York Times*, 450 National Guard troops were called out on March 4 to enforce a 10:30 p.m. curfew; and, earlier in the day, police removed 100 protesters from the Illinois Student Union, where recruiters for General Motors, Standard Oil and the Chrysler Corporation were conducting job interviews. On March 10, two months after the Champaign Police Station was set ablaze, an off-campus Air Force recruiting office was bombed (Hillman, "UI Steers Clear"). Across the country and within hours of Nixon's address, firebombs damaged the Information Systems Building, Music Annex and Downey House at Wesleyan University in Connecticut. It was a punishing year for American universities and, as was the case in Derry and Belfast, bombs and incendiary devices caused much of the destruction.

Mike Davis's intimation of a transatlantic influence provides a useful context for IRA bombings, including "Bloody Friday" on July 21, 1972, in which twenty-six bombs detonated in Belfast caused eleven deaths and over 130 injuries. As Davis suggests, radicals on American campuses might even bear indirect responsibility for the scope of such campaigns by experimenting with and producing inexpensive, yet devastatingly effective explosives. After a splinter group affiliated with Students for a Democratic Society (SDS) at the University of Wisconsin–Madison read a pamphlet advising farmers on how to "excavate duck ponds," it began fabricating devices from cheap, readily available ingredients like fertilizer and fuel oil (55). The resulting Ammonium Nitrate Fuel Oil bomb, ANFO, as it was later abbreviated, "raised the maximum yields of a van or truck bomb to several tons of TNT" (56). On August 24, 1970, activists detonated an ANFO bomb hidden in a van parked by Sterling Hall, in which the Army Mathematics Research Center and the school's Physics department were housed. The explosion decimated one wing of Sterling, damaged two dozen other buildings and killed a young physicist working in his lab. The "Madison gang," Davis remarks, "suddenly found itself with innocent blood on its hands" (54–55).

So did bombers in Northern Ireland, and news of cascading violence there led to the founding of such organizations in America as the National Association for Irish Freedom (NAIF) and National Association for Irish Justice (NAIJ) that, among other things, lobbied President Nixon to act. Yet, the policy of nonintervention was so sacrosanct that mere allusions to Northern Ireland in drafts of Nixon's 1972 campaign speeches were deleted (four years later, Carter purposefully inserted such allusions in his). The Nixon Administration's position was summarized by Alexander Haig in a memorandum to a White House aide: "Thus far," he observed, "we have avoided a hornet's nest" by limiting commentary on the matter to hopes for peace while "at the same time emphasizing that it would be 'inappropriate and counter-productive' to intervene in any way" (qtd. in Sanders, *Long Peace*, 67–68).

While within a decade this position became untenable, adherence to it before then did not necessarily mean that the "cordial" relationship between countries remained unchanged during the Nixon years. Ironically, several disagreements over bilateral policy revealed the shallowness of this cordiality and, albeit awkwardly, brought—in one instance, *pushed*—Ireland and America closer together after Nixon's "forgotten visit" to Ireland in 1970.[18]

Nixon in Ireland, a Burgeoning Economy and The Carter Initiative

Before arriving at Kilfrush House in County Limerick for a formal dinner and two-night stay, President Nixon and his wife Pat were met at Shannon airport on October 3, 1970, by a group that included Ambassador John Moore, Patrick Hillery, who later served as Irish president from 1976 to 1990, and Taoiseach Lynch. After welcoming his guests, Lynch waxed effusively about the "very, very close" ties between the two countries and predicted that the president's arrival would make these ties even closer. For his part, Nixon mused about being the second president to visit Ireland while in office, referring to "a little hitch" in 1960 that prevented him from being the first. He then turned to his family's affection for their ancestral home:

> As is true for millions of American families, there are close and abiding Nixon family connections with Ireland [...]. I hope that my visit will

underscore the great warmth, closeness, and the non-partisanship of American-Irish ties, rooted in our Irish ancestry, in our admiration for Irish traditions, and our dedication in common to work for a democratic and peaceful world. (qtd. in Sanders, *Long Peace*, 47)

The next day, while Pat Nixon met relatives in Mayo, the president repeated these sentiments at a friendly, uneventful gathering at a Quaker cemetery in County Kildare. But his receptions in Dublin and Limerick on October 5 were hardly so tame, as *en route* to Dublin Castle to meet Lynch and his wife for a state luncheon Nixon's motorcade was greeted by demonstrators protesting American militarism, especially that in southeast Asia.

In his 2022 reflections on the president's "less than overwhelming welcome" in Ireland, John Mulqueen assesses the changing ideological landscape in the years between the Kennedy and Nixon visits. The very factors responsible for the change—international student activism, in particular—motivated a reception that was at times more hostile than underwhelming. Nixon's effigy was burned outside the American embassy, and he was targeted by three egg-throwers, one of whom, Máirín de Burca, co-founded the Irish Women's Liberation Movement. Three months earlier, two sailors from the *USS Plymouth Rock* were shot in Dublin— fortunately, neither was seriously wounded—by a member of the Irish-Indo-Chinese Solidarity Front in retaliation for the deaths of "unarmed" Vietnamese peasants. Such events led Ambassador Moore to advise the White House that anti-American demonstrators have "fed on the irritants which have crept into Irish feelings for the US as the old family ties between the countries weaken" (qtd. in Mulqueen).

An advocate for a more robust American-Irish economic partnership, John Moore served as Ambassador to Ireland from June 23, 1969, to June 20, 1975; and from the beginning, he was aware of another strain on the countries' relationship: transatlantic air travel and Irish insistence that Shannon remain its air traffic control center. In 1945, it was determined that all "eastbound air traffic from the United States to Ireland and beyond, shall stop at the Shannon airport as first European port of call"; all westbound traffic on the same route would as well. The agreement was negotiated at international conferences in Chicago, Havana and Montreal in 1944 and 1945, consistent with the stipulation that each country could "restrict the freedom of aircraft using the skies above it" (Furlong, *Irish Tourism*, 99). Seán Lemass and his colleagues parlayed this into an economic strategy to develop the western counties, and in 1947 Shannon was designated a "Customs Free Airport" with goods flown to and stored in newly constructed warehouses. Yet, however "legal," this dispensation continued to rankle American carriers.

So, when the Irish government sought permission for Aerlinte Eireann to land in New York, Boston and Chicago, American officials requested a reconsideration of the mandatory stop in Shannon. It was denied.

By 1961, and in kerfuffles before then, American solicitation for landing rights in Dublin grew more vocal, unnerving Limerick-based travel agencies and car rental companies. Politicians who ascribed Limerick's ascendant economy to the establishment of Shannon as an international airport and industrial center also opposed the idea (Sanders, "Landing Rights," 151). While Dublin Airport was lengthening its runways to accommodate larger jets and adding departure piers (a new terminal was opened in 1972), tensions seemed to ease—but not for long. Other solutions were considered. In 1966 Lemass, searching for a compromise, had suggested that U.S. planes might be allowed to land in Dublin if they stopped at Shannon first, but by 1968 a feisty memo from Secretary of State Dean Rusk's office to Walt Rostow at National Security Affairs revealed ongoing acrimony over the issue:

> Since 1961 we have participated in a fruitless dialogue with the Irish [...]. The Irish have refused to make the slightest concession on the landing rights problem [...]. (qtd. in Sanders, 155)

"Fruitless dialogue" and refusals to grant even the "slightest concession" threatened to undermine the cordial and "very, very close" relationship between countries.

In August 1971, the luster of President Nixon's newly burnished Irishness having faded, the State Department advised the Irish government that "unless settlement was reached on its request for USA carriers to serve Dublin in addition to Shannon, the right of Aerlinte to serve New York would be terminated in August 1972" (Furlong, *Irish Tourism*, 107). As reported in the *New York Times* (August 19, 1971), this ultimatum marked "a sudden break in 25-year-old negotiations" and "was said to be related to President Nixon's new economic doctrine and its insistence on 'fair competition' in foreign commerce." In response, a spokesman for Irish Airlines called the demand "a threat to its existence," as 65% of its North American travel was based in New York (Lydon, "Irish Planes to be Barred"). Eventually, Nixon's hard line resulted in a mutually beneficial understanding. As the *Times* put it on June 12, 1973— the deadline for an agreement having been extended by a year—after 27 years of "haggling," the dispute was settled ("After Twenty-Seven Years"). Shannon *and* Dublin were now open to American carriers.

With his determination to resolve the landing rights dispute and a keen economic interest, John Moore, an exceptionally competent envoy to Ireland, helped usher in a new era of cooperation. His obituary in the *New York Times*

(September 13, 1988) cites his key role in the 1963 founding of the Ireland–United States Council, an organization that, as its website clarifies, focuses "on activities that will develop communications, dialogue and improved understanding between leaders in business and government on both sides of the Atlantic." As an example, in 2021, the Council's website reprinted editorials from the *Wall Street Journal* critical of the Biden Administration's proposal for a global minimum tax. In "Ireland's Tax Lesson for Biden" (May 27, 2021), the *WSJ* Editorial Board reminded readers that the country's low-tax policy has been a "boon to global growth and investment." Its critique ended with a political death wish: "Let's hope Ireland and a few other tax stalwarts hold out and kill the Biden global tax scheme." The Council echoed the *WSJ*, offering a brief history of the moribund post-war Irish economy saved in part by revised, business-friendly tax policies.

Many narratives of this progress foreground developments in the 1970s and 1980s that led to unprecedented growth in the 1990s, a remarkable feat considering the severe global recession as the 1980s began and the increased international concern over Northern Ireland. In 2015, Henry McDonald in the *Guardian* related the good news that "almost one new US plant per week has opened [...] over the past two years" in Ireland, a record of continuing investment "still growing dramatically." He estimated that the country had "benefited from $277bn (£182bn) of US direct foreign investment in the past two decades—gaining more from American firms than Brazil, Russia, India, and China combined." Employing some 130,000 workers, the list of over 700 companies in Ireland featured such names as Boston Scientific, Pfizer, Google and Intel. In 2022, RTÉ reported that the roster of companies had grown to over 900, employing 190,000 people directly with 152,000 working in a "related, indirect" capacity. Corporations like Deloitte, Citi Group, Amazon and Starbucks have also found Northern Ireland a profitable place to invest, leading in September 2022 to a record number of workers employed in the private sector. And, as Mimi Murray emphasized in the *Irish Times* in 2018, investment has flown in both directions, as Irish companies have infused some $85 billion into the U.S. economy. In his remarks to the houses of the Oireachtas on April 13, 2023, President Biden celebrated the fact that bilateral trade between countries exceeds $1 trillion and, while alluding briefly to the taxation the *WSJ* opposed, he expressed his confidence in the continuing success of the countries' "thriving economic relationship" ("Remarks by President Biden").

It would be naïve, however, to overlook the unfortunate side effects of this partnership. Fintan O'Toole discusses several of these and, while I might quibble with him about distinctions between "Troubles" and "civil war"—and, as I shall discuss later, about his suspicion concerning Bill Clinton's motives for engagement with Northern Ireland—his analysis of the downsides of the Irish-American business partnership is persuasive. In *We Don't Know Ourselves: A Personal History of Modern Ireland* (2021), he discusses two of particular note: first, in addition to creating fictional ways of thinking, the influx of American capital has produced a new form of "compartmentalization" in Ireland; and second, as of 2013 multinationals were responsible for just 15% of the Irish workforce, with 85% of workers employed by "indigenous businesses, most of them small or medium-sized." The result? "There was not an Irish economy—there were two of them" (498). And the former one has evolved (metastasized?) in ways that impair accurate financial accounting (and thus tax liability) through chimeric "profit rates," the invention of companies "that were not companies" and "magical money that could be everywhere and nowhere" (496). Such phantoms surfaced, in part, as a result of Apple's enormous growth in Cork—700 employees working in 1980 ballooned to 6000 by 2019—when it came time to calculate taxable income. Through a series of maneuvers beneficial both to the corporation and the State, O'Toole argues, it was determined that a substantial portion of the profit was generated "in that place that has always been so central to the Irish imagination: elsewhere" (495). And corporate taxes aren't levied there.

Equally discernible are the unhealthy, even libidinal effects of the new prosperity on the 85% of individuals working in the second economy—financial impacts, of course, but also disturbing subjective ones as well. Becoming an "average western European country" was "fabulous," O'Toole concedes, but "its achievement was drowned out by a constant drumbeat of hype." By the late 1990s, he argues, Ireland's chief exports from the big pharma corporations included Viagra, Prozac and Botox, signifiers of the "artificial highs" and "cosmetic enhancements" inherent to this hype (498). In turn, these pharmaceutical prostheses create fictions that seep into the senses of self-worth of those struggling to keep pace, as Dermot Bolger's *Tanglewood* (2015) depicts. Chris and Alice, the middle-aged couple at the center of the novel, have been together for twenty years, but as their story begins they have recently moved to separate bedrooms. Entrepreneurial speculation has been running wild all around them—their neighbor Ronan epitomizes this in his risky acquisition of properties—but Chris "missed out on Ireland's bonanza years, with neighbours exploiting tax incentives to acquire buy-to-let apartments" (11). Viewing himself as a failure, Chris attends property auctions to try and catch up, but he never makes a winning bid; and the "longer the saga of trying to buy a house in this frenzied market went on," the more he seemed "to diminish himself" (15). Driven by the "perfumed aphrodisiac of prosperity" that permeates Main Street in Blackrock in the form of S-Class Mercedes Benz's and lines of cocaine, Ronan "possessed the balls" Chris lacked (52). Maybe he really needed the Viagra Alice discovered in his jacket pocket to "prove himself capable of closing a deal" with a girlfriend (14). Alice's libido is also affected by Chris's emasculation: "If she started thinking about the house for auction, she was doomed to lie awake. It would be almost as bad as if Chris were in the bedroom, tormenting her with figures" (14).

The gestation of this economy was coterminous with the evolving Troubles; and the 1970s ended, as they had begun, with shocking atrocities. Solutions to both Ireland's economic woes and sectarian violence would require far greater bilateral cooperation, more than polite "cordiality." One impetus of this was Ireland's joining the European Economic Community (EEC) in 1973, which not only affected its interactions with regional neighbors but also, as Martin Wall posits, added a "new dimension to its relations with the US" in which "economic considerations became the main focus of Irish foreign policy." Part of this focus was borne from the realization that Ireland's fortune was now bound more tightly to that of its neighbors; as a consequence, the "economic strategy of the Irish government moved from protectionism to free trade" (Wall, 125). Moreover, Ireland joined the EEC at a time when the relationship between Europe and the US was "stormy," the controversy over airplane landing rights partially responsible for this inclemency. But America, Wall argues, came to understand that Ireland would "no longer be able to unreservedly accept US foreign policy." By the summer of 1975, relations had "normalised again within this new context" (126).

The political challenges were just as daunting. Violence in the North throughout the 1970s was impossible to ignore, as Louise Kennedy's novel *Trespasses* emphasizes with bombings, shootings and other horrors defining daily reality in nearly every chapter. As the Carter administration settled in, this factor and the Troubles' impact on human rights led to an even greater revision of American foreign policy. As James Cooper recalls, *candidate* Carter, perhaps in an effort to "capture the Irish-American voter," marched down Fifth Avenue in New York's 1976 St. Patrick's Day parade wearing a lapel badge with the slogan "Get Britain Out of Ireland" ("The Situation Over There"). Contrary to suggestions of his indifference, President Carter took the matter far more seriously.

In the fall of 1976, John Hume accepted a semester-long fellowship at Harvard University's Center for International Relations. The appointment afforded him opportunities to meet with the Irish American "Four Horsemen" and their chiefs of staff, including Tim Russert from Moynihan's staff and Kirk O'Donnell from O'Neill's. Russert, O'Donnell, National Security Advisor Robert Hunter, and Michael Lillis, then a political counselor at the Irish embassy who later played a key role in negotiating the 1985 Anglo-Irish Agreement, "wrestled over six months on a text with the recalcitrant team from the British embassy and the State Department, who were backed by discouraging phone calls from prime minister Jim Callaghan to President Jimmy Carter."[19] This opposition to what eventually became the Carter Initiative on Northern Ireland, predictably enough, originated in America's "special relationship" with Britain and the longstanding policy of nonintervention in its affairs.

Two of Hume's greatest assets were his abilities to critique enervated policies and devise solutions to seemingly intractable problems. He was a prime mover in the Sunningdale Agreement of 1973 which, in Lillis's summary of Hume's legacy, amounted to an "anthology of what later became known as Humespeak: power-sharing within Northern Ireland, North-South partnership, Anglo-Irish partnership, a Bill of Rights" (372). The Agreement, as Marilynn Richtarik recounts, was undone when in May of 1974 the British government "allowed unionist strikers to prevail" and failed "to protect the North's new political institutions" created by the Agreement ("Hume, Heaney, Harvard").[20] This, in turn, motivated Lillis's similar denunciations of Harold Wilson's government and Merlyn Rees, Secretary of State for Northern Ireland, for "endorsing the British army's cowardly refusal to confront the loyalist workers' strike," and of the PIRA, who were just as "ferociously determined to destroy Sunningdale by their deliberately intensified campaign of assassination and bombing as were the killers of the UDA and UVF" (372).[21] These events led Hume to realize, as Richtarik puts it, that "other powerful forces" needed to be recruited: *American* forces. These insights, dedicated work behind the scenes and the lobbying of the Four Horsemen led to the 1977 Carter Initiative.

While the significance of the Initiative's departure from orthodox foreign policy is irrefutable, opinions differ about its genesis. A 2009 *Irish Times* article by Deaglán De Bréadún, former head of the newspaper's Belfast bureau, begins with aspersions both of Carter's fatuity about Northern Ireland and of the intellectual laziness of his staff:

> Top White House staff in the administration of President Jimmy Carter were not just ignorant of the basic facts about Northern Ireland but also apparently unwilling to study the issue or even to take it seriously [...]. However, in a briefing document for the US visit of Taoiseach Jack Lynch from November 7th to 16th, 1979, ambassador Seán Donlon praises Mr Carter as 'the first president to commit his administration on the Northern Ireland issue.' ("Carter's staff")

Indeed, Carter *was* the first president to make such a commitment. This fact and Robert Hunter's participation in negotiations suggest the absurdity of any insinuations that the Carter White House opted for willful ignorance and simply capitulated to political "pressure." The president understood exactly what he was doing, as he did when blocking the sale of American-made guns to the RUC in late 1979.

In a more generous reading, historians P. J. McLoughlin and Alison Meagher argue that the Carter Initiative was "more significant than, or certainly foundational to," the brokering the Good Friday Agreement (671). More obviously, it possessed a "much greater political import" than is typically recognized, in part because of the implications of phrasings that should be read carefully, not merely skimmed over or ignored. For example:

> The United States wholeheartedly supports peaceful means for finding a just solution that involves both parts of the community of Northern Ireland [...] as well as the Governments of Great Britain and Ireland [...]. In the event of such a settlement, the U.S. Government would be prepared to join with others to see how additional job-creating investment could be encouraged, to the benefit of all the people of Northern Ireland.

Two of the Initiative's assertions evolved over the next twenty years into prerequisites: a "just solution" required the approbation of both Northern Irish communities, and the process of reaching it also required the participation of both the British *and* Irish governments.

But there is more, rendering the witticism that the Belfast Agreement was "Sunningdale for slow learners" slightly inaccurate. To be sure, the Sunningdale Agreement anticipated elements of the 1998 treaty, a power-sharing Executive, for instance. Yet the later 1990s were different than the 1970s, in part due to the more vigorous engagements of Britain, Ireland and America described in the following chapter. In depicting the political climate of Northern Ireland prior to the Hunger Strikes of late 1980 and 1981, journalist David Beresford alludes to a prevalent misconception that the British "were looking for a withdrawal and it was only a matter of time before they went" (43). Given the disastrous imposition of internment and the failure of Diplock courts, the supposition that an exasperated Britain was packing its bags might seem understandable. But Britain wasn't going anywhere—and the Troubles were hardly over. In addition to the Carter Initiative proposing the inclusion of the British and Irish governments, two other commitments were equally critical: "job-creating investment" that would benefit all citizens and the moderation of acerbic Irish-American commentary on Northern Ireland by those who supported republican paramilitary organizations.

Work remained to be done.

Notes

1. For comparisons between Donald Trump and Hitler, see Caryl Rivers, "POV: Comparing Trump to Hitler Misses the Point."
2. Goldwater's recommendation about Falwell has been reprinted often. In an editorial celebrating O'Connor's career, Linda Greenhouse notes that although O'Connor was a critic of *Roe v. Wade*, after four justices took a position in *Webster v. Reproductive Services* (1989) that as a "practical matter would have overturned *Roe*," she declined to do likewise. "There will be time enough to re-examine *Roe*," she wrote. Three years later, that moment arrived when she voted to uphold women's right to abortion in *Planned Parenthood v. Casey*.
3. Goldwater and Trump share other similarities, including the former's tendency to give "impulsive" answers to reporters' questions as Trump did at daily news briefings during the pandemic. Like Trump's, Goldwater's statements and addresses were not always "carefully prepared or presented" (Goldberg, 224).
4. The contributions of Patricia McCluskey in "documenting, highlighting and challenging the injustices of the Northern state, and laying the foundation for the civil rights movement" in the early and mid-1960s, as Bernadette (Devlin) McAliskey emphasized, has "never been properly acknowledged" ("A Peasant," 77).
5. The subtitle of one of Dumbrell's articles summarizes this narrative: "The United States and the Northern Irish Conflict 1969–94: from Indifference to Intervention." Dumbrell even quotes a journalist who alleges that from 1969 to the inauguration of Bill Clinton American policy toward Northern Ireland was "wholly baleful," not merely indifferent (107). As Marilynn Richtarik emphasizes in *Getting to Good Friday: Literature and the Peace Process in Northern Ireland*, distinctions between "nationalist" and "republican" are important, and these caused disagreement among many Irish Americans. As Dumbrell notes, "over the years US-born Irish-Americans have found constitutional nationalism an alternative more acceptable than the tradition of 1916" (110).
6. Limerick historian Gearóid Ó Faoleán has questioned the accuracy of estimates of the number of Catholics in the Ulster Defence Regiment. See also Weinraub, "Catholic Member of the Ulster Force is Slain," *New York Times*, October 11, 1972.
7. As Robert Collins points out, the release of the *Compton Report* ten days after Bloody Sunday rankled many, as its inquiry into allegations of British brutality in conducting interrogations raised questions about the barbarism of British forces in Northern Ireland (39).
8. Weinraub's reporting refutes accusations made by Irish-American nationalists that reporters wrote about the Troubles from the comforts of their London hotels. Weinraub also undermines the notion that the *Times* was a pro-British paper, leading to the punning aspersion that it favored "All the News That's Brit to Print." See Andrew J. Wilson, *Irish America and the Ulster Conflict, 1968–1995*, 181–88.
9. In the front matter of *JFK in Ireland*, Tubridy reproduces Jacqueline Kennedy's note thanking Éamon de Valera for attending her husband's funeral. In it, she emphasizes his affection for Ireland, affection deepened by his trip which "meant more to him than any other in his life."
10. See Bixby. As she, Zuelow and others note, by the end of 1998 cooperative agreements were made between Northern Ireland and the Republic. Tourism Ireland was founded in 2000, with Tourism Brand Ltd. to follow.

11 Wheatley and Krobb, 3. Their Introduction to Richard Arnold Bermann's *Ireland [1913]* stresses both this point and the concern that Irish entrepreneurs exploited tourists. In the debate over tourism fifty-seven years later, both objections were resurrected, suggesting the ongoing challenge of balancing tradition with the demands of modernity.

12 Bridling at analogies between her and figures like Joan of Arc, Devlin in her "Foreword" to *The Price of My Soul* clarifies her intention to present in her account a "real flesh-and-blood" person before being "submerged" by such "fancy labels" (vii–viii).

13 In his Introduction to *Twenty Years On*, Farrell describes the organization of the Peoples Democracy before the October 5, 1968 March on Derry. Like Bernadette Devlin, he acknowledges the influence of figures like Martin Luther King and Che Guevara (11).

14 Alexander wrote this retrospective following Paisley's death. On November 11, 2023, Trump told a New Hampshire audience, "We pledge to you that we will root out the communists, Marxists, fascists and the radical left thugs that live like vermin within the confines of our country [...]." Two days later, Trump spokesman Steven Cheung defended the former president's comments: "Those who try to make that ridiculous assertion are clearly snowflakes grasping for anything [...] and their sad, miserable existence will be crushed when President Trump returns to the White House."

15 McClements reports that while in 1971 only 26,000 residents of the Republic were born in Northern Ireland, by 1981, the number had risen to over 40,000. She regards this increase as the result not only of violence but also of a "class judgment" whereby working-class Catholics were denied employment in the North. Devlin's father was one of these, deemed "politically suspect" and forced to seek work in England (Devlin, 24).

16 See Carroll, *Killing Thatcher*, 55.

17 The incident at Jackson State was also motivated by rumors of the assassination of a local political figure. None of the shooters was prosecuted or convicted.

18 One of these is Branagh Dempsey who, in his catalogue for a 2022 exhibit "Famous Faces," an installation of photographs and artifacts collected from the arrivals of world leaders and celebrities at Dublin Castle, describes President Nixon's visit as "forgotten."

19 Lillis, 373. In *John Hume in America*, Maurice Fitzpatrick similarly emphasizes that the Carter Doctrine didn't simply materialize one providential day, but rather required six months of hard work and negotiation. See Fitzpatrick, 56–60.

20 See also Richtarik's *Getting to Good Friday*.

21 Bew, Gibbon and Patterson note that the UWC "had clear links with the main Protestant paramilitary organizations like the Ulster Defence Association and the Ulster Volunteer Force, and its success was clearly dependent on the intimidatory tactics of these organizations in the strike's earliest stages" (198).

Provocation 2

A "CAREENING CIRCUS OF PRATFALL EMBARRASSMENTS": DONALD TRUMP IN IRELAND

> And you have promised me that when I come here in the evenings to meditate upon my madness; to watch the shadow of the Round Tower lengthening in the sunset [...] you will comfort me with the bustle of a great hotel, and the sight of the little children carrying the golf clubs of your tourists as a preparation for the life to come.
> —Peter Keegan in Bernard Shaw, *John Bull's Other Island* (1904)

On her June 6, 2019, show, MSNBC's Rachel Maddow characterized Donald Trump's visit to Ireland as "a careening circus of pratfall embarrassments." Most of the wince-inducing mortifications surfaced in the president's meeting with Taoiseach Leo Varadkar the preceding day during which Trump's ignorance and hubris were on full display. But the trip also exhibited more than low comedy. In the context of American presidents' appearances in Ireland—Joe Biden's trip to Ireland in 2023 marked the seventh such occurrence—Trump's stay was uniquely disturbing and ironic, especially so given Peter Keegan's vision in Bernard Shaw's *John Bull's Other Island* of a tranquil and beautiful country transmogrified by the "bustle" of tourists populating expensive hotels and playing golf assisted by child caddies. Prior to his arrival in Shannon, members of fifty political, human rights and anti-racism organizations that formed the Stop Trump Ireland coalition organized to protest his visit. The coalition includes Friends of the Irish Environment, which collected 100,000 signatures for a petition decrying the methods used by the Trump International Golf Club in Doonbeg to prevent erosion.

Such disdain, even outrage, is not unprecedented, as not every American president has basked in the Céad Mile Fáilte (100,000 welcomes) extended to Presidents Kennedy and Obama from huge audiences in Dublin, or felt the "rousing enthusiasm" Bill Clinton, the first president to visit Northern

Ireland while in office, enjoyed in Belfast (Mitchell, *Making Peace*, 26). Richard Nixon and Ronald Reagan in, respectively, 1970 and 1984, were greeted warmly in the homes of their ancestors but, as I have described, demonstrators in Dublin hurled eggs at Nixon while others burned his effigy at the American embassy. In an impromptu ceremony, eight graduates of Galway's University College set fire to their degrees, and three holders of an honorary doctorate of law degrees returned or "de-conferred" them, in response to Reagan's receipt of his honorary degree (Booth, "Reagan Booed"). In both cases, Cold War tension and American foreign policy—that regarding southeast Asia in Nixon's case, Central America in Reagan's—combined to elicit loud censure of the leaders of one of Ireland's oldest and closest friends.

Joe Biden's popularity in the Republic is not shared by Northern Ireland loyalists, demonstrating the impact of foreign policy on the close, but fragile, American-Irish relationship. While serving as Vice President in June 2016, Biden spent six days in Ireland, receiving an honorary doctorate from Trinity College, addressing its 2016 class, delivering a speech to a large crowd outside Dublin Castle and much more. He met with Taoiseach Enda Kenny, with whom he played a round of golf, also meeting with President Michael Higgins and his wife Sabina to discuss such global topics as the rising number of incidents of violence against women. Four years later, Biden's election victory was wildly celebrated in Ballina in County Mayo, his family's ancestral home. One large poster humorously speculated that "Mayo Joe's" win might qualify Ballina as an American state. American flags waved on street corners, and photographs of the "beaming" president-elect—"Our man in the White House"—adorned shop windows (Neely and Suliman, "Joe Biden's Irish ancestral hometown"). His view of Brexit, however, angered some unionists. Members of Orange Lodges rejected Biden's endorsement of the Northern Ireland Protocol, an agreement that allows the North to remain in the European Union in part by creating a customs border in the Irish Sea between Britain and Northern Ireland. This proposal, as NBC News reported in the summer of 2021, enraged loyalists who fear that the imaginary partition "pulls" Northern Ireland closer to the Republic; thus, the president's approval of the idea exposed his Republican "bias" (Abbas et al., "Biden becomes a divisive figure").

Two years later, things *seemed* to have improved. Described in a *New York Times* headline (April 9, 2023) as the "most Irish president since J.F.K.," Biden experienced enthusiastic welcomes and displayed his obvious happiness to be in his ancestral home (the *Irish Daily Mirror* captured both in a massive April 13 headline "Biden Joy" and the *Irish Examiner* proclaimed on its front page "Beaming Biden savours return 'home'"). But in Britain, as Edward

Luce complained in the *Financial Times*, this visit signified more than an opportunity to celebrate the signing of the 1998 Good Friday Agreement:

> His decision to attend the Good Friday anniversary and skip the London coronation sends a message to Britain, Europe, and beyond. The UK will get no trade deal with America if it jeopardizes the peaceful border between Ireland's north and south. Rishi Sunak, Britain's prime minister, has taken that to heart [...]. ("Joe Biden's Long Good Friday")

Indeed he has, as the prime minister greeted the president at the Belfast airport on April 11. They had a friendly conversation and later met with leaders of Northern Ireland's five major political parties. As *Reuters* reported, Biden arrived at a "delicate time" in Northern Ireland, as the "largest pro-British party continues to boycott the devolved power-sharing government, a key part of the 1998 Good Friday Agreement" (Holland and Humphries, "Biden arrives").

That "largest pro-British" party is the Democratic Unionist Party (DUP), whose obstructiveness to the peace process in the North is the stuff of legend. On the eve of the Good Friday Agreement's signing on April 19, 1998, as Glenn Patterson quips in *Backstop Land*, "the DUP were—literally—outside the tent as the world's press crowded in to talk to the signatories of the Agreement" (36). His optimism getting the better of him, Patterson confessed that he "honestly thought that that night" the DUP was "gone" forever, "consigned to history" (37). Twenty-five years later, it was still there, on this occasion insisting that Biden's visit "will not pressure it" to mute its opposition to post-Brexit trade rules that "treat the province differently" than the rest of the United Kingdom (Holland and Humphries). And, at the time of the president's visit, the power-sharing, devolved government brought into being by the Agreement was once again in turmoil. As Eimear Flanagan calculated in 2022, since devolution began "Stormont has been without a functioning government for 35% of its lifespan" ("Stormont without NI leadership").

By contrast, other than meeting with Taoiseach Varadkar, Donald Trump did none of the things presidents before him have done during their visits: no public speeches or university addresses; no trips to smaller towns and villages (and thus no statues created for him like those of President and Michelle Obama in Moneygall); no conversation with entrepreneurs or Belfast metal workers as Bill Clinton scheduled in 1995; no address to the Irish Parliament as Kennedy, Reagan, Clinton and Biden did; no receipt of an honorary degree. As Trump had intimated, his stay in Ireland, the last segment of a longer trip following a formal state dinner in London, was not entirely "official" and his statement on May 30 that "We'll be meeting with a lot of the Irish officials" was hardly accurate (Lynch, "Trump in Ireland"). He didn't. In *Business Insider* (June 8, 2019), Ellen Cranley recalled his comment that the trip was "very important" to him because of "the relationship I have with the people and with your prime minister." It wasn't. In a brief chat with the president at the Shannon Airport, Clare TD and Minister of State Pat Breen didn't hear much about meetings with leaders or "the people." Instead, as he told the *Irish Times*, a "very pleasant" Trump was "looking forward to playing a round of golf" and staying at his resort which, Breen emphasized, played an important role in the local economy.

As the Trumps landed at Shannon at 4:42 p.m. on June 5 and departed on June 7, how could the president (or anyone, for that matter) play a round of golf, make a day trip to Normandy on June 6 to speak at an event commemorating the seventy-fifth anniversary of D-Day, *and* confer with "a lot of Irish officials"? Or cultivate relationships with the Irish people? He couldn't. But his sons Eric and Don, Jr. did, "coming down to say hello" to the habitués of Doonbeg pubs on June 6 (Byrne and Blaney, "Donald Trump's Ireland visit 2019"). As Bess Levin describes in *Vanity Fair*, now emancipated from the cartoonish tuxedos in which they were straitjacketed at Queen Elizabeth's state dinner a few nights earlier, Eric and Don hit the bars like "frat boys on spring break." In the process, they "didn't miss a chance to attack the media" and, when asked if their cavorting was an effective way to spend taxpayers' money, Eric is reported to have said, "We're just trying to have a good time" (Levin, "Of course Eric and Don Jr."). The boys were clearly more interested in having a little fun than talking to "buzz-killing" reporters.

After photographs were taken at Shannon Airport on June 5, the president and his wife Melania were whisked away by helicopter, arriving at their resort at 6:25 p.m. to experience, as its website touts, the "luxury accommodations, breathtaking views, and unparalleled service" at Trump International Golf Links & Hotel Doonbeg. The plan *not* to meet lots of people and political leaders was actually revealed earlier when, prior to the president's arrival, a senior White House official confirmed that the conversation with the Irish Prime Minister was the only public event on his schedule. The president's gushing enthusiasm about speaking with Irish officials and the Irish people— that was just part of the grift. The Trump team wanted his conversation with Varadkar to be held at his resort, but the Taoiseach's Office declined, countering with an invitation to convene at a nearby castle converted into a conference center. Trump refused. Instead, their conversation was conducted at an improvised space at the airport. Less than an hour after the Trumps arrived at Doonbeg, the *HuffPost*'s S. V. Dáte posted this notice: "President Donald Trump finally began his taxpayer-funded trip to his Irish golf resort

Wednesday after dispensing with a 65-minute airport lounge meeting with the prime minister that was added at the last minute to avoid a vacation-only foreign visit." Dáte's sense of the rushed timing of things was echoed by the Taoiseach, who described their meeting as "coming out of the blue."

How much did this belated stop in Ireland cost the American taxpayer? *Business Insider* calculated it to be around $3.6 million, the same amount Peter Wade reached, who in a June 8, 2019, article for *Rolling Stone* set $105.8 as the total cost of Trump's tours of his properties during his administration. Without accounting for every cent, some of the expenses of the Irish trip are reflected in the filed contracts Ellen Cranley reviewed. These include:

- $1,023,940 to rent cars and limos for staff.
- $10,866 to install temporary phone lines.
- $16,325 to rent golf carts for the Secret Service agents protecting Trump on the golf course. (As a golfer who has rented *hundreds* of carts or "buggies," as they are called in Ireland, I am perplexed by this figure—not by Trump's extraction of fees from the Secret Service, which he did frequently, but by the amount.)

Although these and other contractual obligations were deemed "within the usual purchases for presidential travel measures," the added price of one other element was not: Trump's insistence on making the trip to Doonbeg in the first place, which he described as "convenient." It wasn't. In fact, it added well over 1,000 miles of air travel to the trip and thus hundreds of thousands of dollars to its cost. Trump flew 370 miles from London to Doonbeg, so his trip to Normandy the following day meant "retracing his flight 440 miles east and then flying another 440 miles west back to Ireland hours later" (Cranley, "Here's How Trump Spent $3.6 Million"). How much additional expense was incurred? Using data obtained from the Air Force estimating the cost of flying Air Force One, a converted Boeing 747–200, Joseph Trevithick in 2021 set the hourly average cost of its use at $177,843, down from over $200,000/hour in 2015. Trump should have been aware of this expense, as he was briefed on air travel costs before taking office ("'Air Force One' 747s Now Cost $177K an Hour").

What benefits did taxpayers accrue from the junket? Disingenuous self-congratulation from the president and embarrassment, as Rachel Maddow suggests, much of which surfaced at the press conference at Shannon Airport. After introducing the president and observing that he was the sixth American leader to visit Ireland during his term of office, Varadkar turned to Trump, who exaggerated his friendship with the Taoiseach, praised his job performance and expressed his affection for both Ireland and Irish America.

He also correctly predicted that their conversation would involve Brexit and mentioned that while in London he conferred with some "very good people who are very much involved" with the issue. Assuring Varadkar that Brexit would "work out very well" for Ireland "with your wall, your border," the president compared the partition to America's southern border and reiterated that "it's all going to work out very well" ("very" being indispensable to the rhetoric of Trumpism). His comment about a border wall in Ireland elicited audible gasps from the pool of reporters in attendance, and the Taoiseach responded immediately with "The thing we want to avoid, of course, is a border or a wall." Unfazed, Trump replied, "I think you do, I think you do." His allusion to a wall, however, inspired a variety of mocking headlines the next day. Under a photograph of Trump exiting Air Force One, for example, the *Daily Mirror* placed the pun "Border will be Wall Right" over a line in smaller print that read "Trump compares Brexit woes with Mexico plans."

To be fair, let's concede that presidents make mistakes both at home and abroad. As I noted earlier, in addressing the Irish parliament President Kennedy misquoted lines from Joyce's *Ulysses* and misattributed a quotation from Shaw's *Back to Methuselah*; while speaking about a rugby-playing relative, President Biden confused the New Zealand All Black rugby team with the Black and Tans mercenaries that terrorized Ireland a century ago. While the Irish press variously described the misstep as minuscule and unimportant, the *New York Post* predictably damned it as "yet another cringeworthy gaffe" from a president prone to parapraxes. But, let's get real—it's so much small beer compared to Trump's ignorance of a century-old partition, or his suggestion in 2017 that Frederick Douglass was still alive, a howler for which he blamed the counsel of Secretary of Education Betsy De Vos.

His performance didn't improve when the press had an opportunity to pose questions. The first concerned Brexit, with Trump reiterating that it will be "good for Ireland" and "the border will work out" without explaining any basis for his optimism and supplying yet more fodder for mocking newspaper headlines. Another questioner mentioned Irish criticism of America's environmental policies to which Mr. Trump, apparently forgetting about or oblivious to the water crises in Jackson, Mississippi, and Flint, Michigan, boasted that America has the "cleanest" air in the world and "crystal-clean water," an enviable record achieved by his administration, which was "setting records environmentally." The 100,000 signatories of the Friends of the Irish Environment's petition against the Trump Golf Club might have reason to investigate these claims, and in 2020 Yale University's *Environmental Performance Index* ranked the quality of America's sanitation and drinking water as twenty-sixth among the world's developed countries. When asked if his visit was intended to promote the struggling resort he acquired in 2014—in January 2022, *IrishCentral* calculated that it had lost $18 million since it opened—Trump deflected the question, returning to his relationships with the UK, the Taoiseach and the Irish people as the reasons for his visit.

Perhaps most disturbing, and most easily overlooked, is not Trump's exceptional ignorance or self-congratulation, but rather the ways in which his popularity in Doonbeg is the result of an enduring economic dilemma described in the previous chapter and envisioned by Shaw's melancholy priest in *John Bull's Other Island* over a century ago. Indeed, the emigration of young people posed a major challenge in the postwar years—at the time of Ireland's First Programme for Economic Expansion (1958–63), some 45,000 people per year left the country—and was particularly acute in agrarian Ireland. By contrast, today the Irish economy, even after the fall of the Celtic Tiger, is highly successful: hundreds of multinational and American companies have invested in Northern Ireland and the Republic, employing hundreds of thousands of workers directly and indirectly. This investment continues and the Republic's GDP as measured on a per capita basis is one of the most productive in Europe.

But this thriving economy has not benefited everyone, as Michael Staines observed in *Newstalk* during the 2020 American presidential election, when Doonbeg residents supported Trump's candidacy even though an Irish national poll put his disapproval rating at 82%. The anomalous support in Doonbeg is based on one issue: jobs. In several televised segments and news releases detailing the president's visit, BBC interviews there explain why the village is, as one headline renamed it, "Trump Town." Kathleen Whelan, a shopkeeper, said she was looking forward to the president's visit and hailed his arrival as a boon for local business. Her enthusiasm has deep historical and economic roots: "There's no investment in rural Ireland. Everything goes to Dublin," she explained. "It's tough for people to earn a living, and we recently lost the post office in the last year." The president's "presence here is great publicity for West Clare, so he would be very welcome in my shop." Tommy Tubridy, a local publican, agreed, telling the BBC that he hoped Trump would make an appearance in the village, which would "roll out the red carpet" for him. "We might get a tweet this evening saying he's on his way" (McCracken, "Doonbeg: Welcome to 'Trump Town'"). They didn't. Gerard Corbett, a Doonbeg resident, estimated that Trump employs 300 people in the summertime and 200 in the winter; if the Trump resort didn't exist, "people would be on the airplane" to America and elsewhere looking for work. But perhaps the most telling comment came from businessman Tommy Comerford who, while acknowledging protesters' rights to express their disdain for the American president, stressed the villagers' "right to live [in] and protect our townland." In Doonbeg and small rural villages, the most urgent priority hasn't changed much since the post-war years: keeping young people in the community. Without jobs, this would be impossible.

In other words, the "careening circus" replete with pratfalls possessed unsettling connotations that transcend mere buffoonery. Trump's reference to a border wall, for example, laid bare MAGA's cavalier indifference to the histories of our closest allies, while also demonstrating his staff's failure to prepare him adequately for informed diplomacy. The trip also foregrounded the unethical behavior of the president himself, who promoted it as a meaningful engagement with Irish political leaders and the general public when it was nothing of the kind. And it reinforces two of the emphases of this book: the importance of economic development in the relationship between America and Ireland, and the continuing schism in both countries between town and country, multicultural cities and small towns or villages. On a more personal level, the trip was a missed opportunity for the president: because his resort is so vital to the West Clare economy, Doonbeg villagers, unlike the majority of Irish citizens critical of his administration, would have showered him with the adulation he craves. Perhaps he should go there sometime.

Postscript

Or maybe not. Maybe the time to be welcomed as the munificent, or at least indispensable, "playboy of the western world" has passed. Returning to Doonbeg in May of 2023, as *Politico* reported, while Trump received a "typically warm reception" from employees inside his resort, "fewer than a dozen fans greeted him as his motorcade arrived in the village," and the "smattering of U.S. flags and MAGA hats among people standing by the roadside were greatly outnumbered by Secret Service and Irish police" (Pogatchnik, "Police outnumber fans"). As is the case in the United States, pratfalls and comic schtick eventually get old.

Chapter 3

THE LONG ROAD TO GOOD FRIDAY, II: FROM REAGAN TO CLINTON

> The essence of the economic problem of Northern Ireland is that it is an economy with a rapidly growing labor force tied to a slow growing national economy [...]. Equally worrying is the fact that recovery in the national economy since 1982 has largely excluded Northern Ireland.
> —Northern Ireland Economic Research Centre,
> qtd. in Frank Gaffikin and Mike Morrissey,
> *Northern Ireland: The Thatcher Years* (1990)

> Prior to the 2007–09 recession, the 1981–82 recession was the worst economic downturn in the United States since the Great Depression.
> —Tim Sablik, "Recession of 1981–82," *Federal Reserve History* (2013)

The story of American investment in Ireland that Charles Haughey related to the Economic Club of New York in May 1982 must have amazed many listeners. Because, as Tim Sablik of the Federal Reserve Bank of Richmond characterizes it, the implementation of tight monetary policy to contain soaring inflation between July 1981 and November 1982 ignited the "worst economic downturn" since the Great Depression. Here, "downturn" denotes the "largest cumulative business cycle decline of employment and output" in America's post-World War II period (Goodfriend and King, 1). When Paul Volcker was named Chairman of the Federal Reserve on August 6, 1979, inflation had already risen to over 13% and the unemployment rate stood at 7.5% as manufacturing, residential construction and automobile sales languished. In the latter two sectors, unemployment reached levels of 22% and 24%, respectively, and mortgage rates in 1981 climbed to 18.63% in October. By 1989, they were still over 10%. However, eventually Volcker and the "Reagan recovery" brought inflation under control. During the president's two terms, the Standard and Poor 500 Index more than doubled; new jobs were created, and mortgage rates came down (though, speaking from personal experience, a 30-year fixed mortgage of nearly 12%

in 1985 was hardly a panacea for first-time homebuyers). As economists Marvin Goodfriend and Robert King put it, Volcker's eventual victory over inflation made the "inflation peak" of early 1980 "stand out dramatically in the U.S. experience" (1).

In 1981 and 1982, the twin menaces of unemployment and inflation—like a high cost of living and failures of regional banks similar to those that induced market jitters in 2023—were difficult to vanquish without adversely affecting the housing industry in particular and domestic production in general. This dilemma moved the Federal Reserve to deploy a nimble "stop-go" strategy that alternated between combating high unemployment on the one hand and attacking the rising costs of everything from grapefruit to gasoline on the other. As Sablik explains, during the "stop" periods, when inflationary pressures intensified, the Fed raised the interest rate; during the "go" periods, lower rates loosened the money supply in an attempt to curb unemployment. By 1983, in a remarkable outcome given the anxiety that high prices would pose a permanent challenge for consumers, inflation had eased. And, for the most part, the output losses some had predicted did not materialize (Goodfriend and King, 2).

In the summer of 1981, America's new president—cultivating allies from both political parties—enjoyed legislative victories in addressing many of these issues. In July, Reagan's team persuaded Congress to pass its budget, which featured both spending reductions and tax reforms, the latter a theme of the 1980 campaign. As a 2021 *Forbes* retrospective of Reaganomics foregrounded, the Economic Recovery Tax Act (ERTA) signed into law in August was the "biggest tax cut in American history," eclipsing both the "mammoth" reductions enacted after World War II and Donald Trump's Tax Cuts and Job Acts of 2017. Yet, soon after Reagan signed the bill, his advisors sought "ways to unravel it," and eventually the president acceded to minor tax hikes (Thorndike, "Reagan's Tax Cut"). Even so, ERTA established his *bona fides* as a tax reformer, and elements of the Act—lowering the rate in both higher and lower brackets—enhanced the president's popularity outside of the Capitol.

Cutting spending proved just as difficult. As Chris Matthews, who in July 1981 became Tip O'Neill's Administrative Assistant, saw it, the Speaker suffered a "crushing defeat" when his House colleagues supported the Administration's request for an "up-or-down" vote on the entire package of spending cuts rather than a review of each line item individually. One potential casualty was the minimum Social Security benefit of $122/month provided to the country's poorest recipients, a measure certain to induce panic in Republicans and Democrats alike who voted for the bill "once they'd realized what they'd done" (Matthews, 146). And in presidents as well.

In an article for *Brookings*, Paul C. Light writes that "despite his best efforts to convince the public that Social Security was going broke, Ronald Reagan got exactly nowhere." In May before Reagan's summer triumphs, budget director David Stockman proposed a "deep cut" in the early-retirement stipend available to recipients at age 62; and in September, word "leaked out" that a three-month freeze in the annual cost-of-living adjustment was being considered. Once the proposal to reduce minimum Social Security benefits became public, Reagan did "what any beleaguered president would do: he proposed a bipartisan national commission to study the issue" (Light, "Crisis Last Time").

During his commencement address and honorary degree conferral at the University of Notre Dame that May, the president signaled that other changes were imminent. After thanking his hosts, acknowledging his shared Irish heritage with fellow degree recipient Pat O'Brien and reliving some of the pair's experiences filming *Knute Rockne, All American* (1940), he launched into a blistering critique of contemporary Federalism:

> Central government has usurped powers that properly belong to local and State governments. And in so doing [...] government has begun to fail to do the things that are truly the responsibility of a central government [...].

Overregulation, a favorite Reagan target, exemplified this failure:

> You are graduating from a great private, or, if you will, independent university. Not too many years ago, such schools were relatively free from government interference. In recent years, the government has spawned regulations covering virtually every facet of our lives. ("Address at Commencement")

Over "439 separate laws" at the "college level alone," he continued, regulate everything from the hiring of faculty to "recordkeeping, fundraising and, to some extent, curriculum and educational programs." (In its banning of books, attacks on women's reproductive health, and other measures, so-called conservatives today seem to have forgotten they're supposed to be against overregulation.) Such "burdensome" oversight, "inflated currency and prohibitive taxes" created a moribund economy Reagan was eager to revive.

As the 1980s began, Britain's economy suffered from similar maladies and the Thatcher government prescribed similar remedies: reduced public spending, lower tax rates and deregulation. In the process, it is hardly surprising that they diagnosed the same socio-economic ills in implementing their plan, one that after a particularly fractious interaction with Democratic House committee chairs David Stockman identified when dubbing them the "Politburo of the Welfare State" (qtd. in Matthews, 144). As I suggested earlier when describing Trumpism's authoritarian populism, Thatcherite antagonism to social support programs was in part rationalized by a blinkered conception of Victorian values in which self-reliance, initiative and hard work occluded the era's colonial misadventures, social inequality and Dickensian squalor. In *The Downing Street Years* (1993), Mrs. Thatcher lauds Victorian "virtues," preeminent of which was the ability to distinguish "between the 'deserving' and the 'undeserving' poor." The "problem with our welfare state," she observed, was that "we had failed to remember that distinction"; as a result, help was rendered to "those who had simply lost the will or habit of work and self-improvement" (627). Oblivious to the plights of Britain's working poor and Northern Irish Catholics—though aware of the "discriminatory past" of unionists (Bew et al., 216)—the Prime Minister apparently believed that some citizens *deserve* to be poor, a verdict that informed her "free market gospel" (Gaffikin and Morrissey, 11). Yet, as Ian Gough observes, spending on the poor barely changed in the early years of her government; instead, greater funding for unemployment and benefits programs led to "serious cutbacks in local authority services—education, personal social services and especially housing" (150). Two rounds of budget adjustment and balancing were undertaken in late 1980 and 1981, and a "Budget and Public Expenditure White Paper" in March 1982 stressed that public expenditures should be "planned solely in cash terms which allowed for no cost increase outside those budgeted for" (150). Writing in 1983, Gough regarded the welfare state as clearly "under attack" as evidenced by the privatization of airlines, energy production facilities and other public entities (152).

Mrs. Thatcher's meeting with President Reagan on February 26, 1981, was crucial to the development of a warm, yet complicated relationship that, at times, positioned the President on a political tightrope stretched between America's "special" relationship with Britain and Irish America. It was not their first meeting. They *may* have met in July 1972 at a luncheon given in his honor at 10 Downing Street, although biographer Charles Moore found "no evidence" that she and Reagan actually spoke then (according to the Margaret Thatcher Foundation, a menu from the luncheon can be found in her collected papers, so she was present at the event). Three years later, they gathered at her office for a conversation scheduled for forty-five minutes that lasted for an hour and a half. As Mrs. Thatcher later wrote, "I was immediately won over by his charm, directness and sense of humour" (qtd. in Moore, 314). In *Killing Thatcher*, Rory Carroll references their meeting in California in the late 1970s where she appears to have discovered a "soul mate" in the governor, an ally "of like mind" (34). Although several of his senior advisors at the White House in 1981 were critical of the Prime Minister, Reagan was determined to make the partnership work. He insisted that Thatcher call him "Ron" and, though uncomfortable with such familiarity, she agreed to be called "Margaret," addressing him as "Ronald" at a meeting of G7 leaders in Ottawa later that July. It was perhaps his "effortless amiability" and use of leaders' "Christian names" that induced conferees to dress casually for gatherings, an informality to which the Prime Minister made "almost no concession" (*Downing Street Years*, 164).

Such occasional discomfiture aside, Mrs. Thatcher recognized that she and the president were battling common fiscal enemies, including deficit spending, high taxes and unemployment, although they didn't always agree on how to defeat them. She recalls being "at odds" with Reagan over growing deficits, particularly in their early years. Favoring a "very firm hand on the purse strings," she felt Reagan was at times too willing to "temporarily put up taxes" to whittle down the deficit, a strategy that she believed encouraged more spending (165). Over time, the pair found other topics upon which to agree, the importance of international trade and security from terrorism, for instance. Their partnership may have led his administration to cast a blind eye to the sale of 3,000 Ruger pistols and some 500 rifles to the RUC. Meeting with Jimmy Carter on December 17, 1979, Mrs. Thatcher lobbied for the sale to proceed—having fired the Ruger .375 handgun and its replacement, she deemed the American weapon to be superior—but, while remaining on good terms with the prime minister, Carter followed Congress's lead in blocking such transactions (O'Dowd, "Carter and Thatcher Clashed"). Things may have changed, however, when Reagan took office. Reviewing declassified documents in 2012, security analyst Joseph Fitsanakis concluded that "thousands of American-made weapons, as well as spy equipment, ended up in the hands of Northern Ireland's police force in the 1980s, despite a strict ban enacted by Congress" ("U.S. Gave N. Ireland Police Weapons").

Northern Ireland's fiscal house was in no better order than Britain's, as Gaffikin and Morrissey assert in the epigraph above, referring first to the stagnant economy to which it was tethered, then to a recovery in 1982 that failed to extend from London to Belfast. Progress was also complicated by the fact that Thatcherite homilies on the free market were received very differently by nationalist and unionist communities. Gaffikin and Morrissey quote Labour Party MP David Marquand to preface this argument:

> A society of atomistic individuals, relating to each other only through the mechanisms of free exchange, in which intermediate associations are seen as conspiracies to distort those mechanisms and treated accordingly, is easy meat for state power. (18)

Aware of the role British subvention played "in maintaining their incomes and employment"—and that a Protestant regime was the beneficiary of "military and financial support" from London—Northern unionists were predisposed to endorse Thatcher's free market ideology (Bew et al., 192, 201). Nationalists, however, perceived these matters differently, and in a study of Northern Irish unemployment, Queen's University scholars Neil Rowland, Duncan McVicar and Ian Shuttleworth explain why. In addition to unemployment rates in the 1970s being over two and a half times higher for Catholic men than for their Protestant counterparts (17.3% versus 6.6% in 1971), Catholics were also "under-represented in upper tier occupational groups and industries," routinely taking "roles of lesser status in the same occupational class" (2). Where Catholics lived and how they were educated may account for some disparities, but Rowland and his colleagues contend that the "unemployment gap" cannot be explained by only "observable characteristics" or other "econometric data" (1).

Some of these "observable characteristics" are more psychological than material, as Julia Obert explains in mapping the postcolonial psychogeographies of residents in postcolonial cities like Belfast. In this built environment of paradoxical "subjection and subversion," the grandeur of Stormont, with its "elaborate ornamentation," bas-relief carvings and lofty perch on a hilltop in east Belfast, epitomizes the city's "enterprise and success" while papering over its divisions (*Making and Unmaking*, 31). For Obert, Stormont's "monumentality," its bronze statue of Sir Edward Carson for instance, hardly represents the lived experiences of Northern Catholics—just the opposite given Carson's staunch unionism. The result, in an inventive echo of Freud, is an "architectural uncanny" both congenial and familiar, but for young Catholics something also cloaked and dangerous. Bobby Sands's Rathcoole, for example, where the Vigilante Defense Associations armed with crowbars and guns roamed the streets, convinced Sands that he could no longer pursue a "normal life" there (O'Hearn 12). Graduating from secondary school in 1969 at age fifteen, he enrolled at Newtownabbey Technical College to train as a bus builder. He landed a job at the North Belfast Bus Works in the spring of 1970, earning a steady wage and enjoying the perquisites a reliable income affords. But after two years as an apprentice builder—and after tensions with Protestant coworkers began to mount—he discovered a death threat in his locker at work and was laid off from the "only real job" he ever had (14). So, while Rowland and his colleagues argue that by 2021 the religious differential in employment had "largely (if not completely) disappeared" (2), for decades Catholics like Sands, at home and work if they could find a job, lived in an increasingly threatening world.

Like a philosophy rationalized by a myopic sense of Victorianism, Mrs. Thatcher's response to the 1981 hunger strikes may have originated from her misapprehensions about Ireland. Prior to his first meeting with the Prime Minister on May 20, 1980, Taoiseach Haughey benefited from the counsel of John Hume, who had conferred with her a week earlier. Historian Stephen Kelly notes that while, from Hume's perspective, Thatcher seemed "willing to foster a stronger relationship between Dublin and London," the history of Northern Ireland seemed to be "a closed book" to her (qtd. in *'A Failed Political Entity,'* 136). To her credit, she seemed aware of this failing and, while preparing for a holiday in July 1980, requested a list of books on Irish history to take with her (Moore, 596–97). Her knowledge of Northern Ireland may have been equally shallow. While publicly refusing to negotiate with paramilitary groups who perpetrated or countenanced the taking of innocent lives, she seemed indifferent to the murder of 107 Catholics in the wake of internment in 1972 (Collins, 38), or to the July 1975 executions of members of the Miami Showband.[1]

Happily, the torrents of bombings and shootings in the 1970s slowed in the 1980s, although the decade was hardly free of violence, particularly in its beginning years. Paul Bew, Peter Gibbon and Henry Patterson calculate that deaths "from political violence" in 1972 and 1973 alone comprised a quarter of all Troubles-related fatalities between 1969 and 1990 (196). Citing governmental, academic and corporate studies, and employing data from the *Northern Ireland Annual Abstract of Statistics, 1989,* Gaffikin and Morrissey similarly observe that between 1980 and 1987 shootings dropped over 80% from the preceding decade; explosions declined by 60%; and civilian deaths fell from nearly 1,300 to 372. To be sure, *any* spilling of innocent blood is unacceptable, and the destruction of housing and infrastructure continued. Damaged some thirty-three times between 1971 and 1993, for example, Belfast's Europa Hotel didn't earn the reputation as the "most bombed hotel in Europe" for nothing (McClements, "Europa Hotel").

Demographic factors also exacerbated economic woes. By 1987, Northern Ireland had the highest birth rate and the largest population of residents under fifteen of any region in England or Wales; the highest rate of unemployment; and "for a region with a long industrial history [...] a low proportion of employment concentrated in production" (Gaffikin and Morrissey, 45). One consequence of these factors, other than a low GDP to which younger children could obviously not contribute, was that the public sector began to drive employment, creating over 40% of all new jobs (45). Another ramification, according to a 1989 Coopers & Lybrand Deloitte study of England and Northern Ireland, was that while expenditure on Agriculture, Trade and Employment, Transport and Housing declined sharply, spending rose for Health and Personal Social Services and Social Security programs (47). As a result, a 1988 critique in the *Economist* argued that the Northern Irish economy more closely resembled that of "an Eastern European country than Margaret Thatcher's privatizing Britain." That is, as the ratio of public spending to GDP was falling in England, it was "rising inexorably" in Northern Ireland, where many households had realized negligible economic gains and 42.3% were classified as "low income" (48, 51).

Ironically, the welfare state Thatcherism sought to dismantle became even more necessary. Desperation and a sense of futility are powerful motivators, and in the early 1980s, they not only heightened the stresses of daily life but also moved republican inmates at the Maze Prison like Bobby Sands to plot a course of action that led to their martyrdom—and to changes of policy on both Downing Street and Pennsylvania Avenue.

Hunger Strikes, An Invalidated Visa and the Friends of Ireland

> Northern Ireland [...] lacked direction for the first few months of Mrs Thatcher's time in office [...]. What changed matters was the assassination on 27 August 1979 of Lord Mountbatten and, on the same day, the murder of eighteen British soldiers.
> —Charles Moore, *Margaret Thatcher: The Authorized Biography–From Grantham to the Falklands* (2013)

Three weeks after Paul Volcker was appointed chairman of the Federal Reserve, Lord Louis Mountbatten was enjoying a summer day on his boat with his extended family off Mullaghmore in County Sligo. Without warning, a fifty-pound gelignite bomb concealed in the ship's engine compartment was detonated by a radio signal, reducing the *Shadow V* to splinters and killing Mountbatten, his fourteen-year-old grandson Nicholas, and Paul Maxwell, a fifteen-year-old working as a boatman.[2] Lady Doreen Brabourne, 83, died the next day from the injuries she sustained, while Mountbatten's daughter Patricia; her husband, John Knatchbull; and Nicholas's twin brother Timothy survived. The PIRA claimed responsibility, stating that Mountbatten's death and the "tributes" he received would be seen "in contrast to the apathy of the British Government and English people to the deaths of over 300 British soldiers and the deaths of Irish men, women and children at the hands of their forces." Asked about the assassination by Joan Boyd, a reporter visiting the Maze, Bobby Sands, a "grotesque looking figure with filthy shoulder-length hair and a long scraggly beard," regretted the loss of life but felt no remorse over Mountbatten's death as he had once been a cog in a "British war machine" that had perpetrated "injustices" in British colonies "around the world" (qtd. in O'Hearn, 250–51).

At a ceremony marking the tragedy's fortieth anniversary, Prince Charles reflected upon losing Mountbatten, "the grandfather he never had," someone from whom he sought advice "about everything from leadership to romance" (Westenfeld, "Lord Louis Mountbatten").

The incident initiated what Leslie Kennedy terms a "raw, dark period" for England and Northern Ireland, although the car bomb that killed Thatcher ally Airey Neave five months earlier had already augured what was to come ("The Assassination"). But reports of the ambush of British paratroopers on August 6—granular, horrific accounts of decapitation and mutilation caused by two enormous ANFO-type bombs—proved decisive. Charles Moore alludes to a lack of "direction" in British policy concerning Northern Ireland in the early days of the Thatcher government, but in Rory Carroll's estimation the crisis revealed a more "humbling truth about policy on Northern Ireland. She didn't have one" (*Killing Thatcher*, 29). After Mrs. Thatcher wrote notes of condolence to the families of the paratroopers massacred in the August explosions, she was determined to address this omission.

By contrast, news of the two August 6 attacks was greeted with "euphoria" by some prisoners in H-Block, though as he describes in *Blanketmen* (2005) Richard O'Rawe, serving an eight-year sentence for armed robbery, was disturbed by aspects of the Mountbatten assassination:

> Unlike the elation I had felt on hearing of the ambush of the Paras (whom I regarded as my enemy and a bunch of bloodthirsty killers of innocent people), I found nothing to cheer about in the killing of this elderly lady and two innocent schoolkids [...]. I have always felt that killing non-combatants was unacceptable [...]. (58)

The attack on the paratroopers was also ironic. For just seven years earlier, as I have described previously, British "Paras" killed thirteen people on "Bloody Sunday" (a fourteenth victim died months later), seven of whom were teenagers just a few years older than the boys on the Mountbatten boat. None of the "many photographs" of Bloody Sunday shows any "civilian holding an object that can with certainty be identified as a firearm or bomb" (*Widgery Report*, 69). Of the teens killed that day, two were shot running away, one in the shoulder and the other through the elbow with the bullet passing to his chest (72); one, suspected of possessing a nail bomb, was shot in the stomach and posthumously cleared of the charge (79); one was wounded in the buttocks while crawling on the ground before being struck by other rounds (79–80); one was hit in the face and another in the chest. No residue from explosives was detected on the clothing of eleven of the thirteen casualties, and one victim's clothing was exempted from analysis due to contamination at the hospital.

The Paras suffered no fatalities.

Less than four months later on May 8, 1972, inmates at Belfast's Crumlin Road Jail, angry at being treated like common criminals and not political prisoners, demanded that Secretary of State for Northern Ireland William Whitelaw acknowledge the distinction. Whitelaw refused. In response, the prisoners threatened a hunger strike and eventually began refusing food. Starting with five inmates, with five more added each week and prisoners at the Armagh Women's Prison joining the protest, the strikers forced a brief truce between June and July that led to the introduction of the Special Category Status which afforded both republican and loyalist prisoners "the right to wear their own clothes; to abstain from prison labor; to associate freely; to participate in recreational and educational activities; and to have full remission of sentence restored" (qtd. in Wilson, *Irish America*, 170).

The calm was short-lived, however, and several points of contestation remained flashpoints. In his introduction to Bobby Sands's *Writings from Prison* (1994), Nobel Prize winner and founding member of Amnesty International Seán MacBride indicts Britain's abrogation of "ordinary laws," its installation of a "police-state regime" and the regime's disregard of conditions at the Maze (16). In September 1976 Kieran Nugent, who three years earlier at age fifteen had been shot eight times, was convicted of hijacking a bus. When Britain expanded its counterinsurgency plan by revoking nationalist prisoners' special category status and required them to wear prison uniforms, Nugent refused, stripped, and wrapped himself in a blanket, initiating the blanket protest (23). In MacBride's view, this change in policy was designed to undermine any notion that the PIRA and Irish National Liberation Army (INLA) were participants in a freedom movement and as such formed part of a larger strategy to reduce the presence of British soldiers in the North (24). Local police arrested suspects and, if necessary, coerced confessions out of them, then no-jury Diplock trials presided over by a British magistrate took them off the streets.

Protesting these procedures, prisoners maintained their opposition to wearing uniforms and wrapped themselves in thin blankets. And this is only one of the hardships they endured, an unhappy fact that rebuts rosy assertions about prison life in Mrs. Thatcher's autobiography. Defending the treatment of prisoners to Michael Foot, leader of the opposition, Mrs. Thatcher praised the conditions in the Maze as "among the best in any prison anywhere" (*Downing Street Years*, 391). Denis O'Hearn's account of prisoners' daily torments rebuts this fiction, as does Bobby Sands's *Writings from Prison*. In "One Day in My Life," he relives a "restless torturous night" sprawled on a "damp foam mattress" on the floor with intense cold tormenting his naked body (*Writings*, 25). The next morning, after suffering the abuse of warders and before picking at his breakfast—a crust of dry bread and a dollop of porridge—he wondered, "Suffering Jesus, can it get any worse?" His answer was painfully obvious: "You know bloody well that it will" (28).

And it did. The "No Wash" protest evolved into the "dirty protest" in March 1978. The latter, in which bodily products were splashed through cracks and smeared on walls, created the "shit-filled world" which, as O'Rawe describes, "screws" (guards) so resented being forced to enter that "they resorted to what screws everywhere know best: the wholesale use of brutality" (33). O'Rawe's sense of being "buried alive in a sewer" eased somewhat when forced washing in tubs of freezing water produced a modicum of cleanliness, but these were typically followed by abuse that "increased significantly on H3, H4, and H5" in an "all-out offensive" intended to "break the spirit of the republican prisoners" (46). "Horrific beatings" could be heard "almost every hour" (65). So much for Mrs. Thatcher's fable about life in a Maze "flowery dell"—prisoner slang for a dank, joyless cell at Dublin's Mountjoy Prison in Brendan Behan's *The Quare Fellow* (1954).

The 1981 hunger strike was a last, desperate tactic, a spectacle that attracted an international audience just as it had earlier in the century in both the Irish nationalist and women's suffrage movements. In August 1920, Terence MacSwiney—playwright, Lord Mayor of Cork and Commandant of the First Cork Brigade of the Irish Volunteers during the Irish War of Independence—was convicted of possessing seditious documents and sentenced to two years in prison. Initiating a seventy-four-day hunger strike while confined in Cork, he completed it in the Brixton prison in South London to which he was transported and in which he died on October 25. As Paige Reynolds observes, although MacSwiney may have "struggled to define the terms of masculine heroism" in his plays, he embraced the notion that "the male iconic body characterized by its publicness and consistency might inspire the masses." The result is hardly a "strongman" masculinity, but rather "an essentially passive model of Irish identity" that melded seamlessly with martyrdom (*Modernism*, 129).

If the Thatcher government was ignorant of this history, more recent protests might have alerted it to the performative efficacy of self-sacrifice. After sisters Dolours and Marian Price were arrested for planting bombs in a March 1973 attack in London, their trial and conviction attracted international attention which increased after announcing their decision to go on strike until they were granted the status of political prisoners and remanded to a Northern Irish facility. In May 1980 Gwynfor Evans, an MP and leader of Plaid Cymru, the Welsh nationalist party, announced his intention to begin a hunger strike in October when his project to launch a Welsh-language television channel, an innovation promised by the Conservative Party, faltered. That same spring

Martin Meehan, incensed at being convicted of spearheading the kidnapping and torture of a seventeen-year-old boy believed to be an informer, began a sixty-six-day hunger strike that was halted by the intervention of Cardinal Tomás Ó Fiaich, the Archbishop of Armagh. Heralded as a champion of the peace process after his death on November 3, 2007, in such newspapers as the *New York Times* and the *Los Angeles Times*, Meehan afforded the British government a "practice run" for a larger protest that "appeared inevitable" (Beresford, 23). Sadly, the practice did not prove sufficiently instructive.

On October 10, 1980, Sinn Féin announced a hunger strike to begin later that month, prompting innumerable pleas for humane responses to the prisoners' grievances. An editorial in the *New York Times* on November 27 "Don't Let Clothes Make the Martyr," for example, urged restraint:

> If Mrs. Thatcher's government can end the present confrontation on humane terms, that may not of itself bring out the better angels among ancient adversaries. It would, however, be a salutary setback for the politics of hate.

The *Times* bristled at the prime minister's inflexibility over such "bureaucratic fine print" as clothing, a stance that "has only gained sympathy for the hunger-strikers among moderates." On December 1, three women at the Armagh prison joined the strike; two weeks later, twenty Maze prisoners followed. On December 18 after fifty-three days on strike, Sean McKenna's condition was grave, necessitating his relocation to a hospital. Behind the scenes, the Foreign Office offered a "possible settlement" which was accepted, bringing the strike to a close (Beresford, 29). "Almost immediately," however, a new one was being planned (31).

The Sands-led strike, depending upon one's point of view, was brought to conclusion either by genuine concessions or mere doodling with "fine-printed minutiae" traceable back to August 1979 when Mrs. Thatcher met with Taoiseach Jack Lynch, in London for Lord Mountbatten's funeral. Their dialogue grew "heated" when she challenged the Irish delegation to "get down to brass tacks" about improving security measures, her "vehemence" eliciting the retort, "You may not like the idea but some people have a quantity of sympathy with the men of violence." The comment provoked both her fury and an accusatory question, "Are you condoning murder?" (qtd. in Moore, 592). Ironically, "the very thing which made Mrs. Thatcher so angry— the feebleness of the Irish Republic towards terrorists operating from within its borders"—eventually became "the factor used to push forward" a much-needed conciliation (592). The acuity of this thesis became evident in the aftermath of the 1981 hunger strikes.

The period between 1980 and the signing of the Anglo-Irish Agreement on November 15, 1985, demonstrates at least two political truisms: partnerships succeed only if both sides evince at least a smithereen of flexibility, and public sentiment can be quickly swayed. Hoping that a niggling accession to the prisoners' demands might suffice, the Government agreed to provide "civilian-type" clothing issued by the prison, but not to allow anyone to wear his own clothing. As Charles Moore notes, and at the risk of succumbing to the *post hoc, ergo propter hoc* fallacy, this conciliatory gesture was made on October 23 after the prime minister received a communication from Haughey predicting "serious repercussions" if the hunger strike was allowed to proceed (598). Thatcher and Haughey had met earlier on May 21 but only after members of her government encouraged her to do so.

Although once resistant to Ireland's participation in dialogue concerning Northern Ireland—and after "ruling out" objectionable terms like "unification, confederation and joint authority" (*Downing Street Years*, 400)—Mrs. Thatcher at times was more willing to consider an "Irish dimension" in addressing the Troubles. As Stephen Kelly emphasized in a 2014 *Irish Times* editorial on the Thatcher-Haughey "Love/Hate" relationship, this change was aided during their first summit by a "glint" in Haughey's eye that Mrs. Thatcher found "attractive." The charm was short-lived. By March 1982, when Haughey returned briefly as Taoiseach only to be replaced by Garret FitzGerald later that year, his nationalist leanings and condemnation of Britain's sinking of an Argentinian vessel during the Falklands War were not well received.[3] Looking back on this moment from the perspective afforded by forty years, John Downing labeled that spring a low point in Anglo-Irish relations in part caused by the "dramatic offense" taken in London over Haughey's May 4, 1982, urging of the UN Security Council "to seek an immediate end to hostilities and the withdrawal of EEC sanctions against Argentina." Such positions reduced the leaders' relationship to "no contact at all" save for a few perfunctory courtesies (Downing, "Haughey, Thatcher and the Falklands").

Fortunately, this damage was inflicted *after* the leaders met on December 8, 1980, in a summit that exerted a "lasting effect on the state of Anglo-Irish relations" (Kelly, "Love/Hate"). One view of the meeting's importance is that while some members of the Thatcher government, like many American politicians, believed that Irish, British and American involvement was of crucial importance in resolving the Troubles, Mrs. Thatcher was less sanguine about the prospect—and so, initially, was the Reagan administration. On July 14, 1981, Garret FitzGerald in his first term as Taoiseach asked the President to intervene with the Thatcher government to avert the death of hunger striker Kieran Doherty, and Seán Donlon emphasized to Michael Deaver, White House Deputy Chief of Staff, the "need for an early response" (qtd. in Cooper, 104). *Nine* days later, Reagan wrote FitzGerald to express his sympathy but, concerned about America's "special relationship" with Britain, declined to intervene even though in a meeting with Ted Kennedy in June he seemed willing to do so (103). Doherty died on August 2.

During his first term, however, the Reagan administration's engagement with Northern Ireland was increasing in intensity. Initially, as I have mentioned, the hunger strikes elicited shocked editorials; similarly, articles on the efforts of DUP leader Ian Paisley to enter the United States were accompanied by criticism of both Northern Irish unionists and, among Christian fundamentalists, the Reagan State Department. Two months after the conclusion of the 1980 strike, and three weeks before Bobby Sands began his protest on March 1, 1981, five journalists were loaded into a van and driven into the hills outside Belfast. In *Ten Men Dead*, David Beresford describes what they saw:

> They came into a clearing to find a bizarre scene: 500 men standing under a flapping Union Jack, being addressed by the huge figure of the Reverend Ian Paisley [...]. A whistle blew and the 500 men, in rows of ten, raised their right arms, brandishing pieces of paper above their heads. They were firearms certificates. (49)

Addressing this ragtag army, Paisley accused the British and Irish governments of plotting a reunification plan that he vowed to fight, even if it necessitated violence: "It is not for men who have such stake as we have to trouble about the costs" (49). Nine months later, it *was* up to the State Department to "trouble about the costs" of his entry into the country and, as the *New York Times* reported on December 22, 1981, his visa was invalidated. Apparently forgetting his incitement of the gun owners outside Belfast, Paisley "utterly repudiated" the allegation that he had encouraged violence ("U.S. Cancels Visa"). When he again experienced visa difficulties the following spring, Bob Jones, Jr., Chancellor of Bob Jones University, condemned Secretary of State Alexander Haig's Catholic bigotry, disparaging him as a "monster in human flesh" and praying that God would "smite him hip and thigh, bone and marrow, heart and lungs [...] and destroy him quickly and utterly" (Taylor, "Bob Jones Jr.").

While its chancellor was praying for Haig's dismemberment, Bob Jones University was appealing to the Supreme Court to "grant it tax-exempt status despite the fact that it practice[d] racial discrimination" (Taylor). The university's history of discrimination long preceded the appeal (it didn't admit black students until 1971 and banned interracial dating until 2000). As Richard L. Jordan calculates, 106 hours before Martin Luther King, Jr.'s assassination in the spring of 1968 conservative clerics gathered in Greenville, South Carolina to launch the annual Bob Jones Bible Conference. Paisley was one of these "militant clergy" convinced that "God's plan was under attack from an alliance of the civil rights movement, international communism, and liberal clergymen who wanted to secularize, socialize, and integrate American society." As was the case with 1960s civil rights marches in America broadcast on Belfast televisions, Paisley's arrival in Greenville "indicated that the reappraisal of American racial relations had acquired an international audience" (40).

Like American segregationists entrenched on the wrong side of history, Margaret Thatcher seemed to cede the ethical high ground in 1981 to the hunger strikers. Inaugurated by Sands's refusal of food on March 1, the strike ended on October 3 after Bernard Fox, in failing condition, and Liam McCloskey ended their fasts on September 24 and 26, respectively, the latter doing so after his mother persuaded him that she would intervene when he lapsed into a coma.[4] Well before the strike's conclusion, however, Phillip Knightley in the *London Sunday Times* perceived that "world opinion has begun to shift away from the British government and in favor of the IRA." The "general opinion," he suggested, was that the "time has come for Mrs. Thatcher to begin negotiations with Dublin." A *Wall Street Journal* article declared British policy in Northern Ireland "bankrupt," and Colman McCarthy in the *Washington Post* labeled the strikers' demands as "modest," particularly so considering that many of their convictions were "suspect" in the first place (qtd. in Wilson, *Irish America*, 183, 184–85).

The most damning evidence of the Thatcher government's culpability in the strike came from the prime minister herself. In *The Downing Street Years*, she insists that her government "had done everything in our power to persuade [strikers] to give up their fast" (391). After falling into a coma, Bobby Sands died on May 5 with Frank Hughes following on May 12. The next day, John Hume traveled to London, hoping to persuade Mrs. Thatcher to seek a resolution. Describing the deaths of the strikers as self-inflicted, she continued to refer to them as criminals and labeled their passing a "significant defeat for the IRA" (393). Some supporters in the British press agreed, praising her "magnificent obstinacy" and "firm moral purpose." Even the *Guardian*, typically more sympathetic to the nationalist cause, commended her "resolute determination not to be bullied" (qtd. in Beresford, 331). But, in his conclusion to *Ten Men Dead*, David Beresford denounces the Thatcher government's hypocrisy, for just three days after the strike's end Jim Prior, Secretary of State for Northern Ireland, announced new concessions, including the right of prisoners to wear their own clothing. Like the Player Queen in *Hamlet*, Mrs. Thatcher seems to have protested her innocence "too much."

Her intransigence was earlier decried by the Friends of Ireland on St. Patrick's Day, 1981. Covering the bipartisan group's fortieth anniversary for RTÉ in 2021, Brian O'Donovan spoke with co-chair Richard Neal (D-MA), who recalled the group's origins: "The idea of the Friends of Ireland was to generate a competing narrative of what could happen peacefully [...]. It was a direct challenge to much of the gun-running that had been taking place in the United States." An editorial in the *New York Times* (March 17, 1981) put a finer point on this challenge: "Joining in [the Four Horsemen's] appeal are 20 other prominent Americans, Democrats and Republicans, Catholics and non-Catholics. This is an open challenge to the Ad Hoc Congressional Committee for Irish Affairs, led by the clamorous Mario Biaggi of New York" who, regrettably, "has yet to find words to emphatically disavow the bomb and bullet." By stark contrast, the Friends called on the United States to play "a healing diplomatic role in finding a workable solution" for Northern Ireland. "Better still," the editorial continued, "they are establishing a new forum for the responsible discussion of what Americans can and should do to help" ("Ireland's Friends").

The debate over what America *should* do acquired greater urgency when bombings wracked London in the early 1980s. On July 20, 1982, the PIRA detonated two explosive devices packed with four- and six-inch nails during military ceremonies at Hyde Park and Regents Park, killing eight and wounding over fifty, the majority of whom were civilians. On Sunday, November 20, 1983, thirteen days after Mrs. Thatcher met for a second time with Garret FitzGerald, INLA gunmen burst into the Pentecostal Gospel Hall near Darkley in County Armagh, killing three church elders and firing on some sixty to seventy worshipers that included twenty children ("Darkley, Armagh: Shootings"). While Mrs. Thatcher viewed her meeting with FitzGerald as "the origin of the later Anglo-Irish Agreement" of 1985, she was moved deeply by the horror and incongruity of the Darkley attack: "In spite of all the fine words about the need to defeat terrorism which I had been hearing from the Taoiseach, the Irish Justice minister refused to meet Jim Prior to review security co-operation and the Garda Commissioner similarly refused to meet the Chief Constable of the RUC" (*Downing Street Years*, 396).

A month later on December 17, 1983, a PIRA unit positioned a car bomb near a side entrance to Harrod's, detonating it in the early afternoon. Although a telephone warning preceded the explosion, no evacuation of the large holiday crowd was completed. In the *New York Times*, Jon Nordheimer painted the scene: "remnants" of the car and "others caught in the explosion burned fiercely," while "some of the wounded, covered with blood and stunned by the explosion, sat numbly, waiting for help." Six people (not five as was originally reported) were killed, three shoppers and three policemen, and over ninety people were injured in what Prime Minister Thatcher condemned as a "wicked crime against humanity and a crime against Christmas, too" (qtd. in Nordheimer, "5 Killed"). One of the fatalities was Kenneth Salvesen, an American out shopping before his family arrived the next day; another was a young woman shredded by shards of flying glass. The father of Mark McDonald, a twenty-eight-year-old Michigan geologist who was injured by the blast, wondered aloud what many must have been thinking. Rushing to London with his wife, he "expressed amazement" that any of his fellow Americans donated to "the Northern Ireland Aid committee [NORAID], which raises money for the Irish Republican Army [...]. People back at home surely must be misguided if they are supporting this type of activity" ("Prince Charles Denounces"). Many Americans shared his incredulity. And, well before the IRA attempted to assassinate Mrs. Thatcher at the Grand Hotel in Brighton on October 12, 1984, in a bombing that killed five and injured thirty-one, the Friends of Ireland and President Reagan were weighing the same question Mark McDonald's father raised: Why are some Americans supporting such atrocities?

The stage was set for the Anglo-Irish Agreement. It is an oft-heard speculation that America *made* the Thatcher government meet the Republic at the bargaining table; Mrs. Thatcher is said to have confessed as much to one of her advisors. But "made" is an unyielding term with little room for nuance. Softening this charge, Mary Alice C. Clancy refers to Reagan's application of "some pressure" (156), the pressure he hesitated to wield in the summer of 1981 when requested to do so. In a 2015 article for the *Irish Times*, Conor O'Clery prefers the term "leaned"—the president *leaned* on the prime minister—even as O'Clery's subtitle suggests that he only "encouraged" her flexibility. In *The Making of the Anglo-Irish Agreement of 1985*, a memoir published in 2022 but written thirty years earlier, David Goodall, a Thatcher cabinet member, regards American pressure as a consideration but not a "decisive factor" in sparking a serious dialogue about cooperation. When he asked Mrs. Thatcher, she responded, somewhat "dismissively," that a conciliatory approach "helped a lot with Reagan" (3).

A greater obstacle in brokering a cooperative agreement may have been the prime minister's own aversion to working with the Republic. After reading a draft of Goodall's memoir in 2018, Robert Armstrong, Thatcher's Cabinet Secretary who also played a key role in negotiations, wrote to Goodall's widow Morwenna inferring from what he read that "David was obviously wondering, just as I was, whether she really wanted an agreement, and whether she would see it through" ("Introduction," xiii). Yet, at times Mrs. Thatcher seemed more positively inclined. Goodall recalls enjoying a postprandial nightcap at 10 Downing Street in December 1982, six months after joining the Cabinet, with the prime minister and her private secretary, John Coles. Their conversation began with the Falklands before moving to her "outspoken distaste" for Jim Prior's advocacy of rolling devolution in Northern Ireland. The concept, outlined in a 1979 white paper and promoted by Humphrey Atkins, Prior's predecessor as Secretary of State for Northern Ireland, involved the election in 1982 of a Northern Ireland Assembly whose initial role would be consultative to Parliament and potentially be expanded if ratified by a vote (rolling devolution was attempted in 1980 but was undone by the Ulster Unionist Party [UUP] and the DUP). After the hunger strikes, however, the political landscape had changed. Goodall was impressed by Thatcher's seriousness and her comment that if "we get back next time"—that is, if her government wins reelection in 1983—"I would like to do something about Ireland" (qtd. in Goodall, 5). This "something" centered around security and cooperation, although "anything that smacked of 'joint independence' must be excluded" (12).

In September 1983, Goodall and Irish negotiator Michael Lillis met in Dublin to begin mapping a path forward. Speaking for Taoiseach FitzGerald, Lillis underscored the Republic's acceptance of the Union and a revived Stormont Parliament, concessions requiring a revision of Articles 2 and 3 of the Republic's Constitution in which the nation's territory was defined as encompassing "the whole island of Ireland, its islands and territorial seas." In return, Britain would permit Irish security forces to patrol with British troops, and Irish judges to sit with magistrates in the trials of suspected terrorists. Goodall suspected that the addition of Irish troops in Ulster would be viewed with disdain in London, but nevertheless the Republic's acceptance of the Union necessitated a positive response. Armstrong, busy negotiating with an Irish counterpart, agreed. Besides, Goodall writes, the NIO (Northern Irish Office) had "run out of fresh ideas," and FitzGerald's "overtures, however unacceptable they might be, marked a sea change in the attitudes of successive Irish governments." To "simply turn them down" could be to miss "an unrepeatable opportunity" (11).

They didn't. Over two years later, on Friday, November 15, 1985, Mrs. Thatcher and FitzGerald signed the Anglo-Irish Agreement, the prime minister reiterating that in doing so "there was no derogation from the sovereignty of the United Kingdom" (*Downing Street Years*, 402). Within a few months, however, she grew anxious about unionist reaction to the Agreement and invited Jim Molyneaux, MP for Antrim and UUP leader, and Ian Paisley to London for a late February conversation during which she "made it plain" that she would not accept even a "temporary suspension" of the Agreement and that a proposed general strike in opposition to it could do irreparable damage (as it had done with Sunningdale). "It was a reasonably successful meeting," she concluded, but after Molyneaux and Paisley "consulted their supporters in Northern Ireland they came out in support of the strike" (404). John Hume and the SDLP also expressed concerns, especially about joint security; as many observed at the time, British forces patrolling within the Republic's border seemed destined to generate anger, not enhance safety.

In the aftermath of the hunger strikes and bombing campaigns, the Friends of Ireland were also busy lobbying for new political initiatives in Ulster, echoing Hume's advocacy of nonviolence. So was President Reagan, who in remarks at the Irish Embassy on St. Patrick's Day in 1983 proclaimed both his pride in "our Irish heritage" and his "strong condemnation of all acts of terrorism and violence." "A lasting solution," he added, "can only be found in a process of reconciliation" ("Remarks on St. Patrick's Day"). With Tip O'Neill at his side in 1985, he praised the Anglo-Irish Agreement as a "great breakthrough" and pledged his assistance in restoring sound economics" in Northern Ireland and encouraging "private investments that will provide prosperity and employment" ("Remarks on the United Kingdom-Ireland Agreement"). In a later congratulatory note to FitzGerald he added, "We hope and pray that the enterprise will be successful" (Edwards, "Anglo-Irish Agreement").

In the months after the signing, Reagan considered the details of U.S. economic support, prompting a *Chicago Tribune* editorial to ask, "How Much Aid for Ireland?" (January 22, 1986). The *Tribune* speculated about the size of a funding package—mentioning, incorrectly, $1 billion—and enumerated obstacles to the president's plan. Chief among these was a growing budgetary deficit, exacerbated by the tax cuts of ERTA five years earlier and his administration's controversial commitment in 1986 to supply Nicaragua with $100 million of humanitarian aid. Congress had already responded to the deficit in 1985 by passing the Gramm-Rudman-Hollings Balanced Budget and Emergency Deficit Control Act (popularly known as "Gramm-Rudman"), which the President signed into law in December 1985.

In March, the administration proposed a five-year, $250 million aid package to Northern Ireland: $50 million per year, with $20 million disbursed as direct aid and $30 million to incentivize private investment. As John M. Goshko reported in the *Washington Post* (March 6, 1986), although Congress eventually supported the plan, "sharp differences" existed about the "conditions under which the funds would be distributed." Some feared they would not be disbursed equitably; others worried that money might be diverted to police or intelligence operations. The Friends of Ireland opposed the awarding of guarantees or loans to businesses, arguing that the entire package should be directed toward the people (Wilson, *Irish America*, 254). Complicating the debate, policy concerning the extradition of criminals arose, culminating in President Reagan's signing of a Supplementary Treaty he defended as "essential in the battle against world terrorism." This issue first surfaced in late 1985 with Senator Joe Biden (D-DE) lodging "particularly vocal" criticisms and asking "awkward" questions about legal abuses in Northern Ireland (Wilson, 254). When the issue reemerged in 1986, Senator Richard Lugar (R-IN) persuaded the Friends of Ireland to "moderate their position" (255). As the *New York Times* reported on March 7, the five-year package was passed by Congress with $20 million per year earmarked for direct aid and $30 million leveraged to encourage investment.

However imperfect, this legislation confirms that cordial diplomatic relationships were maturing into more impactful partnerships. Yet, recognition of the actors responsible for this narrative has been decidedly uneven. As James Cooper argues, while Bill Clinton's role in the Northern Irish peace process has been the subject of "considerable discussion, both journalistic and scholarly," Reagan's role has received comparatively little attention (97). I agree. And, when he took office in 1981, he was hardly typecast for the major role he played. While covering the Republican primaries in 1979 and introducing himself to the future president as a writer for the *Irish Times*, Conor O'Clery discovered how little candidate Reagan knew about Ireland:

> "Your paper is [in] Dublin? That's south of the Border, right?" This was Governor Ronald Reagan, in an interview in Baltimore, Maryland, on October 10th, 1979, when he was campaigning for the Republican nomination for president [...]. It wasn't a propitious start. ("Reagan in the White House")

Recall, too, that Reagan was advised to downplay his heritage in the 1980 election, and that during his visit to Ireland in 1984, he revealed his relative ignorance of his genealogy. Yet even in 1979, he revealed his commitment to be of service: "Anything that would help end the bloodshed," he said, "the United States should put itself on the line in whatever way it could." By his second term, O'Clery theorized, Reagan "had developed an emotional bond with Ireland and the Irish, reinforced by a visit to his ancestral village of Ballyporeen [...]." He had also developed strong relationships with the Irish and Irish American politicians with whom he worked.

So, while Jacqueline Kennedy, Dave Powers and others marveled at President Kennedy's transformation after visiting Ireland, Reagan's Irishness may have been the more consequential. In this regard, O'Clery and

Cooper's observations are right on at least two counts: Reagan's facilitation of the Northern Irish peace process *has* been underappreciated, and his growing attachment to Ireland—and an Irish-American community in Congress—motivated his intervention in matters that many presidents before him avoided. His commitment to Ireland was also personal. Famously characterized by his wife Nancy as not letting anybody "get too close" and by colleagues as an "unfailingly warm but rarely intimate" man, his affection for Ireland evolved during his presidency.[5] He forged this bond during his 1984 visit, however tumultuous his arrival there. He revealed as much in his remarks to the Irish parliament on June 4, for as his plane landed at Shannon two days earlier, he felt as if "something deep inside began to stir" (qtd. in Matthews, 332). This is precisely why Tip O'Neill's son Tom observed that while his father's advocacy for Ireland at times put both Reagan and Thatcher in difficult positions, the president never "resented it and she did" (qtd. in Matthews, 335).

This chapter's long trek to Good Friday is nearing an end, and its closing section outlines the Clinton administration's engagements with Northern Ireland and, in brief, those of George W. Bush and others that, like the Carter Initiative and Reagan aid package to Northern Ireland, have too often been overlooked. Also, because one of the Friends of Ireland's charter members was Joe Biden, the young senator who occasionally posed awkward questions, this conclusion serves as a preface to the next chapter. That is, Irish ambassador Daniel Mulhall's compliment of Biden in 2021 as having "40 years of immersion in Irish affairs" is hardly hyperbolic: "He understands Ireland [...] and that can only be a good thing."[6] If the Friends of Ireland laid "the groundwork for the lobbying of the Clinton administration," the group's concerns also influenced the Biden 2020 presidential campaign and his stance toward Brexit (O'Donovan, "Forty Years"). The paragraphs that follow survey this groundwork.

Good Friday and Beyond: Clinton, Peace Dividends and Envoys

> The next day [November 30, 1995] I flew to Belfast as the first American President ever to visit Northern Ireland. It was the beginning of two of the best days of my presidency [...]. After the tree lighting, we attended a reception, to which all the party leaders were invited. Even the Reverend Ian Paisley [...] came. Though he wouldn't shake hands with the Catholic leaders, he was only too happy to lecture me on the error of my ways. After a few minutes of hectoring I decided the Catholic leaders had gotten the better end of the deal [...]. It was the end of a perfect day.
> —Bill Clinton, *My Life* (2004)

"Creating a new yardstick [to measure American foreign policy]—a Post-Cold War doctrine—is no easy task. The Bush administration's 'new world order' was never fleshed out [...]; still, foreign policy was relatively consistent under President George Bush, focusing mainly on managing relations among the great powers, protecting those few U.S. interests deemed vital and promoting open trade [...]. President Bill Clinton's foreign policy is less easy to define."
—Richard N. Haass, "Fatal Distraction: Bill Clinton's Foreign Policy" (1997)

Bill Clinton's account of his first day in Northern Ireland is almost masochistic, as an abrasive "hectoring" hardly seems part of a "perfect day." Yet even Ian Paisley's accounting of the error of the president's ways at a late-evening reception—"I didn't get a word in edgewise for twenty minutes, but I didn't care," Clinton would say later—couldn't dampen his exhilaration. By the holiday season of 1995, as he took in the lights of Belfast and the beauty of a Christmas tree flown in from Nashville, Clinton was excited by what had been accomplished and what more might be done (Figure 4). Many in his audience shared his optimism, as a long-dormant emotion—hope—began to awaken: an American president had

Figure 4. Bill Clinton Meets with Ian Paisley, November 1995. William J. Clinton Presidential Library. Photographer: Robert McNeely.

come to pledge his support. Niall O'Dowd placed the scene's refulgence in both historical and personal contexts: "Ireland would never be the same again," he said. "I vividly remember that moment, one of the highlights of my life" ("On This Day").[7] The wisdom German Chancellor Helmut Schmidt imparted to young senator Biden years earlier illuminates one source of O'Dowd's exuberance. "Miffed" at Jimmy Carter, Secretary of State Edmund Muskie and the American ambassador, yet needing an American interlocutor to prepare for a summit with Leonid Brezhnev, Schmidt, who had gotten to know the senator and appreciated his candor, requested that he fly to Bonn to participate in his rehearsals. Biden later asked about the request, to which the Chancellor replied, "Joe, you just don't understand. Every time America sneezes, Europe catches a cold [...]. Words matter. They do" (qtd. in Witcover, 318).

Especially the words of an American president, an assertion that reappears throughout these pages. In his remarks earlier at West Belfast's Mackie Metal Plant, Clinton told a large audience, which included a bipartisan Congressional delegation and two hundred local schoolchildren, that "at this holiday season all around the world the promise of peace is in the air." And this promise was affecting the daily lives of Belfast's citizens for the better:

> Soldiers have left the streets of Belfast. Many have gone home. People can go to the pub or the store without the burden of a search or the threat of a bomb. As barriers disappear along the border, families and communities, divided for decades, are becoming whole once more.

A more prosperous and equitable economy, a "peace dividend," was much in evidence:

> The economic rewards of peace are evident as well. Unemployment has fallen here to its lowest level in 14 years, while retail sales and investment are surging. Far from the gleaming city center to the new shop fronts of Belfast to the enterprise center in East Belfast business is thriving and opportunities are expanding. With every extra day that the guns are stilled, business confidence grows stronger [...]. ("Mackie Plant Keynote")

Acknowledging the many leaders, local and international, whose efforts facilitated this expansion—Prime Minister John Major, Taoiseachs John Bruton and Albert Reynolds, David Trimble, John Hume, Gerry Adams, David Irvine, Gary McMichael and others—the president announced his commitment to help "secure the tangible benefits of peace."

His elation was well-founded. A year earlier, after a long-awaited IRA ceasefire was initiated, the Clinton Administration had launched a series of programs to bolster investment in Northern Ireland. Nancy Soderberg, head of Irish affairs at the National Security Council, began organizing an advisory panel of government officials and business leaders as the White House sought to encourage bilateral trade. The centerpiece of the initiative was economic opportunity, and Secretary of Commerce Ron Brown led a delegation to Belfast in December to attend a conference focusing on this opportunity (Wilson, "Doing the Business," 156). The president appointed George Mitchell as Special Advisor for Economic Initiatives in Ireland, which evolved in 1996 into his chairmanship of a group of ten Northern Irish political party leaders, British negotiators and Irish officials to find ways to bring the violence to an end. The process was far from simple—or always civil. In *TransAtlantic*, Colum McCann's fictional George Mitchell, like his real-life counterpart, ponders the gnarled skein of the texts that eventually constituted the Agreement:

> What they have is a sixty-page draft [...] a little less than two weeks [from the deadline]. Strand One. Strand Two. Strand Three. None of the strands yet set in stone. The incredible weave of language. All the little tassels still hanging down [...]. The rumor of a rewrite. The suggestion of a delay. (127)

Endless rewrites and delays, however, would make it impossible to meet the deadline of May 1998 imposed by Tony Blair soon after he succeeded John Major as Prime Minister. His patience worn to a nub, Mitchell supported Blair's ultimatum—"without a hard deadline these people would just not decide anything" (*Making Peace*, 126). More haggling would not only be "unbearable," but also unwise: "A deadline would not guarantee success, but the absence of a deadline would guarantee failure" (126). An even earlier completion date was set, and the Agreement was announced on April 10.

Organizing agendas for meetings and establishing procedures occupied Mitchell for much of the spring of 1996 after the release of the six "Mitchell Principles" (the report of the International Commission on Arms Decommissioning) in late January. The first all-party meeting convened on June 10, at which Paisley's obstructionism was on full display; he would later abandon the negotiation process and spearhead the DUP's opposition to the Agreement. By September 1997, Mitchell was also concerned about developments outside the meeting rooms: "Every time we're on the verge of progress," he complained, "a bomb goes off or someone is shot. Will we ever be able to work it out?" (*Making Peace*, 117). In spite of these obstacles, advances were made: David Trimble and his UUP delegates sat across from Gerry Adams and Sinn Féin for the first time. Equally important, "substantive discussions" were made possible after Paisley and Robert McCartney of the United Kingdom Unionist Party (UKUP) walked out in July "vowing to wreck the process" (63). From Mitchell's perspective, their exodus was a godsend; reaching an agreement without them "was extremely difficult," but "it would have been impossible with them in the room [...]. There would have been no agreement" (110).

Throughout 1997, he worried that the enterprise of peace was in jeopardy. One of the most serious threats to this project occurred as the year ended on December 27, when Billy Wright, head of the Loyalist Volunteer Force (LVF), was assassinated by INLA gunmen. Both groups opposed the peace process, and many feared that the talks were destined to fail. In the wake of Wright's shooting, however, yet another unheralded figure, Marjorie "Mo" Mowlam, appointed by Prime Minister Blair as Secretary of State for Northern Ireland, stepped forward. In early 1998, this "intelligent," "outspoken" and "unpretentious" politician took the controversial step of visiting loyalist prisoners at the Maze to rally their support for the peace process (*Making Peace*, 102). As the *New York Times* reported on January 8, she announced the reason for her decision "just hours after soldiers defused a 500-pound bomb in Banbridge, a predominantly Protestant town southwest of Belfast": she was concerned that negotiators representing the outlawed UDA and the UVF would withdraw from the meetings. Her meeting with 130 convicted bombers and gunmen prompted calls for her resignation. MP Ken Maginnis accused her of ignoring IRA culpability and asking loyalists to do the same by standing down: "The time has come for her to go [...]. She has shown for some time a predisposition to side with Sinn Féin" (Breen, "Unionist MPs"). Mitchell viewed her actions very differently: "With a combination of skill and daring," she "kept the process intact" (132).

Concerns over the future of the negotiations preceded her trip to the Maze. In July 1997 Prime Minister Blair reportedly advised Taoiseach Bertie Ahern that the meetings could "lose all credibility" if the dialogue didn't proceed; for his part, Ahern pointed to the decommissioning of weapons and the disposition of prisoners as yet unresolved problems. Mowlam, responding to Blair's insistence that Sinn Féin's participation could be considered only if they agreed to a genuine ceasefire, countered that "we have allowed the loyalist parties to be in and remain in the talks, even though their linked paramilitaries were engaged in punishment beatings all the time" (qtd. in "Tony Blair Warned"). The talks must be fair to all sides, but as Mitchell advised at the outset, expectations of their outcomes must also be realistic: if unanimous consent is required, "if every party's approval was to be necessary for every decision," then "this process could not possibly succeed; indeed, it would never get off the ground" (49).

In 1995, however, when Clinton arrived in Belfast, the Agreement belonged to the future. Yet, like it, advances in security, investment and employment to which he alluded in his remarks at the Mackie Plant did not materialize out of thin air. The 1994 ceasefire was crucially important, achieved in part by the Clinton administration granting Gerry Adams a temporary visa, a decision that in some quarters set things in a broil.[8] Adams had previously sought a visa in April 1993, but it was denied. A month later, Clinton told a reporter that, after being asked to take a second look at the request, everyone in his administration, "including officials at the State Department," recommended that it be denied (O'Clery, *Daring Diplomacy*, 70). Six months later in October, the political terrain was changing. David Dinkins, seeking reelection as Mayor of New York, was asked if he would consider inviting Adams to the city. "I'll do it tomorrow," he answered. On October 25, he sent the White House a letter requesting another review of the visa request, basing his appeal on Adams's participation in Sinn Féin's dialogue with John Hume (O'Clery, *Daring Diplomacy*, 69).

Deliberations over the request coincided with the bombing of a fish and chips shop in Protestant Belfast on October 23. The Shankill Bombing, as it was later called, made Dinkins's request impossible to honor and, as O'Clery notes, National Security Advisor Tony Lake dismissed it almost immediately. In the wake of the atrocity, with the image of Adams carrying a coffin "fresh in people's minds," there was little support for his appearance in New York (*Daring Diplomacy*, 71). The details of the bombing, as James F. Clarity outlined in the *New York Times*, also shattered whatever optimism existed about an imminent resolution to violence. Four women and two girls were among the ten fatalities with fifty-seven people sustaining injuries, many of them serious, in a bombing for which the IRA failed to provide advance warning. Admitting that things went "tragically wrong," the IRA apologized, blamed a faulty timing device and emphasized that some of the casualties were its own operatives. The attack was aimed at the Ulster Freedom Fighters, a loyalist paramilitary unit headquartered above the shop, but none of its members were killed (Clarity, "I.R.A. Bombing").[9] John Major condemned the IRA as the embodiment of "sheer bloody-minded evil," and both Taoiseach Reynolds and President Clinton expressed their outrage. On the twentieth anniversary of the tragedy, Chris Kilpatrick in the *Belfast Telegraph* sketched biographies of the bombing's victims (no IRA operatives are mentioned). They include shop owner John Frizzell and his twenty-nine-year-old daughter Sharon McBride, who often worked there; Michael Morrison, Evelyn Baird and their seven-year-old daughter Michelle, whose deaths left a nine-year-old son and six-week-old daughter without parents and a sister; and Leanne Murphy, thirteen, out shopping with her mother, who later identified her daughter's body at the morgue ("Shankill Bomb").

Opposition to Adams's visa roiled outside of Washington as well. As Éamon Phoenix reported in 2018, recently released confidential files trace several NIO attempts to block the approval. Nevertheless, Adams was eventually invited to speak at a one-day conference in New York a month after the Downing Street Declaration, an invitation Major's private secretary predicted would cause more destruction: "It would surely be embarrassing for the Americans if they let Adams in, only to find IRA violence was increasing" (Phoenix, "State papers"). The ceasefire needed to be settled first, a mandate opposite that of a chief reason for Adams's New York appearance in the first place—to help him sell the Downing Street Declaration to the "hard men in the Provisional IRA." Ted Kennedy, Chris Dodd, John Kerry and others endorsed this argument, but as Clinton recalls, a "heated debate" continued with the State Department, Warren Christopher and Ray Seitz, American ambassador to the United Kingdom, all of whom opposed the idea. "It would make us look soft on terrorism," they countered, and it "could do irreparable damage to our vaunted 'special relationship' with Great Britain" (*My Life*, 579).

Fortunately for Adams, he had a champion in his corner. In a June 19, 2020, essay, he celebrated his friendship with Ambassador Jean Kennedy Smith (Figure 5), calling her "pivotal to the development of the peace process" and to his obtaining the controversial visa:

> Her strength of character shone through on many occasions but none more so than when I applied for a visa in January 1994. [She] sent a cable to the State Department endorsing the visa application. Some members of her staff sent a dissenting cable to express their opposition. She removed the staff and faced the wrath of the State Department and of Secretary of State Warren Christopher [...]. ("Gerry Adams Remembers")

Consistent with Adams's description, after being confirmed in 1993 Smith replaced the Dublin Embassy's deputy chief of mission, Tom Tonkin, whose "tone and disposition" often aggravated Irish politicians, particularly when discussing intervention in Northern Ireland (*Daring Diplomacy*, 79). But her skill and political connections allowed her to do more than put the Embassy's house in order, as the fracas over Adams's visa demonstrates. And this acrimony roared on both Pennsylvania Avenue and Downing Street after Tony Lake informed Major's government on January 22 that if Adams agreed to promote nonviolence, commit to negotiations, and accept the joint

Figure 5. Gerry Adams and Jean Kennedy Smith, *Fresh American* Magazine Party, 1995. Photographer: Ed Geller/Globe. Courtesy of Alamy.

Declaration as a basis for discussion, the visa would be approved. Ambassador Smith, like John Moore before her during the Nixon administration, demonstrated that envoys to Dublin needed to be competent and knowledgeable about Ireland,—and care about it. Moore cared about Ireland enough to be buried there alongside his wife and daughter who preceded him in death. Similarly, as Smith's critics inside the Embassy grumbled, she "was more attuned to Irish rather than US interests" (qtd. in O'Clery, 90). To be an effective diplomat, that's not always a bad thing.

So, while it is true that the Clinton administration's role in the peace process has garnered considerable attention, diplomats like Smith and members of the president's staff—Nancy Soderberg, for instance—have not. Nor is it the case, as many have argued, that the contributions of the Carter, Reagan and George W. Bush administrations have been sufficiently appreciated. It is also true, however, that not all the attention lavished on Clinton has been positive. For although Niall O'Dowd, founder in 1987 of the *Irish Voice*, a weekly New York-based newspaper, and of Irish Americans for

Clinton in 1991, regards the president's inaugural trip to Belfast as a watershed event in Northern Ireland's history, other commentators have been less impressed, some even questioning the sincerity of his interest.

Richard N. Haass, nominated by George W. Bush as Envoy to Northern Ireland in 2001 and named Special Envoy in June 2003, published a pair of critiques of Clinton's policy initiatives during the president's second term. As John Dumbrell phrases it, Haass's appointment as the Bush administration's "point-man for Northern Ireland" was a significant event in at least two respects: Haass was a respected, "high-profile academic commentator" who served as director of policy planning at the State Department; and his appointment indicated the Bush administration's intention "to maintain an active interest in Northern Ireland" without being "especially concerned to distance their approach from that of the Democrats" ("New American Connection," 360). Widely respected in Northern Ireland, in July 2013 Haass returned there with Meghan O'Sullivan, professor of practice at Harvard's Kennedy School, as the co-chair of roundtable discussions with five political parties (DUP, UUP, SDLP, Sinn Féin, and Alliance) and representatives of the governments of Britain and Ireland. Their goal was to reach a consensus about strategies to reduce tensions caused by, among other perennial irritants, flag waving and Orange Lodge marching through Catholic neighborhoods. Regrettably, as the BBC reported, by the end of 2013 although progress had been made, months of talks addressing "some of the most divisive issues that have hampered the Northern Ireland peace process" ended without reaching an agreement ("Northern Ireland: Richard Haass Talks"). Reactions to this result were mixed. Alliance party deputy leader Naomi Long saw a "huge sea change in the level of political agreement," while her colleague David Ford blamed unionists who "failed to face down the extremes over flags," extremes they "rely on […] to sustain their vote." Journalist Henry McDonald agreed that "unionist parties' failure to support a legally binding code of conduct on loyalist marches" was "one of the main reasons" for the talks' outcome ("Northern Ireland talks collapse"). As they have done for decades, flags and parades continue to provoke tension.

While John Dumbrell inferred from Clinton's policy directives a "new insouciance about upsetting the working norms of the US-UK 'special relationship'," he also recognized other, less conspicuous goals: a "strong effort to include moderate loyalism" in his priorities, for example, and a larger aim to forge "in conditions which did not risk the loss of American lives, internationalist precedents for American peace promotion in the post-Soviet era" (358). Somewhat less generously, Haass published the first of two articles on Clinton's foreign policy in 1997, emphasizing its incoherence. Fashioning a pun from the title of the hit film *Fatal Attraction* (1987), Haass contended that Clinton too readily succumbed to "fatal *dis*tractions," "selective preoccupations" like the expansion of free market democracies and nation-building, while failing to produce policy-relevant guidelines for engaging such unstable hotspots as Bosnia, Iraq, North Korea and Somalia (112–13). In addition, Haass foresaw security risks in a growing globalist economy:

> The expansion of trade opportunities and the free movement of capital have created a complex framework of economic codependencies that do not always mesh with national security objectives. (117)

He recommended the consideration of a new set of priorities for the president's second term starting with China, Taiwan and North Korea; an expansion of NAFTA; and more concerted attention paid to developments in the Middle East. Four years before the September 11 attacks on America, this last recommendation seems stunningly prescient.

In the spring of 2000, Haass published a second article characterizing the Clinton tenure as a "squandered presidency" insofar as policy is concerned. Beginning on a positive note, Haass conceded that "U.S. foreign policy in the Clinton era was not a disaster." It may even be regarded as a "modest success," although the "overriding theme of recent U.S. foreign policy is underachievement and squandered potential," a "preference for symbolism over substance" and "short-term crisis management over long-term strategizing" ("Squandered Presidency," 136–37). Still, NAFTA "contributed to a near doubling in trade volume with America's two largest trading partners" and "helped insulate Mexico from what would otherwise have been a deep recession and political instability." Clinton also achieved "significant milestones in arms control" and demonstrated a "steady hand" during the 1998 Asian economic crisis. Curiously, in his only reference in either essay to Northern Ireland, Haass commends the "significant diplomatic progress" gained there, though in an aside he suggests that the "bulk of the credit" should be given to courageous local leaders (137). In sum, the "ad hoc-racy" of Clintonian policy reflects not only the influence of "special" interests but also the "extraordinarily low status that Clinton accorded international affairs" (140).

Given the experience he acquired in Belfast *after* these critiques were published—both the success he realized there as Bush's envoy and the later frustrations of 2013—Haass might make different assessments today. But what about the historians, political scientists and writers who have been influenced by his critiques? In a study of the years following the Agreement, particularly 2001–06, Mary Alice Clancy develops two lines of argument: the first praises Haass's impact on post-Agreement politics and, after him, that of Mitchell Reiss; the second disputes the Clinton and Bush administrations' claims to be "honest brokers," as both tended to "side with the Irish government" when disagreement rose between Dublin and London (156). The former goal of recognizing Bush's importance partially reflects her disaffection by the "pomp and circumstance" that attended Clinton's "involvement in the Belfast Agreement" (155). That is to say, Clancy complains that Clinton, "apparently feeling foreign policy was not his *métier*," initially "delegated much foreign policy responsibility to officials in the State Department, Pentagon and National Security Council" (156–57). Such charges grow in severity as her argument unfolds, leading to the insinuation that Clinton's investment in Northern Ireland was largely transactional in the crassest sense of the term. Bearing the brunt of "a series of foreign policy *debacles*" and "disasters," Clinton saw Northern Ireland as a "win-win situation," a "low risk initiative with domestic benefits, as it was likely to appease both Irish-American congressional Democrats in general and Ted Kennedy in particular" (157). He needed a victory, and Northern Ireland gave him the best chance to score one.

More recently in *We Don't Know Ourselves*, Fintan O'Toole revisits Clinton's arrival in Belfast for the Christmas tree lighting, commenting that "Objectively, Clinton's great interest in what was now being called the peace process made no sense," especially when juxtaposed to the violence raging in the former Yugoslavia and the casualties suffered annually in major American cities (477). O'Toole's skepticism about the president's motives for involvement in the peace process resembles Clancy's:

> But the most important truth about the Northern Ireland question was that it was, in fact, answerable. For Clinton, and for Tony Blair who came to power in the UK in 1997, there was something to be won. (478)

In politico-economic terms, the Troubles were as contradictory as they were "anomalous." Perhaps this contradiction marked a point of entry for a politician needing a victory:

> While the IRA was bombing the factories, shops and warehouses that provided work, Sinn Féin politicians were demanding jobs for Catholics. While Sinn Féin politicians were denouncing breaches of human and civil rights by the authorities, the IRA was torturing alleged informers [...]. (479)

Reasonably enough, O'Toole wonders, "What, though, did any of this have to do with the United States?" Answer: "America's role was to supply the drama," which had the effect of lifting "local deal-making into a stratosphere of global importance" (482).

In this assertion, O'Toole gestures, however unintentionally, to Paul Dixon's provocative thesis about the Troubles providing a pan-national script in which American presidents could take center stage after standing in the wings of noninvolvement for too long. For Dixon, Clinton's role involved the "greening" of the White House and "was designed to help Gerry Adams deliver republicans to the Good Friday Agreement in 1998." However, the larger scripting of the peace process "dramatized the apparent weakness of British pan-unionism […] and the international isolation of unionism." One result of this script was an "Orange" George W. Bush administration more "readily accepted by unionist audiences" (62).

Given O'Toole's distinguished career as a theatre critic, his foregrounding of the performative qualities of Clinton's 1995 trip isn't surprising. But I would push back slightly against the implication of Clinton's shallowness and the charge that he added only "drama" to the peace process. Instead, in 1995, he did what most political figures do when visiting another country: he *performed* the part of a leader, in this instance, an American president displaying a masculinity appropriate to the role. Unlike the entries of melodramatic stars on the Victorian stage, of "strongmen" like Adolf Hitler in Leni Riefenstahl's film *Triumph of the Will* (1935) or Benito Mussolini in Salah el Moncef's dazzling novella *Benghazi* (2023), Clinton arrived in a far more restrained fashion. In *Benghazi*, el Moncef depicts Mussolini's spectacular entrance to the city's Piazza del Municipio in 1937 after his "fascist gang" stationed in Tripoli began pushing Libya into the "fourth shore of Italy." A band, "starchy" and solemn in their stiff uniforms and black helmets, played martial music while a crowd shouted "DU–CE! DU–CE! DU–CE!" (76). Astride a magnificent Arabian stallion in his uniform and eagle-emblazoned cap, Mussolini waits for the precise moment to unsheathe the "Sword of Islam" and wave it triumphantly over his head (77). Lacking such military paraphernalia, Clinton turns on the holiday lights of an impressive Christmas tree flown in for the occasion while "Catholics and Protestants came together to wave plastic American flags and blow-up baseball bats decorated with the Stars and Stripes" (O'Toole, 476). In *Benghazi*, a "gigantic cardboard face of the Duce rose from among the crowd," which had evolved into a mob "mad with enthusiasm" (76); in Belfast, Clinton's audience showed its appreciation, not their frenzied (in some cases, feigned) adulation of a bloated, larger-than-life *poseur* from a musty hippodrama. That night in Belfast, an American president, represented by the Stars and Stripes, played the starring role, but not the part of a cardboard dictator towering over his subjects.

After the Belfast Agreement was finalized, America and its president continued to play this part when George W. Bush announced a support package in August 2001 and visited Northern Ireland in 2003 and 2008.

The package in 2001 underscored the importance of nonviolence in sustaining a more democratic government:

> The package allows the people of Northern Ireland to sustain devolved government and establish a police service with broad public support [...]. The proposals also recognize that a commitment to democratic governance [...] requires all parties to renounce violence and deal decisively with paramilitary weapons. Consequently, substantial progress on de-commissioning is an essential part of today's package. (qtd. in Smyth, "Bush stresses").

As Dumbrell notes, an administration that initially seemed "committed to a foreign policy of 'not-Clinton'," quickly demonstrated its continued engagement with Northern Ireland ("New American Connection," 359). And, like Bush, Joe Biden has recognized that the long road to fulfilling the promise of Good Friday is, in some respects, never ending.

So have the Clintons, albeit in a far different way. On September 24, 2021, for example, Hillary Clinton was inaugurated as the first woman Chancellor of Queen's University Belfast (she was actually appointed in January 2020, but her formal ceremony was delayed by the pandemic). An unsalaried and ceremonial office, as many similar positions at universities in the United Kingdom are, she presides over formal events and, as Queen's president Professor Ian Greer added, she will also serve as a "key advocate for Queen's on the international stage." The "Hillary Rodham Clinton Early Career Fellowship" is given to outstanding young researchers, and the "Hillary Rodham Clinton Award for Peace and Reconciliation" is awarded annually to help American women receive postgraduate training in politics, conflict transformation or human rights. Not surprisingly, some students and staff protested the appointment, a demonstration more squarely directed at American foreign policy than her; and in 2024—as was the case across American college campuses—students and staff protested her support of the Biden administration's policy on Israel. The road to peace is indeed never-ending.

But this discursive road to Good Friday and beyond *is*. And by now, I hope it is clear that the prospect of peace in Northern Ireland continues to require the leadership of major Northern political parties, British Tories and Liberals, American Democrats and Republicans, presidents and prime ministers, and lesser-known diplomats committed to progress, social equality and economic opportunity. History, like the peace process, needs to remain vigilant as both are "living" texts in constant need of attention and revision.

And if, as I mentioned in the Introduction to this book when quoting Jan Kott, the writing of history and cultural criticism shares the goal of illuminating relevant contemporary concerns, Richard Haass has usefully furthered this ambition in a recent essay. In "What Northern Ireland Teaches Us about Ending the Ukraine War," he emphasizes that the "most fundamental" lesson from the peace process in Northern Ireland is that "diplomacy can succeed only where and when other tools cannot." Violence, he adds, "could not be prevented from disrupting lives, but [it] was not allowed to create political facts." Equally important, channeling George Mitchell's observation in summarizing the results of his work, Haass noted that "while no party in Northern Ireland achieved everything it wanted during these negotiations, every faction could realize some of what it sought—and more than any could hope to accomplish through fighting" ("What Northern Ireland Teaches Us"). In the end, this wise counsel applies equally well to addressing the causes of our American Troubles.

Notes

1 In *Bobby Sands: Nothing but an Unfinished Song*, Denis O'Hearn describes "the concerted campaign" of "the Kai" to rid Rathcoole of Catholics. These vigilantes also received financing from the MP of the area, John McQuade of Ian Paisley's DUP. See O'Hearn, 17–24.
2 In *Killing Thatcher*, Rory Caroll outlines the increasing sophistication of the IRA's radio-controlled bombs, "prepacked, easy-to-operate bombs," "long-delay timers" and other technologies (100–03).
3 See De Bréadún, "Falklands a ridiculous war, said Haughey." The majority of the 368 Argentinian sailors who died on June 11, 1982 were in their teens after a British submarine sank the *General Belgrano*. Shortly thereafter, the Irish government "withdrew its support for European sanctions" imposed on Argentina, an action that "precipitated a massive rift in British-Irish relations."
4 See Maggie Scull, "Timeline of 1981 hunger strike," *Irish Times*, March 1, 2016. See also the Bobby Sands Trust, "Death of Liam McCloskey."
5 Reagan's maintenance of personal distance has often been noted. In *Power Players: Sports, Politics, and the American Presidency* (2023), and after citing Nancy Reagan's observation that her husband "doesn't let anybody get too close," Chris Cillizza quotes H. W. Brands's *Reagan: The Life* (2015) that the president "had almost no close friends" (150). See also Jeff Shesol's review of Brands's biography in the *New York Times* (June 1, 2015) that emphasizes this point.
6 Jules Witcover describes Biden who, after having recently lost his first wife and child, was asked by his friend Jimmy Kennedy to speak that spring at a St. Patrick's Day event held by the "Friendly Sons of Ireland, or whatever the hell it is [...]." "You're an Irish kid," Kennedy said. "You're the guy" (108–09). Biden's friend is most likely referring to the Friendly Sons of Saint Patrick and he kept the engagement.
7 O'Dowd alludes to the twenty-third anniversary of Clinton's arrival, but the date on his *IrishCentral* essay reads "2015," the twentieth anniversary.
8 I have borrowed "set things in a broil" from a voiceover narration in Orson Welles's 1967 film *Chimes at Midnight*.
9 Writing the next day, Clarity reported that nine fatalities and fifty injuries had occurred.

Provocation 3

IMAGINED COMMUNITIES AND HISTORICAL MEMORY, TROUBLES TIME AND "TRUMP TIME"

There is an incisive exchange about history and collective memory in Bernard MacLaverty's *Cal*, a novel (and, later, film) set during the Troubles complete with Orange Lodge parades, deadly ambushes and the firebombing of Catholic homes. Over his career, MacLaverty has written several novels and short stories portraying in often excruciating detail the emotional toll of living through such violence, with *Cal* being, arguably, the most poignant. When discussing the novel, critics often point to similarities between the dilemma of its main characters and that of Shakespeare's "star-crossed" lovers Romeo and Juliet, as its protagonist Cal McCrystal (McCluskey in later printings), an unemployed, working-class Catholic, falls in love with Marcella Morton, the young widow of a Protestant policeman in whose murder Cal was complicit. In this "love across the barricades" story, as in Shakespeare's play, a sense of tragic foreboding is occasionally relieved by glimmers of possibility—for example, when Cal finds fulfilling work on the Morton family farm and makes a new home there to be near Marcella. His days of living on the dole may be over, and his new job hints at a better future. Unlike the protagonists of *Romeo and Juliet* whose fates are tied to family lineages and histories they cannot alter, Cal seems convinced that he possesses the agency to escape his connection to sectarian violence. Sadly, in the novel's closing scene, his arrest and imminent punishment destroy any possibility of a future with Marcella. But the question remains unanswered, to recall Haines's observation in James Joyce's *Ulysses*, of how "history is to blame" for Cal's fate. Perhaps it isn't. Perhaps historical *memory* and the at times nefarious uses to which history is put are the culprits (Figure 6).

Unlike *Cal*, MacLaverty's later novel *Grace Notes* (1997) develops tensions between memory and aspiration that lead to a happier, even refulgent conclusion. The novel begins with a fledgling composer, Catherine McKenna, returning to Northern Ireland from Scotland to attend her father's funeral.

Figure 6. Orangemen Marching in Derry, 1996. Courtesy of Robert W. White.

At the cemetery where he is interred, she passes the grave of a boy she once knew who "gave his life for Ireland," as an inscription beneath his name on his headstone clarifies. Reading the epitaph, Catherine wonders what musical composition might best represent the militant nationalism for which her former classmate sacrificed his life. Eventually, she writes a symphony on this theme, which is performed with spectacular success in the novel's conclusion.

The inscription on the young man's headstone, however, was only one determinant of her project, for Catherine had studied with a Ukrainian mentor who escaped the massacre at Babi Yar in 1941 when Nazi troops murdered over 33,000 Jews. Just as her teacher Melnichuck transposed this horror into the spiritual register of his music, Catherine, battling depression, hopes through her music to answer a related question, "How did the mind heal?" (122). In the final chapter, she is buoyed by the response to her composition as she rises to acknowledge the audience's standing ovation. Like her mentor's work, Catherine's symphony *Vernicle*, as the word connotes, is an imprint or image, the wound of a prior injury. She invites four Orangemen from Portadown to play Lambeg drums at the symphony's climax, thereby transforming an object of her fear as a child and of her father's ire—earlier she recalled his hatred of the massive drums' rumblings in the July parades that disrupted their neighborhood—into something almost therapeutic. Fascinated by both "clusters of short notes"—hence, the novel's title—and melodies that seemed to wander and express "two or more things at once," Catherine's aesthetic privileged a multi-tonal composition with sounds only these giant drums could produce (84, 275). The invitation for the Orangemen to play was thus, like Freudian dream content, overdetermined, emerging from a constellation of political, psychological and aesthetic sources.

Historical memory in *Cal* does not promote such healing. Instead, it is most often refashioned into a recruiting device to persuade poor, unemployed teens to fight, kill or die in a seemingly never-ending battle. Desperate to leave the active service to which he has been drafted, Cal goes to see Skeffington, a teacher and the leader of his cell, who asks, "Do you still want to—refuse to help?" When Cal replies, "I'm afraid so" (72), Skeffington recites "The Mother," a poem Padraic Pearse wrote on the eve of his execution by the British after the 1916 Easter Uprising. The speaker of the poem is an avatar of Mother Ireland who, though "weary, weary/Of the long sorrow" of losing her sons, endorses the physical force tradition and the sacrifice it demands: "And yet I have my joy:/My sons were faithful and they fought." Albeit unsuccessful, the 1916 rising marked the birth of the Irish Free State some six years later. In the process, patriot blood became sanctified in works like "The Mother" and Lady Gregory and William Butler Yeats's play *Cathleen ni Houlihan* (1902). And here is where memory enters the dialogue about history and nationalist sacrifice, for undaunted by Skeffington's recitation of the poem, Cal exclaims, "But it is not like 1916." Skeffington quickly responds, "It wasn't like 1916 in 1916" (73).

He's right. 1916 and 1776; January 6, 2021, in Washington and January 30, 1972, in Derry—these dates have been redefined by memory and political discourse in ways participants at the time could hardly have foreseen. In *Imagined Communities: Reflections on the Origin and Spread of Nationalism* (revised edition, 2006), Benedict Anderson underscores the "ghostly *national* imaginings" with which such monuments as the tombs of Unknown Soldiers are "saturated," constructions with a "strong affinity with religious imaginings" (9, 10). In times of civil discord, dates also function as monuments, many becoming *memorials* concretized in and sanctified by such imaginaries. Some, like December 7, 1941, live in infamy; others, those that celebrate great triumphs or advances, reside in sanctuaries. But, as Paul Muldoon notes in *Rising to the Rising* (2016), a volume of poems and short prose pieces commissioned to commemorate the centenary of the Easter 1916 Rising, all are susceptible to hijacking by groups or individuals like Skeffington with ulterior motives.

To complicate matters further, as Muldoon acknowledges, borrowing an observation from Keith Jeffrey's *1916: A Global History* (2017), both Catholics and Protestants have canonized the same year as marking a glorious chapter in their very different histories. That is to say when the 1916 Easter Rising of nationalists in Dublin is counterbalanced by the blood sacrifices of the 36th (Ulster) division fighting for Britain at the Battle of the Somme. Both sides of the Northern Irish impasse thus justified their actions through historical memory—one reason a portrait of the heroes of the 1916 Rising is displayed in Skeffington's home—citing their connection to nation-building or ancient heroism, and this valorization seems almost always steeped in blood. As Anne McClintock argues, "All nationalisms are gendered; all are invented; and all are dangerous" (89). MacLaverty's narrator in *Cal*, sounding a little like Anderson and McClintock, recognizes the power of nationalism and the mythologies that seem always to define it:

> People were dying every day, men and women were being crippled and turned into vegetables in the name of Ireland. *An Ireland which never was and never would be.* It was the people of Ulster who were heroic, caught between the jaws of two opposing ideals [...]. (92; my emphasis)

Nationalism in twenty-first-century America is sustained by and susceptible to similar manipulations of collective memory, as Nick Bryant explains in regard to Donald Trump's 2016 presidential campaign. Albeit more disturbingly tinged with Messianic allusions, Trump's 2024 campaign promulgated similar imaginary constructions of the nation as a community. For Bryant, Trump's slogan "Make America Great Again," particularly the addition of "*again*," encourages speculation about when that moment of greatness was last realized. That the conceit is not original—Rory Carroll notes in *Killing Thatcher* that, during her spring 1979 campaign, Mrs. Thatcher defined her "business" as trying to "make Britain great again" (qtd. on 34)—is hardly a concern for Trumpism. Instead, the slogan affords Trumpists "the historic license to conjure up kingdoms of the mind, places that existed only in the abstract, for the country to revisit" (Bryant, 8). A British journalist whose imagination was always "fired" by America, Bryant views Los Angeles in the 1980s as the last time the United States "lived up to its billing": from its "multi-lane freeways to the cavernous fridges; from drive-in movie theatres to drive-through burger joints." For him, steaks "the size of frisbees" epitomized an American greatness of speed, calories and consumerism (15).

But in recent years, more serious ideological disputes over an imaginary past have torn the country apart: the Supreme Court's 2022 decision in the *Dobbs v. Jackson Women's Health Organization*, for example, transports the country back in time before *Roe v. Wade*. In states like Texas, the recuperation of mythic greatness starts with the prosecution of victims of rape, incest or poverty seeking medical attention—and with medical professionals who try to help them.

As the Trump presidency pursued its anti-globalist, "America First" and at times America-only agenda, it became obvious that the nation's "greatness" depended upon more than the efficiency of the drive-through lane at In-N-Out Burger. During the Trump administration, international cooperation and multinational initiatives to address everything from immigration to COVID-19 to climate change gave way to an imaginary "nation-ness," which, as Anderson describes, is an aggregation of fantasies of sovereignty and community "regardless of the actual inequality and exploitation that may prevail." Ultimately, he concludes, this mythology of nationhood has made it possible, "over the past two centuries, for so many millions of people, not so much to kill, as willing to die for such limited imaginings" (7).

Central to such imaginings in the Northern Irish context, as the narrator of *Cal* realizes, is a nation that never existed and never will, implying that the nation is both a fiction and discursive phenomenon, not a material fact. Instead, "nation" acts as a "provisional framework" that disappears once its leadership is revealed to be mortal and therefore fallible (Franco, 133). In *Rising to the Rising*, Muldoon features a poem qua rap performance entitled "One Hundred Years a Nation" that applies pressure to the process of nation-building, highlighting its darker operations. Returning to his observation about the memorialization of 1916 by both nationalists and loyalists, dates can be transformed by memory into self-justifying rationalizations. Such was the case when the Confederate battle flag was carried by members of the mob that attacked the Capitol on January 6 and later by a supporter of Virginia gubernatorial candidate Glenn Youngkin at an October 13, 2021, rally. In both instances, insurrection is re-narrativized as a legitimate protest—or a hallowed lost cause. That October night in Virginia, the crowd pledged allegiance to a flag carried by someone described as having attended a "peaceful rally with Donald J. Trump on January 6." As such, both events at some later date can be folded into a mythology about nationhood, with January 6 and Youngkin's election forming chapters in a revised "New Lost Cause" narrative in which the Confederate side of the American Civil War has long occupied a privileged position (Graham, "New Lost Cause").

Troubles Time and "Trump Time"

> Trump time [...] was nothing more than a clever and deceptive sales pitch.
> —Governor J.B. Pritzker, quoted in Carol Leonnig and Philip Rucker, *I Alone Can Fix It: Donald J. Trump's Catastrophic Final Year* (2021)

> Even for dedicated news junkies, it is remarkable how much we can forget, in the shock of the moment, about the previous shock of the moment.
> —Carlos Lozada, *Washington Post*, March 16, 2018

For a Trump acolyte like Peter Navarro, "Trump Time" is as fantastical as Benedict Anderson's imagined community. Promoting his book *In Trump Time: My Journal of America's Plague Year* (2021), Navarro touts "Trump Time" as a feature of the president's nimbleness in responding to any and all crises. In his effusion, Navarro praised the president for working "night and day for the American people," and his spearheading of a vaccine initiative to fight COVID-19 "literally at warp speed" reflects this astonishing ability. How fast warp speed *literally* moves is never defined, nor is it clear how the president could work night and day on the nation's most daunting challenges while practicing to clobber those 280-yard drives about which he likes to boast (after smashing a drive at the Pro-Am of the 2022 LIV Tour Team Finals, he asked, "You think Biden can do that?"). These diversions notwithstanding, "Trump Time" is shorthand for "amazing competence" and "superb leadership," the result of years of experience in the real estate business navigating issues that would bring mere mortals to their knees.

Or is "Trump time" something else? As Carol Leonnig and Philip Rucker report in *I Alone Can Fix It*, this lightning-quick efficiency Navarro applauds didn't always function quite so brilliantly, as when J. B. Pritzker, the Democratic governor of Illinois, visited the White House in the early weeks of the pandemic. In late 2018, Pritzker along with other governors met with the president, who greeted him with unusual warmth and congratulated him on his gubernatorial victory. He also promised the governor immediate attention should Illinois ever require his assistance. And soon thereafter it did. By late March 2020, as COVID began to overwhelm hospitals across the country, Illinois faced a shortage of Personal Protective Equipment (PPE) and ventilators, so Pritzker telephoned the president asking for help. The president then called Navarro, who contacted the governor and assured him that 300 ventilators and 300,000 N95 masks could be heading his way. And he could get them to the Governor in "Trump time," six days later.

Six days later, nothing arrived. Several days after that, the ventilators appeared, but the masks were not what Navarro described and what Pritzker needed. Some weeks later, unable to locate N95 masks, Navarro called to offer the governor hand sanitizer. So much for warp speed efficiency, leading Pritzker to conclude that "Trump Time" was merely a "clever and deceptive sales pitch" (Leonnig and Rucker, 90–92).

But more than a roster of desperately ill patients, inadequately equipped medical professionals and hoodwinked governors fully accounts for the connotations of Trump time. Carlos Lozada describes one of the most dangerous of these when observing that in the "shock of the moment" over Trump's egregious blunders or thoughtless asides— each assault on the press or FBI, each character assassination of a public servant simply doing her job— it becomes easier to forget the previous shock of the moment. In other words, if MacLaverty's Skeffington appropriates the events of 1916 and refashions them into a recruitment or retention pitch, the Trump administration's prodigious record of assaults on democracy undermines or short-circuits the operations of memory itself. The effects of such an onslaught transcend the specific instance—*this* firing of a staffer, *that* subversion of a constitutional norm—and contribute to a more general weakening of both collective memory and the social contract.

More than memory is imperiled, however, as our experience of time itself is altered. Reviewing Amy Siskind's *The List: A Week-by-Week Reckoning of Trump's First Year* (2018) for the *Washington Post*, Lozada theorizes a freighted sense of lived time in Trump's America in which "every day feels like a week, every week a month, every month a year." But the effects hardly end there. As Trump's first year in office progressed, the "outrages" to civility and democracy grew so overwhelming in number that even the most voracious consumer of news couldn't keep up with the barrage. Consider the "Stop the Steal" narrative, which grew more convoluted and absurd with each passing day. Bombarded by such an onslaught, memory falters, eventually allowing subsequent outrages to "pass" as instances of a "new normal." Lozada's conclusion? "President Trump comes at you fast, and the whiplash of firings, tweets, shake-ups, indictments and alternative facts can be a lot to take" ("Think You Can Remember"). Too much to take. Forgetting some of these outrages may function as a balm to the psyche, but this amnesia allows Trumpism more latitude to pursue its destructive mischief.

How different is the memorial overload caused by Trumpism from the impact of daily violence during the Troubles? Anna Burns's novel *No Bones* (2001) begins with her young protagonist's obsessively precise memory of when the violence began: "The Troubles started on a Thursday [in 1969]. At six o'clock at night. At least that's how Amelia remembered it" (11).

Some pages later, however, in a chapter entitled "Somethin' Political, 1977," Amelia struggles to remember even recent events and their sequencing: "Somethin' happened political. No what was it? Was it the hunger-strikers? No, not yet. Was it a Butcher killing? No, not this time." She concludes that it was a shooting of a girl she once knew sitting by the fire in her own home. Loyalist gunmen invaded it and started firing because it was rumored that the girl had once been an IRA operative, although Sister Mary Fatima at the school she once attended "wasn't having any of it" (95). The impossibly precise chronology of the Troubles with which *No Bones* begins—they started in the late afternoon on a Thursday in 1969—devolves in the space of barely eighty pages into a collage of kidnappings, murders and dates. The 1981 hunger strikes jostle in the memory with the brutal attacks in 1975 of the Shankill Butchers which then merge with the shooting of a neighbor who once attended a Catholic school nearby. The cascade of shock after shock batters the memory of previous atrocities into an indecipherable blur, as names are forgotten and replaced by those of new victims. "Troubles Time" parallels "Trump Time" in its engendering of confusion, uncertainty and memorial overload.

These are the effects of both civil wars and Troubles, conflicts waged in the name of imaginary nations and sacred dates, that both disrupt time and alter our perception of it. And these often begin before we recognize them, as Robert Kagan has argued: "The United States is heading into its greatest political and constitutional crisis since the Civil War, with a reasonable chance over the next three to four years of incidents of mass violence, a breakdown of federal authority, and the division of the country into warring red and blue enclaves" ("The Constitutional Crisis"). For Kagan, our American Troubles, or Civil War as some call it, a conflict grounded in imagined communities, memorial lapses and distorted senses of time, are already well underway.

Chapter 4

READING OUR TROUBLES: SEAMUS HEANEY AND THE BIDEN PRESIDENCY

> History says, *Don't hope*
> *On this side of the grave.*
> But then, once in a lifetime
> The longed-for tidal wave
> Of justice can rise up,
> And hope and history rhyme.
> —Seamus Heaney, *The Cure at Troy: A Version of Sophocles' Philoctetes* (1990)

> Where do you turn in times like these? The answer for most people is probably not to novels. More's the pity [...]. A novel, my contemporary Robert McLiam Wilson once wrote, is 'shoe-swapping on the grand scale.' To read one is to engage in repeated acts of empathy, to accept the invitation to see the world as it appears to people other than oneself.
> —Glenn Patterson, *Here's Me Here: Further Reflections of a Lapsed Protestant* (2015)

It was a blustery July night in Galway, as if somehow November had finagled a new home on the calendar and banished summer for the remainder of 2017. Savoring the warmth of a banquet hall on the NUI-Galway campus, members of the Eugene O'Neill International Society and their guests gathered to dine; to honor Jessica Lange and Gabriel Byrne for their star turns in O'Neill's plays, particularly in *Long Day's Journey into Night* in 2016; and to enjoy President Michael D. Higgins's account of memorable evenings in the theatre viewing O'Neill's masterworks.[1] Sitting with my wife, daughter and fellow banqueters—and having enjoyed speaking with President Higgins before—I recalled President Mary Robinson's learned remarks twenty-five years earlier at a convocation of Joyceans at Trinity College in Dublin. Irish presidents are expected to be well-read. And, much like a president's words, his or her reading matters.

Listening to President Higgins, my American friends and I felt more than a twinge of envy that our Irish colleagues could claim such a cultured man as their leader (fifteen months later, they *reclaimed* him when he won a second seven-year term). More than a published poet and theatregoer, Higgins is also a perceptive commentator on modern Irish literature, revising his 2012 remarks at a Dublin conference dedicated to Bernard Shaw's work to introduce the anthology *Shaw and the Making of Modern Ireland* (2020). Suffice it to say, his welcome to Shavians earlier was hardly the arid formality to which conference-goers have become inured. Instead, he highlighted Shaw's work as a public man, citing his investigations of tenement housing and denunciation of the business magnate who locked out desperately poor workers in a 1913 Dublin strike. Higgins's argument emphasized that as a public intellectual, Shaw assumed several identities—moralist, essayist, dramatist, lecturer, advocate, ironist—and seemed always poised to fulfill his "civic responsibility" (12). Committed to improving the modern condition, particularly the modern urban condition, he exposed the squalor of working-class tenements, the larger societal effects of poverty and the commodification of women, topics that inform such plays as *Widowers' Houses* (1892), *Mrs. Warren's Profession* (1902), *Major Barbara* (1905) and many others.[2]

After Higgins had spoken and dinner was over, Gabriel Byrne and Jessica Lange were summoned to the stage to receive their awards. Grinning puckishly and aware of a significant American contingent in the audience, Byrne thanked the O'Neill Society before relating his pride in listening earlier to President Higgins's erudite account of his experiences in the theatre, a pride, he feared, many in attendance that night might never feel when hearing their recently elected president. Like his portrayal of the tortured, guilt-ridden James Tyrone in *Long Day's Journey into Night*, in his improvisation as a soothsayer Byrne proved exceptional (Figure 7).

By the end of 2019, his drollery seemed even more ironic after Matthew Dessem compiled a list of Donald Trump's book recommendations from his posts on social media. No titles by Joyce, Shaw or O'Neill—no drama or poetry, no fiction save for a children's book—graced the list. Instead, the former president recommended such titles as *The Case Against Socialism* by Rand Paul, *The Case for Trump* by Victor Davis Hanson, *Exonerated: The Failed Takedown of President Donald Trump by the Swamp* by Dan Bongino and—in a nod to the writers' guild at Fox News—*Radicals, Resistance, and Revenge: The Left's Plot to Remake America* by Jeanine Pirro and *Power Grab: The Liberal Scheme to Undermine Trump, the GOP, and Our Republic* by Jason Chaffetz.[3] As Glenn Patterson maintains in the epigraph above, engagement with a skillfully

Figure 7. President Higgins Welcomes Mr. Joe Biden, President of the United States, at Áras an Uachtaráin, April 2023. Courtesy of President Higgins's Office.

crafted novel—much like viewing a well-wrought play—is to "accept the invitation to see the world as it appears to people other than oneself" (6). Such an invitation isn't tendered by books in which you're the principal subject. Empathy, the imaginative act of walking in another person's shoes, shares this quality with hope: more specifically, with Christian conceptions of hope. That is, as Paul Corcoran argues, the "possibility presents itself that the message of hope that rings across the centuries in Heaney's *Cure at Troy* is in important ways, a Christian one" (435). Why? Because a "meaningful vision of hope must be communal, it must extend beyond the concerns of the individual" (437).

On January 21, 2021, the society of empathetic presidential readers welcomed a new member who, like Higgins's characterization of Bernard Shaw, is a "public man." Following Joe Biden during the final months of the 2020 campaign, Evan Osnos introduces his account with a startling image of a nation in need of just such a leader:

> At the very moment that his country was lying spread-eagled before the eyes of the world, Biden had arrived at his season of history. (4)

Splayed helplessly on the ground America, American democracy, in particular, has been overwhelmed by authoritarian populism. This assessment is hardly radical as, among other studies, the "Democracy Index" of the *Economist* Intelligence Unit since 2006 has charted the downward spiral leading to this point, indicating that in 2016, the line separating "full" democracies from damaged ones had been crossed ("Why America is a 'flawed democracy'"). In 2022, David Meyers indicted Trumpism for exacerbating the problem: "For the past six years, Americans have lived in a 'flawed democracy,' one dragged down by high levels of polarization, gerrymandering, and events like the Jan. 6, 2021, insurrection [...]" ("U.S. remains a 'flawed democracy'").[4] In 2023, Julia Kirschenbaum and Michale Li at the Brennan Center for Justice, who described gerrymandering as a "thorn in the side of democracies for centuries," warned that with more severe redistricting "it's a bigger threat than ever" ("Gerrymandering Explained").[5] More generally, voter suppression, as Dan Balz and Clara Ence Morse explain in the *Washington Post*, has already led to one unfortunate demographical fact:

> Today, a minority of the population can exercise outsize influence on policies and leadership, leading many Americans increasingly to feel that the government is a captive of minority rule. Twice in the past two decades, the president was elected while losing the popular vote—George W. Bush in 2000 and Trump in 2016. That had happened only three times in the previous 200-plus years.[6] ("American democracy")

Biden's "season of history" will indeed be shaped by daunting challenges.

Given the tenor of these challenges, Tess Taylor's exuberance after the 2020 election that "We are going to have a president who quotes poetry" is more meaningful than it might appear (*CNN Opinion*). And not just because First Lady Jill Biden happens to teach courses in both writing and literature. It means that, like Irish voters, we have elected a president who not only reads the poetry of William Butler Yeats, Seamus Heaney, Langston Hughes and Robert Graves but also appreciates the wit of Mark Twain, the wisdom of Steven Levitsky and Daniel Ziblatt's *How Democracies Die* (2018), and the historical relationship between Ireland and America (Ryan Tubridy's *JFK in Ireland*, for example).[7] It means that he is a leader with a deep reservoir of empathy that the readerly imagination replenishes, a quality essential to the cultivation of hope. In the same editorial, Taylor embraced the election of an elegant and well-read Vice President, Kamala Harris, who is fond of quoting, among other writers, Toni Morrison and Richard Wright. A "great sea-change," to borrow a phrase from *The Cure at Troy*, has restored literacy to the White House without the need for insurrection or divine intervention. For that's what it would have taken to turn Biden's predecessor into a reader, as Jennifer

Weiner complained in the *New York Times*: "It is appalling to me that the man in the White House seems to read absolutely nothing—not literature, not best sellers, not his security briefings, not even, if his co-authors can be believed, the books he has ostensibly written" ("What's Your Favorite Book"?).[8] Her point is even more arresting when contextualized with the sophistication of Trump's predecessor. As the *Guardian* reported, Barack Obama's "19 favorite books for 2019" featured titles on subjects ranging from "surveillance capitalism and the attention economy to feminism and race in Britain." Two of these concerned Ireland and Northern Ireland: Sally Rooney's novel *Normal People* and Patrick Radden Keefe's account of violence during the Troubles in *Say Nothing*.

The significance of such literacy obviously extends well past the composition of reading lists. Donald Trump's "sub-literacy," comedian Bill Maher's deprecation when proposing a "new rule" that "if you can't read, you can't be president" ("Sub-literate America"), identifies one of contemporary America's most worrisome trends. For if, as Robert Maynard Hutchins, longtime president of the University of Chicago, insisted in *The University of Utopia* (2nd edition, 1964), the "object of the educational system [...] is not to produce hands for industry or to teach the young how to make a living. It is to produce responsible citizens" (3), then we are drifting into perilous straits. This peril is evident in a state like Florida where high school classes in American History represent slavery as providing black Americans with marketable skills; courses in Psychology exclude considerations of gender and sexuality; and, as the 2023–24 school year began, syllabi in English literature were inoculated against the deleterious effects of Shakespeare's plays.[9] The education for which Hutchins advocated, one grounded in a common experience of the Great Books and supple enough "to take into account the philosophical diversity characteristic of our time," is under attack (54).

While business luminaries like Berkshire Hathaway's late Vice-Chairman Charlie Munger, who claimed never to have met an intelligent person who didn't read—"not one, zero"—would have celebrated the ascendance of a literate leader, many Americans wouldn't notice or care. Some have grown so cynical that the idea of a well-read politician seems either a fraud perpetrated by public relations flacks or an irrelevancy. The former suspicion surfaced in 2019 when Pete Buttigieg was asked what books he would take if, like Philoctetes in *The Cure at Troy*, he was marooned on a desert island. He mentioned *Ulysses*, a title that elicited a wary incredulity from Jennifer Weiner: "When a politician or other public figure is asked to list his or her favorite books, it's never just a list. It's an answer to the question '*Who do I want people to think I am?*'" Finally conceding that Buttigieg might be telling the truth—his father, after all, was a professor of English and a Joyce scholar—Weiner turned to the (non)reading public and literature itself:

> Somewhere along the way, between *Beowulf* and Chaucer, people learned that reading was a slog and that literature consisted of books about characters who looked and sounded nothing like them, living in worlds that were nothing like their own [...]. As soon as no one was forcing them to do it, they stopped. ("What's Your Favorite Book?")

However unpersuasive—Americans really have little curiosity about characters different from themselves? Marvel Studios take note—this thesis hints at one potential outcome of Buttigieg's bookishness: although progressive voters might be wowed by it, few others would be. Ten days later in *The Chronicle of Higher Education*, Steven Johnson supported this contention when noting that "just 31 percent of college graduates were considered proficient readers in 2003, down from 40 percent in 1992" ("The Fall and Rise"). These data suggest that more than the convenience of tweets and other social media is responsible for the trend: Americans are forsaking books because they no longer possess the skills to navigate them.

But leaders *must* possess these skills, even if presidential reading lists in the past have provoked controversy. When Hugh Sidey in "The President's Voracious Reading Habits" (March 17, 1961) calculated that President Kennedy could consume "1200 words a minute" and attached a list of the president's favorite titles that included Ian Fleming's *From Russia with Love* (1957), detractors were quick to pounce. Some ascribed Kennedy's interest in Fleming to James Bond's sexual license which, if imitated, would damage the president's reputation and office. One biographer detected the "dark side of Camelot" in this revelation, while another half-mockingly proposed a link between the president's fascination with the British aristocracy and fantasies of "naked women" emerging "from silver dishes at their banquets" (Willman 186–87).[10] Biden's enthusiasm for Heaney's writing is neither so scholarly as Michael Higgins's study of Shaw, nor so controversial as JFK's enjoyment of Fleming, but it is also more than a public relations contrivance or return to his recitation of poetry as a remedy for stuttering.[11] On the contrary, I want to argue that Biden's reading of *The Cure at Troy* not only constitutes evidence of his self-proclaimed Irish identity, but also contributes to an ethics and worldview well-suited to emancipate American democracy from its spread-eagled abjection.

Stated another way, democracy requires empathy before Hope (with a capital "H") can rhyme with History. Both principal characters in *The Cure at Troy*—Philoctetes and Neoptolemus, the young Greek who arrives on Lemnos to secure the famous bow in the elder Greek's possession—enter the play suffering from grievous wounds. As the narrative progresses Philoctetes's impulse to avenge those responsible for his injuries seems to intensify, and before his entrance, Neoptolemus learns that he has been "Behaving like a savage" and "Howling wild like a wolf," cues that actors playing the role routinely follow when making their entrances (13).[12] Upon first meeting Neoptolemus, the aggrieved "savage" concedes that he indeed looks "like a wild animal," a bestial appearance he attributes to the "traitors" who abandoned him (15). "Gods curse them all," he later shouts. "I ask for the retribution I deserve" (19).

But vengeance, as Heaney's play reiterates, also conduces to *national* pathologies. In examining these matters in Heaney's text, I hope to identify parallels between troubles in contemporary America and those in Northern Ireland while, at the same time, avoiding an allegorical reading of *The Cure at Troy*. As Marilynn Richtarik observes, Heaney's "foremost concern in writing it had been to be faithful to the original while rendering it more accessible to those who would see it on tour [in 1990]" (*Getting to Good Friday*, 45). But this aspiration does not make him a political writer nor does it make a Sophoclean character a stand-in for someone else. After interviewing him before the play's October 1990 premiere, Eileen Battersby inferred that Heaney "would be impatient with the idea that there is a coded message about Northern Ireland" in it (qtd. in Richtarik, 54). Obviously, there is no encoded critique of the United States in Heaney's play either. So, rather than constructing univocal and allegorical bridges from fifth-century BC Athens to 1970s Belfast and twenty-first-century Washington, I hope to use Philoctetes's story to illuminate the challenges Joe Biden will face as he undertakes his "season of history."

Time, Identity and the Psycho-political Atmosphere

> O look, look in the mirror,
> O look in your distress;
> Life remains a blessing
> Although you cannot bless.
> O stand, stand at the window
> As the tears scald and start;
> You shall love your crooked neighbour
> With your crooked heart.
> —W.H. Auden, from "As I Walked Out One Evening" (1937)

Before a line is uttered in *The Cure at Troy*, before the three women who comprise its Chorus "*stir and move, like seabirds stretching and unstiffening*" at the beginning of the prologue (1), a reader of the play's text encounters this epigraph from a poem in W. H. Auden's 1940 volume *Another Time*. For someone familiar with Philoctetes's fate, these stanzas might be seen as a précis of the play's narrative: like his Greek predecessor, the figure addressed in Auden's poem is "in distress"; like Philoctetes, he can see only his misery and cannot "bless"; and, like the play's woeful hero, he is admonished to forego his looking glass of self-absorption for a window that affords him a more capacious view of the world around him. At first glance, Auden's and Heaney's emphases would seem to privilege the spaces of selfhood; when the mirror becomes a window, introversion is supplanted by *caritas* allowing the addressee to love a "crooked neighbour." Yet, while these excerpts from Auden's poem don't make this clear, these admonitions are in fact not made by the poem's speaker, by the "I" walking down a crowded street; instead, he hears them in the "whirr and chime" of "all the clocks in the city." The exhortation to exchange the mirror for a window is thus connected to the poem's opening line—"O let not time deceive you"—as such deceit has rendered the "you" unable to imagine a fuller life:

> O plunge your hands in water
> Plunge them in up to the wrist;
> Stare, stare in the basin
> And wonder what you've missed. (*Collected Poems*, 134).

"Another Time," the title poem that accompanies "As I Walked Out One Evening" in Auden's collection, advances a complementary thesis on the relationship between time and human subjectivity. In it, the poem's speaker insists that "It is to-day in which we live," not yesterday:

> So many try to say Not Now,
> So many have forgotten how
> To say I Am, and would be
> Lost, if they could, in history. (276)

Conceptions of "I Am" and "to-day" can only be distorted or diminished by a fixation on the past. The future is another matter. As Ernst Bloch explains in *The Principle of Hope* (1954), hope is the expression of an "anticipatory consciousness" oriented toward newness or "Becomeness" (203); and, as Paul Corcoran defines it, Hope also pertains to both desire and *"performance*: we change our way of life to work towards that for which we hope" (437). History, conversely, denotes a past "Doneness" that complicates reconciliation and impedes progress.

Another way of understanding the role of history during the Troubles is reflected in the title of David Lloyd's *Anomalous States* (1990), which yokes the past to two very different senses of identity:

> The anomalous character of recent Irish history derives from the fact that, unlike most other Western European states, the moment of nationalist victory did not constitute a moment of apparent national unification, but rather institutionalized certain racial and sectarian divisions. The treaty of 1922, which [...] established the Irish Free State, did so only at the expense of also establishing the Northern Irish state, a self-governing enclave with a deliberately and artificially constructed majority of Protestant citizens. (18)

One result, as Lloyd's occasionally bruising reading of Heaney's poetry suggests, is that "Irish identity," something celebrated when a President Biden or Obama is welcomed in Dublin—or, after Bill Clinton, in Belfast—is inherently plural and often vexed.

Why? Because the "identity of the individual, his integrity, is expressed by the degree to which that individual identifies himself with and integrates his differences in a national consciousness" (Lloyd, 15). This implies, among other things, that mirrors and solipsism do not define identity because they neither gesture toward nor express themselves through a larger community, national or otherwise. In these terms, narcissistic self-absorption is not an identity but a pathology, one that Heaney explores in *The Cure at Troy* through the play's protagonist. For Lloyd, in other words, the 1922 Treaty guaranteed that an "Irish identity" for citizens of the Republic would differ from that of Northern unionists, some of whom, like the deeply troubled Eric Miller in David Ireland's *Cyprus Avenue* (2016), deny possessing any semblance of an Irish identity. "I am exclusively and non-negotiably British," he tells his psychiatrist, and "not now nor never have been nor never will be Irish" (8–9). If Irish culture is "envisaged as performing the work of integration, uniting simultaneously class with class and the primitive with the evolved," that process is undertaken—or resisted—in the present (Lloyd, 15). And a staunch loyalist like Eric Miller will not countenance any such communion.

For many survivors of traumatic events, the present is also susceptible to disruptions by suppressed histories that, like the child's spool in the *fort/da* game Freud observes in *Beyond the Pleasure Principle* (1920), reappear at the slightest tug of the strings of memory. Underscoring the belatedness of the traumatic event, Julia Obert suggests that "sharing stories from both sides" of the conflict may be the best way to salve "old wounds" or "broach the possibility of peace" ("Troubles Literature," 77). In a 2021 article written in the wake of the January 6 insurrection, *Atlantic* writer Anne Applebaum promoted another strategy:

> Drop the argument and change the subject [...]. In the years before and after the peace setlement in Northern Ireland, for example, many 'peace-building' projects did not try to make Catholics and Protestants hold civilized debates about politics [...]. Instead, they built community centers, put up Christmas lights, and organized job training for young people. ("Coexistence Is the Only Option")

Her suggestion of a shared commitment to train workers who have dropped out of the job market or young people struggling to enter it may have merit; so might the partnership in building community centers. But as an unconvinced Sophia A. Nelson wrote in *TheGrio* when accusing Applebaum of being "tone deaf," coexistence is hardly an unproblematic notion. Nelson bridled at the notion of détente with a mob whose trespass of the Capitol was reminiscent of numerous "stories passed down from slavery and Jim Crow" ("Hell no"). Why should she break bread with white supremacists whose forebears murdered her ancestors, razed the Greenwood District of Tulsa, better known as Black Wall Street, in 1921, and two years later wiped Rosewood, Florida off the map?

Traumatic injury—and its re-narrativization originating from the "sorrowful *voice* that cries out [...] *through the wound*"—tends to confound recovery and reconciliation, as today's injury triggers an "inadvertent and unwished-for repetition" from the past (Caruth 2). For this reason, in *Memory, History, Forgetting* (2004), Paul Ricouer insists that "we cannot simply classify forgetting [...] among the dysfunctions of memory alongside amnesia, nor among the distortions of memory affecting its reliability" (426). In assessing the possibility of reconciling past grievances in the present, Ricouer makes a crucial distinction: "Forgetting and forgiveness," he maintains, "each belong to a distinct problematic: for forgetting, the problematic of memory and faithfulness to the past; for forgiveness, guilt and reconciliation with the past" (412). Alluding to the pioneering work of Henri Bergson, Ricouer also distinguishes between "memory which recalls" and "memory which repeats" that operate "sometimes in synergy, sometimes in opposition" (432). "History and hope" in *The Cure at Troy* involves all of these temporalities.

Michael Longley's poem "Wounds" (1972), written at an especially violent moment in the history of the Troubles, reveals the cogency of both Caruth's prognosis and Ricouer's distinction between recalling and reexperiencing. Treading "painful and sensitive ground in its own time and place" and prefacing it with a foray into "another potentially controversial subject area" (Brearton 234)—namely, the sacrifices of Northern Irish protestants at the Battle of the Somme in World War I—the speaker's allusion in "Wounds" to 1916 is connected to the war stories his father told him. As a result, just beneath his response to the IRA's 1971 murder of three young British soldiers, their "bellies full of/Bullets and Irish beer," and the 1972 home invasion and assassination of a bus conductor reside traces of thousands of wartime casualties a half century earlier (40).[13] Wounds speak, some cry out and, as *The Cure at Troy* demonstrates, they do so in several very different registers; some even serve as props, as we shall see, in Philoctetes's howling displays of what Heaney calls the "swank" of victimization.

In "Wounds," in other words, acts of savagery are assimilated into a psyche already freighted with episodes of historical atrocity and triumph *prêt à porter* when summoned by the present. On January 6 at the U.S. Capitol, the Gadsden banner from 1775 with its "Don't Tread on Me" motto, a Confederate flag from the 1860s and a "Camp Auschwitz" hoodie on a rioter brought history into the present. During the Troubles in Northern Ireland, other histories and the artifacts that memorialize them—posters of Che Guevara as part of 1960s youth culture in Belfast or portraits of the leaders of Dublin's Easter 1916 rising displayed in nationalist pubs and on Republicans' walls—were repurposed to supplement ideological commitments or construct personae (martyr, patriot) compatible with them.[14] This layering of histories inheres in what the protagonist of Anna Burns's *Milkman* calls the "psycho-political atmosphere" of the Troubles with its "tribal identification[s]" and strict "rules of allegiance" (24). One of the latter concerns certain practices of reading. While the narrator indulges in what she regards as the harmless routine of "reading-while-walking," a friend views her actions as "creepy" and "perverse." Worse, the narrator's reading of "*whole books*, taking notes, checking footnotes, [and] underlining passages" are "disturbing," "deviant" and "not public-spirited" (200).

In such moments of social disruption places, books and even commodities can be as complexly layered as time. In addition to fetishizing a nation that never was and never would be—fetishism as both a substitution and an object onto which cathexes are projected—tribalism constructs such oppositional spaces as "over the water," "over the road" and "over the border" (*Milkman*, 24). Weary of homilies on the virtues of "ordinary life," the rebellious daughter at the center of *Milkman* ventriloquizes her mother's conflation of gender orthodoxy with spatial regulation into a single maxim: "Marriage, after territorial boundaries, is the foundation of the state" (42). Time is also a factor. By the time they reached sixteen, young women in her neighborhood were expected to be married with children—but not by wandering "over the road" in search of husbands. Many young women's unwillingness to heed this legislation in turn fueled the popularity of "love-across-the-barricades" plots in Troubles novels.[15] In *Milkman*, these barricades are policed by older women who also enforce the laws of domestic economy—"The right butter. The wrong butter. The tea of allegiance. The tea of betrayal" (Burns 25)—and sanction those who violate them.

During the Troubles, artists and scholars also sought other places and times to inhabit so as to gain a purchase on the chaos unfolding around them. In "Place and Displacement: Recent Poetry from Northern Ireland" taken from a 1984 lecture, Heaney considers the efforts of writers to negotiate "the strain of being in two places at the same time, of needing to accommodate two opposing conditions of truthfulness" (125). Three of these writers, Michael Longley, Derek Mahon and Paul Muldoon, "stretched between politics and transcendence," sought out remote locales to which they could retreat where critical perspective might be refined (129). As Helen Vendler underscores while exploring the archaeologies of *Door into the Dark* (1969) and *North* (1975), Heaney also searched for these habitations, the "natural and domestic history" of Irish loughs and bogs, farms and public houses, for instance. In a poem like "Bogland" from the former collection, he "enters [history] willingly, as a 'pioneer [...] striking/Inwards and downwards'" (*Seamus Heaney*, 39).

From the excavation of these sites, a cultural and archaeological digging, Heaney advances "literary and cultural critiques of identity" in Ulster (Russell 291). For example, in "The Grauballe Man" and "Punishment" from *North* Heaney's speakers meditate upon two well-preserved bodies from the distant past—one with his throat slashed, the other drowned with a noose around her neck—exhumed from bogs in Scandinavia and Northern Germany, pairing the latter's victimization with that of a more recent Northern Irish woman.[16] Extending his view across millennia, as Denis Donoghue describes, Heaney circumvented the "immediacies of historical events" (a circumvention that opened him to the criticism of failing to attend sufficiently to the present), uncovering in an "accretion of cultures" evidence of the brutality endemic to human nature (qtd. in Russell, 216). Beginning with an examination of the remains of a mummified corpse thought to have been a fourteen-year-old girl drowned two millennia earlier, "Punishment" demonstrates the strategy to which Donoghue alludes.[17] In the poem's first five stanzas, Heaney's speaker compares the corpse's shaved head, "soiled bandage" of a blindfold and noose around her neck with the public abuse of a beautiful young woman he has seen on city streets. As it had previously done in an act of "tribal, intimate revenge" against the woman's "betraying sisters," a neighborhood mob shaved her head and "cauled" it in tar after convicting her of being a "little adulteress." Tears welling in her eyes, this "poor scapegoat" is a surrogate of the ancient victim described at the beginning of the poem and an indictment of the speaker's silence while witnessing the horrible spectacle (*North* 37–38).

The argument that during the Troubles poems like "Punishment" advanced "literary and cultural critiques of identity" by juxtaposing the modern and the ancient has itself been queried, and in my view, this critique also pertains to Joe Biden's invocation of Heaney before, during and after his 2020 presidential campaign. Writing in 1990, before the Good Friday Agreement was signed, Lloyd summarizes the ramifications of Heaney's juxtaposition:

> The aestheticization of violence is underwritten in Heaney's recourse to racial archetypes [...]. In locating the source of violence beyond even sectarian division, Heaney renders it symbolic of a fundamental identity in the Irish race, as 'authentic.' Interrogation of the nature and function of acts of violence in the specific context of the current 'troubles' is thus foreclosed, and history foreshortened into the eternal resurgence of the same Celtic genius. (31)

In this critique, "race" thus functions not so much as an ahistorical and questionable analytical tool, but as a category that deflects critical inquiry away from the extant social causes of such rebarbative behavior—disenfranchisement, economic inequity and in this case, the violence of one's own tribe against an alleged betrayer—by insinuating that a racial characteristic is at least partly responsible for the horror.

There is little denying that, like his fellow poets' occupying "two places at one time," Heaney's interest in Sophocles's *Philoctetes*, like his turn to archaeology, transports his full critical attention to a historically distant moment. Yet, like Michael Longley's "Wounds," the play was first performed at a time of exceptional violence when the search for solutions grew desperate. While not matching the level of violence of the 1970s, the early 1990s began with a resurgence of IRA killings and bombings, including the destruction in early 1991 of a factory and six shops that threatened the creation of the very employment opportunities for which Sinn Féin had lobbied so vigorously (Richtarik, *Getting to Good Friday*, 56). As Richtarik describes, in 1989 Heaney, who for years had been intrigued by *Philoctetes*, received a postcard from his friend Brian Friel asking him to contribute to the repertory of the Field Day Theatre Company, on whose board of directors both writers served. He began work in early 1990, and *The Cure at Troy* premiered in October, the same month that one of the most heartless atrocities of the Troubles occurred when Patrick Gillespie, a cook at a British military base whose wife and children were held at gunpoint, was forced to serve as a "proxy" or "human" bomb. Strapped into a truck laden with explosives, he drove to an army checkpoint where the bomb was detonated. The resulting explosion was so powerful that his remains and those of five others were almost irretrievable.[18]

Less spectacular episodes had shaken Heaney years earlier, the most devastating of which involved a "murderous encounter" in Belfast between a "Protestant yeoman and Catholic rebel" in the summer of 1969. After this, his conception of poetry changed: "From that moment the problem of poetry moved from being simply a matter of achieving the satisfactory verbal icon to being a search for images and symbols adequate to our predicament" ("From Feeling" 25). Vendler also recognized the effect of recent atrocity on his work: "All this changes when archaeology ceases to be interesting and beneficent, and instead is interrogated for an explanation of violence." Instead, as Lloyd argues, substituting "racial" for "cultural" and objecting to the foreclosure of historical analysis in Heaney's "archaeological" works, ancient and contemporary victims in many of his poems become "emblems of [a] cultural predisposition to tribal sacrifice" (*Seamus Heaney*, 39).

It is hardly a surprise, however, that audiences detected traces of Ulster at war in *The Cure at Troy*. Some of these detections required little intellectual exertion, as Heaney inserted "topical references" in the play which he later judged to be a "mistake." In an interview Dennis O'Driscoll asked him, "Was there not a case for letting the timelessness of the play make its own mark," to which he quickly responded, "there certainly was" (O'Driscoll 421). But such allusions are minimal and mostly confined to a choral ode near the end of the play, preceding the stanza in which hope and history rhyme:

> The innocent in gaols
> Beat on their bars together.
> A hunger-striker's father
> Stands in the graveyard dumb.
> The police widow in veils
> Faints at the funeral home. (77)

As the best-known hunger strikers were associated with the PIRA—most famously, as discussed in the previous chapter, the ten prisoners led by Bobby Sands in 1981—and a largely Protestant constabulary enforced both local laws and those of the British government, this stanza emphasizes that both sides, *all* sides, suffer when the fabric of society is torn by retaliation.

The spiral of reprisals in this stanza, however much Heaney later regretted the references, eventually leads to an abjection similar to that of Philoctetes: hunger strikers, lacking any other effective means to protest their mistreatment, martyr themselves, and the government responsible for their sacrifice must be made to pay. The cycle of revenge and tragedy turns while families in mourning at gravesites and in funeral homes, Catholic and Protestant, can only "stand dumb" waiting for the next car bomb to explode or vacation boat to be reduced to splinters.

Revenge, Wounds and the Swank of Victimhood

The argument against revenge is heard throughout *The Cure at Troy* and if, as I have suggested, the play acts as a kind of primer for President Biden, the imperative to stand against vengeance is one of its most salient lessons. But such resolve is difficult to sustain, as the impulse for reprisal—like the drive in psychoanalytic theory—can prove overwhelming. This dilemma is intimated in the second scene of Sophocles's play when Philoctetes relates the circumstances of his abandonment to Neoptolemus. Venting his anger over his desertion when recalling how Odysseus "shamefully flung me ashore, alone/And abandoned, to waste away with a raging wound" (lines 265–66), Philoctetes reveals how his excruciating physical wound and his desire for revenge have festered together:

> No, I've now
> Been rotting away for nine whole years, in hunger
> And misery, feeding my greedy, insatiable wound.
> That's what Atreus' sons and the forceful Odysseus
> Have done to me, boy. I pray the Olympian gods
> Will make them suffer the like […]. (lines 311–16)

Two inferences might be made from this angry, self-pitying account. First, in a debilitating reciprocity, Philoctetes's emotional anguish—an affect that matches the intensity of his physical pain—*feeds* his wound, just as the wound fuels his rancor; and second, any reprisal for the Greeks' treachery must come from the gods, not men. Philoctetes gestures to the braiding of vengeance and suffering several times; in scene three, for example: "Agamemnon and Menelaus, I wish you both/Could feel this foul disease instead of me/For as long as I have!" (lines 793–95). His injury transcends the physical as the flares of pain in his foot at times disable him, metonyms of the eruptions of traumatic memory.

Such outbursts in *The Cure at Troy* complement Heaney's examination of the larger implications of vengeance. The line in which hope and history rhyme, for example, is followed by a stanza that suggests the impossibility of real change coexisting with the desire for revenge:

> So hope for a great sea-change
> On the far side of revenge.
> Believe that a further shore
> Is reachable from here.
> Believe in miracles
> And cures and healing wells. (77)

Here, Heaney creates a strategic ambiguity about precisely who or what benefits from "healing wells." For just as a miracle will bring about Philoctetes's "self-healing," the Greeks will be empowered to defeat Troy and be healed. This national outcome, this "great sea-change," can be achieved only "On the far side of revenge"—a site located far from the border of reprisal.

The argument against revenge continues in Heaney's revision of the descent of Hercules (Heracles) in the denouement of *Philoctetes*. In Sophocles's play Hercules, now a god, appears above the stage to urge Philoctetes to lay a portion of Trojan spoils at his altar in tribute, concluding his monologue with an endorsement of piety (here, tethered to both reverence and restraint) after the Trojans are defeated and their city is destroyed:

> But when you lay the land
> To waste, remember this: show piety
> Towards the gods, since nothing ranks so high
> With Zeus. For piety does not die with men.
> Men live or die, but piety cannot perish. (lines 1439–43)

This admonition reads differently in *The Cure at Troy* where there is no presumption that the Greeks will ransack their enemy's city; instead, Hercules speaks through a chorus of women, advocating clemency and restraint:

> Go, Philoctetes, with this boy,
> Go and be cured and capture Troy.
> [...]
> Go, with your bow. Conclude the sore
> And cruel stalemate of our war.
> Win by fair combat. But know to shun
> Reprisal killings when that's done. (79)

Philoctetes's and Greece's cure is realized, therefore, not merely when Troy is defeated, but when both tragic hero and nation are merciful in treating their former adversaries. The lesson is clear: hope and history can never rhyme if revenge is exacted and cities are "laid to waste." And the effective suppression of this impulse depends upon the ethics of individuals.

If *The Cure at Troy* evokes the pain of the Troubles, it does so in part by Heaney's replacement of piety to the gods in *Philoctetes* with a focus on human injury and recovery. In the "Production Notes" accompanying performances of the play, Heaney delineates his reasons for revising the "supernatural intervention" of the Sophoclean *deus ex machina* into a manifestation of the "culmination of an honestly-endured spiritual and psychological crisis." But did Philoctetes fully resolve his internal conflict on his own?[19] That is to say, Heaney's protagonist expresses his miraculous healing in what Terry Eagleton regards as an "inarticulate epiphany rather than [a] political strategy" (qtd. in Richards 81). True enough. But the amelioration of the psycho-political atmosphere—borrowing metaphors from Auden, thwarting the narcissism of the mirror and replacing it with the *caritas* of the window—requires both individual epiphanies *and* larger collective action. In the long run, formulating the political strategies to which Eagleton alludes is of course necessary, but pillaging enemy property or banishing opponents to the "other side" of the road will not be conducive to the hard work of negotiation such strategies will inevitably demand.

At the same time, Heaney explores two equally powerful themes relevant to contemporary American troubles, one found in Sophocles and the other unique to *The Cure at Troy*: the necessity of fidelity to one's ethical self and the multifarious nature of "wounds." Neoptolemus communicates the former imperative throughout both *Philoctetes* and *The Cure at Troy*; indeed, as Richtarik emphasizes, Neoptolemus's moral dilemma was what "initially drew Heaney to *Philoctetes*, for reasons that had everything to do with his Northern Irish upbringing" (48). As he explained in an interview with Dennis O'Driscoll, Heaney was intrigued by the "crunch that comes when the political solidarity required from him by the Greeks is at odds with the conduct he requires from himself if he's to maintain his self-respect" (O'Driscoll, 420). Moreover, and again recalling his old friend John Hume's foregrounding of climatic censorship in the Northern psycho-political atmosphere, Heaney regarded the young Greek's internal conflict as one "familiar to people on both sides of the political fence": namely, those occasions when "to speak freely and truly and truly [...] would be regarded as letting down the side" (qtd. in Richtarik, 48). The young Greek's quandary must also resemble those with which Liz Cheney and Adam Kinzinger grappled when deciding to participate in the Congressional investigation of the events of January 6.

The opening scene of Sophocles's play evokes Neoptolemus's internal struggle when Odysseus presses the urgency of seizing Hercules's bow and arrows by any means necessary, while at the same time acknowledging his young countryman's aversion to telling "untruths" or resorting to "double-dealing" (line 80). Still, for Odysseus the national imperative supersedes individual ethical considerations: "But victory's a prize worth gaining. Bring yourself/To do it. We'll prove our honesty later on" (lines 81–82). Uneasy with this ruse, in *The Cure at Troy* Neoptolemus rejects Odysseus's similar endorsement of situational ethics: "I'd rather fail and keep my self-respect/Than win by cheating" (9). Later, after learning that Neoptolemus intends to return the bow to Philoctetes because of the means by which he acquired it, Odysseus scolds him: "Act your age. Be reasonable. Use your head." Neoptolemus responds by asking, "Since when did the use of reason rule out the truth?", a question Odysseus parries by asking him to consider the well-being of the Greek people, whom he claims to represent (*Cure* 66). After this gambit fails, he then insinuates that Neoptolemus has turned himself into a Trojan and threatens adverse consequences if he fails to comply. "So let them come," he responds as Odysseus's hand moves toward the hilt of his sword (67).

There isn't sufficient space to inventory the number of times appeals for citizens to act for the good of the country and threats of violence for failing to do so have been heard in twenty-first-century political discourse. (Trump's "Fight like hell or you won't have a country left" on January 6 comes immediately to mind). Moreover, Heaney seems almost prescient by having Odysseus rationalize his abandonment of Philoctetes in another all-too-familiar way: "Yes, I left Philoctetes here. Marooned him but—/Only because I had been ordered to" (3). Almost any indefensible action can be defended by these two ploys—appeals to the nation's good or the excuse of following commands from superiors. If these ploys don't prove effective, then threats and intimidation are always available.

The most significant difference between Sophocles's and Heaney's versions of Philoctetes's story, however, concerns the signifying potential of wounds, their deployment as means of wresting political advantage through the cultivation of sympathy—or idolatry. At the same time, such displays instantiate a process that operates just the opposite of reading; that is to say, reading involves mental acts of reconstruction and imagination in empathizing with a character's pain, while the audiences of, say, political speeches are too often the passive receptacles of a candidate's false protestations of innocence or victimization. The differences between early lines in *Philoctetes* and *The Cure at Troy* demonstrate this distinction. In the opening scene of Sophocles's play, Odysseus attempts to justify his abandonment of Philoctetes:

> The gnawing wound in his foot was oozing with pus.
> We couldn't pour a libation or offer sacrifice
> Undisturbed. His animal shouts and yells
> Were constantly filling the camp with sounds of ill omen. (lines 7–10)

As this exposition evolves, Odysseus's flimsy rationalization is exposed. Then, he attempts to persuade Neoptolemus to help him secure Hercules's bow, who by the end of the scene seems willing to compromise his ethical objections—"Very well. Confound my scruples, I'll do it!" (line 120). But his pledge is undone after he meets the wretched castaway he planned to dupe; recognizing the depth and misery of Philoctetes's injury, his better nature prevails.

Heaney retains these elements of Sophocles's plot. But more than any other addition to the original, *The Cure at Troy* introduces what in twenty-first-century America has become a familiar device absent from the earlier play: the self-fashioning of victimhood into a manipulative political strategy. Before Neoptolemus meets Philoctetes, the Chorus advises him that, because of the latter's terrible foot and long affliction, the man he seeks has reverted to savagery. Later, like the stanzas from Auden's "As I Walked Out One Evening" in which a mirror is replaced by a window, Heaney's lines imply that personal "distress" can impede clear vision, as Neoptolemus demands that Philoctetes stop wallowing in self-pity: "Stop just licking your wounds. Start seeing things" (74). The effect of such preoccupations with wounds appears in the Chorus's description of "Heroes. Victims. Gods and human beings" in its opening song:

> People so deep into
> Their own self-pity, self-pity buoys them up.
> People so staunch and true, they're fixated
> Shining with self-regard like polished stones. (1)

As products of grievous injury, "self-pity" and a luminous "self-regard" seem incongruous, but as the play's Production Notes suggest, Heaney came to see Philoctetes as "'an aspect of *every* intransigence, republican as well as Unionist, a manifestation of the swank of victimhood, the righteous refusal, the wounded one whose identity has become dependent upon the wound'" (Richtarik, *Getting to Good Friday,* 50–51). The Chorus's reprimand of charlatans who are constantly "Licking their wounds/And flashing them around like decorations" also implies that healing occurs only on the "other side" of suffering just as hope and justice exist on the far side of revenge (2). There exist, in other words, suffering victims continually traumatized by a prior event, and faux "victims" who flaunt their injuries like so many polished jewels. At times, Philoctetes teeters uneasily on the line separating them, on the border between real suffering and the manipulation of wounds to create a new identity and elicit the pity of any audience that will listen.

Without veering any closer to the allegorical reading of *The Cure at Troy* I promised earlier to avoid, let's just say that the contemporary American Troubles, like the violence in Troy and late twentieth-century Northern Ireland, produce real victims, real suffering and real misery. Yet, at the same time, political opportunists, experts at self-fashioning who like to wrap themselves in their country's flag and appeal to its emotional qualities, exploit perceived wounds and incorporate them into their public personae. Genuine healers must be able to distinguish real injury from the swagger and "swank" of *a more performative* victimization—and so do voters. Healers and voters alike also need to realize that some historical moments refuse to fade into oblivion. The attack on the Capitol in January 2021 is one of these, a wound to democracy as agonizing as Philoctetes's swollen foot. Awakening from sleep in the opening monologue of Frank McGuinness's 1985 play *Observe the Sons of Ulster Marching Towards the Somme*, Kenneth Pyper embodies this distinction by addressing the audience angrily about being compelled to retell, and thus relive, an episode from World War I: "Again. As always, again. Why does this persist? [...] Have you no conception of the horror? Did it not touch you at all? [...] I will not talk." Of course, he *does* talk in an outburst punctuated by sudden fits. Pyper, we learn, survived the carnage at the battle of the Somme, while his comrades, "the irreplaceable ones," perished (9). And now, in a metatheatrical complaint to his audience, he must relate the details of this nightmare and its "ocean of blood" all over again (10).

As Freud contemplated in *Beyond the Pleasure Principle*, how does one come to terms with such a history, gone for a moment and then, "as always," back again? I don't know. But learning about—*reading* about—the atrocities in our nation's history is preferable to ignoring them or, worse, erasing them. We must confront these histories together. But because cultural and historical wounds can obstruct our vision, we need a leader qua healer, not a divider or avenger. Maybe, as Anne Applebaum recommends, we also need to change the subject and work as a community on a collective future. But two things are certain: revenge cannot promote healing nor will the canonization of leaders whose swank of victimization includes the wearing of grievances like so many polished stones. *The Cure at Troy* makes all of this exceedingly clear.

One other thing is just as clear. As Lin-Manuel Miranda recited at the Biden-Harris inaugural, "Human beings suffer,/They torture one another,/They get hurt and get hard" (Heaney, *Cure* 77). This hardness is compounded in the crucible of sectarianism and spreads beyond the border separating Northern Ireland from the Republic, perhaps beyond any borders. Now, more than at any time in America since the unrest of the Civil Rights era and the demonstrations against an expanding involvement in Vietnam, seemingly intractable partisan opposition has reemerged. This psycho-political atmosphere must be rendered less adversarial. Seamus Heaney knew this. So do his readers, one of whom is Joe Biden. At times like these, we're all better off if our president is a healer *and* a reader.

Postscript: Biden, Borders and Brexit

> […] only political murders happened in this place. 'Political' of course, covered anything to do with the border, anything that could be construed—even in the slightest, even in the most contorted, even something the rest of the world, if interested, would view as most unlikely—as to do with *the border*. (my emphasis)
>
> —Anna Burns, *Milkman*

The border between Northern Ireland and the Republic is saturated with blood. But that is hardly its only claim of historical influence, as most borders eventually exert larger global ramifications, as they have on the boundary separating Russia and Ukraine. And Brexit, while not engendering fears of militarism and multinational conflict, has nonetheless evoked dark memories of a violent past. A century ago, the partitioning of the island not only tore Irish communities apart but also served as an example for later cartographical experiments by Western powers: the establishment of Israel's borders after World War II, for instance, the antecedent of what a spokesperson for the Israel Defense Forces characterized as "by far the worst day in Israeli history" on October 7, 2023. But like other more imaginary borders—that between social classes, for example—the border also creates and shapes identities. They are personal and constitutive of senses of self, places of birth not death.

In his introduction of President and Michelle Obama to a large, enthusiastic Dublin crowd on May 23, 2011, Taoiseach Enda Kenny alludes to these while noting that "today the 44th American president comes home." Visiting Moneygall on the border of Offaly and Tipperary, the village from which his ancestor Thomas Kearney emigrated in 1850, Obama *does* have Irish roots, as do John F. Kennedy, Richard Nixon, Ronald Reagan, Bill Clinton, the Bushes and fifteen other men who ascended to the nation's highest office.

But there are other sources of Irishness, too, as Taoiseach Kenny noted. Some are "Irish by blood, or by marriage, or by desire," the last source of affiliation recalling President Kennedy's sentiment a half century earlier that although Ireland was not the land of his birth, it is "the land for which I hold the greatest affection." Joe Biden's self-proclaimed Irishness originates in two of Kenny's three provenances, blood and desire. But his Irish identity contains one additional element he references in the closing pages of *Promise Me, Dad* (2017). Mourning the loss of his son Beau to incurable cancer, Biden is reminded of one of his former colleague Daniel Patrick Moynihan's aphorisms "about us Irish":

> To fail to understand that life is going to knock you down is to fail to understand the Irishness of life [...].

Biden confided that he "had been knocked down hard enough by then to understand the Irishness of life, and this past year had reminded me of it all over again." Yet, in a paradoxical afterthought, he quickly adds, "We Irish [...] are the only people in the world who are actually nostalgic about the future" (250). Here his sense of temporality parallels the sentiment of Brian Friel's schoolmaster Hugh in his play *Translations* (1980) when a British officer asks about the nuances of the Irish language: Irish is a "syntax opulent with tomorrows," Hugh says. "It is our response to mud cabins and a diet of potatoes; our only method of replying to [...] inevitabilities" (418–19).

For over a century, the border has played a crucial part in both Irish inevitabilities and the formation of identity, yet this role in both cases has never been simple. Legislated into existence by the Government of Ireland Act in 1920, Northern Ireland could never deliver what its post-World War I proponents in Britain had hoped for: political stability. From England's perspective, as an advisor to Prime Minister David Lloyd George wrote, the partitioning might "at least accomplish two essential things: it would take Ulster out of the Irish question which it had blocked for a generation and it would take Ireland out of English party controversies" (qtd. in Ferriter, *The Border*, 9). As it turns out, the border was such a manifestly imperfect response to the "Irish question" that it reduced its value to what John Donne in another context termed "airy thinness." Particularly during the Troubles, the border and all it represented sparked enormous controversy in Britain, Ireland and the United States.

From Lloyd George's perspective, however, without a border Ulster, heavily populated by a "pugnacious people with a touch of the Scotch about them," might start a civil war at Britain's doorstep which would almost surely "embroil our own people" (qtd. in Ferriter, 13). In voicing this fear, George both resurrected the stereotype of a simianized, bellicose Celt widely circulated throughout the nineteenth century and applied it to Northern loyalists of Scottish descent. In *Born Fighting: How the Scots-Irish Shaped America*, former Virginia Senator James Webb, whose "five-times-great grandfather" traveled from Ulster to Lancaster, Pennsylvania in 1748, ennobles this image through his displays of valor in Vietnam. Stereotyping aside, from the perspective of Anna Burns's protagonist in *Milkman*, "borders" devolve quickly into theatres where political murders are staged. After the Good Friday Agreement of 1998, this particular theatre was supposed to have been closed, and the properties it once employed at major border crossings—searchlights glaring down from towers and guns pointed at the road—relegated to prop rooms.

Sadly, the horror show is occasionally revived. Yet, while Brexit has "undoubtedly contributed to a ratcheting up of tension" in Northern Ireland, Glenn Patterson acquits it and the perennial collapse of Northern governance of responsibility for the emergence of the New IRA, which had "already been going along quite happily, maiming and murdering (including at least two people in internal feuds) for four years before the 2016 referendum" (*Backstop Land*, 99). Before Brexit, in short, the Northern Ireland Assembly produced sufficient instability all on its own. Earlier in *Backstop Land*, Patterson quips that "the whole history of our Assembly reads like a novel by a writer whose desire for plot twists far outstrips any interest in health or education, the mundane business of government" (65). Here Patterson is referring to, among other disruptions, the suspensions of the Assembly in 2002 and again in 2017, the resulting imposition of direct rule, and a myriad of disputes and provisional agreements along the way. As he implies, Brexit has ratcheted up tensions in part by reanimating specters from the past.

After six months on the job, in the summer of 2021, the Biden Administration sallied out to meet old friends and adversaries alike, some created by American withdrawals from the Paris Agreement and the World Health Organization; others, the result of his predecessor's uneven, at times abrasive, relationship with America's friends and allies. After cautioning Russia about the cyber-criminals in its midst and agreeing to donate millions of doses of COVID-19 vaccine to developing countries, the Biden White House confronted two issues smoldering in a deeper ashpit than usual: the immigration crisis at the border with Mexico and the frayed relationships with several allies in the G7, relationships vital to preventing Ukraine from capitulating to Russian aggression. Addressing the former problem, Vice President Harris traveled to Central America and Mexico, pledging Hondurans several hundred thousand doses of COVID vaccine and

Figure 8. President Biden Meets with Taoiseach Leo Varadkar, April 2023. Courtesy of Alamy.

a half million syringes, while also urging desperate Central Americans *not* to embark upon the dangerous trek north (Figure 8).

As the vice president was returning to America, President Biden, long engaged with Ukraine's history and leadership, was on his way to Cornwall to confer with the G7. Prior to doing so, both he and then Prime Minister Boris Johnson renewed the Atlantic Charter first signed in 1941 by Franklin D. Roosevelt and Winston Churchill. The press underscored the symbolic nature of the renewal, some viewing it as a ratification of the "special relationship" between America and Britain. Presidents and prime ministers like Ronald Reagan and Margaret Thatcher, whatever their private disagreements, worked assiduously to represent the stability and warmness of this partnership in public. Biden would add a new, somewhat revised chapter to this old story.

That chapter concerns, among other things, the implications of Brexit, of Britain's decision to leave the European Union (EU) which since 1993 has enacted legislation concerning immigration, customs and other commercial transactions between member and non-member countries. Great Britain is expected to abide by laws intended to ensure food safety, for example, including a prohibition on importing sausages and other refrigerated meats from a non-union member country into its market. Ireland is part of this market. At the time of the G7 meeting, Johnson and the EU were sparring over the particulars of trade rules and standards for goods crossing from Britain to Northern Ireland without calcifying the boundary between Ireland and Northern Ireland into a "hard" border again. A year earlier, the Northern Ireland Protocol was conceived to eliminate this potentially hazardous step backward by implementing checks of goods (eggs and milk, for example) from England, Scotland and Wales at ports where they were received, prompting critics to argue that this in effect created an imaginary border in the Irish Sea (Edgington and Morris, "Brexit").

In the midst of such deliberations, a reporter from the BBC asked Biden for a quick reaction. "I'm Irish," he said and walked away. Almost immediately, as reported in *Daily Beast* (June 10, 2021), some in the pro-Brexit crowd, many of whom had "sworn allegiance to Donald Trump," denounced Biden's comment as both a "grave national insult" and evidence that, the renewal of the Atlantic Charter notwithstanding, the new American president "had little intention of putting Britain above other allies." An unnamed lawmaker from Johnson's conservative party saw it even more cynically as evidence that America was, in fact, not an ally of Britain at all (Ross, "Brexit Brits Freak Out"). Still others chose to promote the issue as yet another example of Biden's senility, as Nigel Farage did on Twitter while also leveling another indictment: "We now have an anti-British U.S. President in the White House. I hope all those who condemned Trump see their stupidity."

The logic that connects these two sentences is as tortured as the evidence that Biden is anti-British: because the American president is concerned about Ireland, every critic of Trump should admit he or she was wrong to doubt him? In his reporting, Jamie Ross *does* note that Biden instructed one of his most important diplomats to relay to a British counterpart his concerns over Johnson's "inflaming of tensions." For Farage, who appeared at an Arizona Trump rally shortly before the 2020 election, and who, as Paul Dallison observed in *Politico* (May 21, 2021), is "clinging like a limpet to the shipwrecked hull of the Donald Trump presidency," Biden's expression of concern about a hard border constitutes yet another reason to disparage "Mayo Joe," as he is affectionately known in Ballina, County Mayo. All of which raises the question of why, in the midst of this imbroglio, Biden proclaimed his Irish identity in the first place. Because his ancestors emigrated from Famine-era Ireland, as he has stated, Irishness is inscribed on his soul? If so, his sense of identity might originate in a more psychically resonant place where notions of identity reside.

As I have mentioned previously, a complex, maniacally guarded identity is on display in David Ireland's *Cypress Avenue* as its central character has suffered a breakdown before the action begins. But, unlike Eric Miller's revulsion at the notion of being Irish, Biden's Irishness is hardly the product of paranoia or animus against England, as Nigel Farage has alleged. It might also originate in something larger than genealogy or "desire," as Taoiseach Kenny speculated when welcoming the Obamas to Ireland: that is, in an awareness of the legacy of violence that borders represent. Jim Sharkey suggested as much in the *Irish Times* (January 20, 2021) when recalling his first meeting with then-Senator Biden forty years earlier during the 1981 hunger strikes. At that time, the alliance between Ronald Reagan and Margaret Thatcher—and a history of noninterventionism in American foreign policy—virtually guaranteed White House inaction. But Sharkey remembers a very different "special relationship" well underway on Capitol Hill by the early 1980s: "This [period] was marked in Washington by the formation of the Friends of Ireland [...] dedicated to peace in Northern Ireland. Together with Ted Kennedy and Tip O'Neill, Joe Biden was a founding father." For them, the hunger strikes underscored the "intolerable dysfunction within Northern Ireland and the urgent need for fundamental reform" (Sharkey, "What can Ireland expect").

The second Catholic ever elected to the American presidency, Irish Joe understands the crucial role America has played and continues to play in both Ireland and Northern Ireland. It is arguable, I think, that this role has only grown in importance since the Kennedy presidency and the achievement of the Clinton administration, even as Glenn Patterson records in a calendar prefatory to *Backstop Land* that by 2019 over 160 "paramilitary murders" had been committed in Northern Ireland since the Good Friday Agreement (xix). Various news agencies have reported a disturbing rise in violence perpetrated by loyalist paramilitary groups, and in "Northern Ireland's Troubled Peace" in *The Atlantic* (May 6, 2023), Charles M. Sennott notes that "In the first 20 years after the Good Friday Agreement, Northern Ireland saw more deaths from suicide than it had from sectarian violence during the roughly three decades of conflict." Still, such bombings and shootings have diminished in frequency in an admittedly imperfect process that Brexit might imperil. And a vigilant Irish president like Joe Biden appears poised to ensure that the hard border so deeply implicated in Northern bloodshed is not reestablished. He understands that even borders without walls are, in the end, political creations and all too often theatres of murder and needless human suffering. The war in Ukraine reaffirms this truth every day.

Notes

1 Jessica Lange, who appeared as Mary Tyrone in *Long Day's Journey into Night* in a critically acclaimed 2000 London production and was nominated for an Olivier Award, won the Tony Award for Best Actress for her appearance in the 2016 Roundabout Theatre Company's revival of O'Neill's play. Also nominated, Gabriel Byrne had previously

won a Tony for Best Actor in a 2000 production of O'Neill's *A Moon for the Misbegotten* and was widely celebrated for his 2008 performance in *A Touch of the Poet*.

2 Higgins also creates a composite picture of modern Irish literature's "five Noras": Nora Helmers from Henrik Ibsen's *A Doll's House*, Joyce's wife Nora and three memorable characters from the Irish theatre: J.M. Synge's lonely character *In the Shadow of the Glen*, Shaw's Nora Reilly in *John Bull's Other Island* and Nora Clitheroe in Sean O'Casey's *The Plough and the Stars* (15).

3 See Dessem for a fuller list of recommendations. In 2019, Trump endorsed Rachel Campos-Duffy's *Paloma Wants to be Lady Freedom*, a forty-page, illustrated book appropriate for young children.

4 See, for example, Nath, "Democracy Index 2023: Understanding the Global Scenarios," for a review of the Economist Intelligence Unit's findings.

5 This analysis of gerrymandering, first released in 2021 and updated in 2023, introduces disturbing statistics. In Pennsylvania, "the congressional map [in 2020] gave Republicans a virtual lock on 13 of the state's 18 congressional districts, even in elections where Democrats won the majority of the statewide congressional vote." In Wisconsin in 2018, Democrats "won every statewide office and a majority of the statewide vote, but thanks to gerrymandering, won only 36 of the 99 seats in the state assembly."

6 As Balz and Morse report, since 1998 Republicans have "had a majority in the Senate a total of 12 years but did not during that time represent more than half the nation's population." Also, "during Trump's presidency, 43 percent of all judicial and governmental nominees were confirmed by senators representing a minority of the population. Under President Biden not quite 5 percent of nominees were confirmed by senators representing a minority of the population."

7 In his biography, Jules Witcover describes Biden closing his eulogy for his first wife Neilia by quoting Milton: "I waked, she fled and brought back my night" (95–96).

8 Discussing Tony Schwartz prior to the 2016 election, Jane Mayer quotes Donald Trump's co-author of *The Art of the Deal* as observing, "I seriously doubt that Trump has ever read a book straight through in his adult life." This accusation parallels Schwartz's observation that while he wasn't certain Trump had ever read the book he supposedly coauthored, he was sure he didn't write it. For a summary of Trump's claims about reading contemporary fiction, see Italie.

9 The ramifications of the Parental Rights in Education Act, signed into law by Governor Ron DeSantis in March of 2022, have been widely assessed. See, for example, Martin Pengelly, "Florida schools plan to use only excerpts from Shakespeare to avoid 'raunchiness'."

10 Willman notes that President Kennedy enjoyed Fleming novels in the 1950s while recovering from back surgery. The two biographers quoted here are Seymour Hersh and Gary Wills.

11 The young Biden's search for a remedy to his stuttering is often regarded as the origin of his interest in poetry. See, for example, Osnos, 32–33; and Teo Armus, who also traces his poetry reading back to his efforts at recitation. Osnos notes that by Biden's sophomore year in high school, partially as a result of this practice, "the stutter was giving way" (32).

12 Reviews of American revivals of the play frequently emphasize this point. G. K. Schatzman begins a review of Philadelphia's Quintessence Theatre Company 2022 production with "A modest audience was drawn into the reeks and roars of a rare

production of Seamus Heaney's *The Cure at Troy*," later noting that Steven Anthony Wright as Philoctetes "snarls and spits as he totes his bandaged foot." Commenting on a December 15, 1997 production by the Jean Cocteau Repertory, Wilborn Hamilton in the *New York Times* refers to Craig Smith as Philoctetes "bellowing offstage like a lion" from the agonized suffering "he is forced to endure."

13 Brearton describes these two specific events in her reading of Longley's poem (231).
14 In 1960s Belfast, republican teenagers were inspired by revolutionaries like Guevara and Fidel Castro (Keefe 15). At the same time, the Provisional IRA leadership sought to improve the image of the IRA *man*, replacing pictures of a besotted "has-been" with that of a more disciplined nationalist or "volunteer," the latter intended to invoke memories of the "doomed heroes of the Easter Rising" (Keefe, 44).
15 For a discussion of romance fiction of the period, see Lehner, 47–49.
16 See Vendler, 38–57, and Russell, 213–36. Russell reads "Punishment" by way of Heaney's biblical and archaeological sensibilities (223–27). In addition, citing both Rita Felski and Susan Sontag, he explores the possibility that a kind of pleasure can be derived from viewing bodies in pain which, in turn, "indicts" readers in much the same way as Heaney's speaker indicts himself in "Punishment" (221–23).
17 "Her" may be an inaccurate pronoun as the "Windeby girl" alluded to in "Punishment" was likely a fourteen-year-old boy. The cause of death is also disputed.
18 I wish to express my gratitude to Marilynn Richtarik for discussing the 1990 production of *The Cure at Troy* with me and for calling to my attention the irony of Patrick Gillespie's murder occurring in the same month as the play's premiere.
19 Quoted in Richards, 79.

Provocation 4

DANGEROUS DEMAGOGUES, FICTIONAL AND OTHERWISE

One hundred percent of my focus is on standing up to this administration. What we have in the United States Senate is total unity [...] in opposition to what the new Biden administration is trying to do to this country.
—Senator Mitch McConnell, *The Wall Street Journal*, May 5, 2021

Part One: Dr. No and the Grim Reaper

As fans of Ian Fleming's redoubtable spy know, Dr. Julius No is James Bond's adversary in *Doctor No* (1958), a novel that when adapted as a film in 1962 launched the most enduring franchise in the history of Western cinema. Since then, and for the most part, films chronicling Bond's adventures—as well as novels by John Gardner, Anthony Horowitz, Sebastian Faulks and others after Fleming's untimely passing in 1964—have flourished, and such phrases as "shaken, not stirred" and "Bond girls" are now part of our vernacular. So, too, are the names of some of Fleming's villains, with "Dr. No" used to lampoon dour politicians hostile to socially progressive legislation. In Northern Ireland and America, the press has employed "Dr. No" as a nickname for Ian Paisley, the late fundamentalist minister and founder of Northern Ireland's DUP and Senator Mitch McConnell, also known as "The Grim Reaper" and "Darth Vader," among other sobriquets. For the most part, McConnell seems amused by these inventions; only "Moscow Mitch," a reference to his indifference to Russia's interference in the 2016 presidential election, appears to annoy him because of its implication that he is an "asset" of the Kremlin (Hulse, "Moscow Mitch"). Both men's capacity for negativism, the most obvious reason for these names, motivates my juxtaposition of them with Fleming's arch-villain—and with each other.

Outlining the Sisyphean labors of brokering the Good Friday Agreement, George Mitchell in *Making Peace* suggests such a comparison when recounting Paisley's recalcitrance during nearly two years of negotiations (which were preceded by some six months of painstaking preparatory work). On occasion, this abrasiveness serves as a structuring motif in Mitchell's narrative. In a chapter entitled "No. No. No. No," inspired by Paisley's outburst at the inaugural meeting of the parties tasked with negotiating the Agreement, Mitchell recalls the DUP leader's "blistering attack" on the British and Irish governments for foisting an American senator on the group. After concluding his screed, Paisley "led his delegates in a walkout," one of several histrionic departures he fomented during the talks (50). Mitchell also recalls Paisley's denunciations of Pope John Paul II as the "anti-Christ, the man of sin in the church"; of Prime Minister John Major for signing the Downing Street Declaration of 1993, which in effect sold Ulster "to buy off the fiendish, republican scum"; and of David Trimble, leader of the Ulster Unionist Party (UUP), whom he disparaged as a "Judas" and "traitor" (51–52). After a protracted debate over the agenda for the negotiations in the fall of 1996, Paisley and fellow Unionist leader Bob McCartney voiced their objections to "the very process in which they were participating," repeatedly calling it "a farce and a sham" (85–86). In his novel *TransAtlantic*, Colum McCann captures the incendiary potential of the group's interactions: "Paisley. Adams. Trimble. McGuinness. Throw a word in their midst and watch them light the fuse" (112). Paisley's rhetorical explosions in those meetings he deigned to attend easily earned him first position in this and most sentences describing the angry volubility of these negotiations.

After spending two months defusing tensions, Mitchell was discouraged that "very little had been accomplished" (*Making Peace*, 87). Yet, in spite of this difficult start, the Agreement was eventually signed and ratified in a May, 1998 referendum, although it took over seven years before the IRA officially agreed to decommission its weapons (in part, because of George W. Bush's phone conversations with both Paisley and Gerry Adams in late November 2004 and his other communications urging them to reach an agreement). Not surprisingly, Paisley and the DUP opposed the Agreement, campaigning, as Glenn Patterson puts it, "vigorously and vociferously—almost Biblically—against" its endorsement in the North-South Referendum (*Backstop Land*, 43). A huge majority disagreed with Dr. No, as 71.12% of Northern Irish voters and nearly 95% of voters in the Republic supported the Agreement. A decade later, in a concession that took many by surprise, Dr. No agreed to a partnership with Martin McGuinness from Sinn Féin to serve as the new government's First Minister. At the time of his death in 2014, as the *Belfast Telegraph* phrased the matter, "it remained a mystery" why the man who "for decades bellowed 'No' to any compromise" wanted his legacy to include his role as a peacemaker ("Divisive 'Dr No'").

Paisley's determination to block progress or ensure that it crawled at a snail's pace has for years been the *modus operandi* of the Grim Reaper, aka Moscow Mitch, aka Turtle Man (see "Horrible turtle man Mitch McConnell has never done a damn thing worth being proud of," *Deadspin*, October 27, 2020). In an example of his legendary obstructionism reiterated in the epigraph above, in early 2021 McConnell announced his opposition to Joe Biden's proposal for an American infrastructure bill, an initiative for which previous presidents, including Donald Trump, had advocated but failed to enact. Aware of the "political calculus in play here," McConnell pledged to lead Republicans in defeating any and all Biden proposals (Abramsky, "McConnell-Led Opposition"). But, in this case, he couldn't. On August 10, 2021, nineteen Republican senators, including the Reaper himself, joined Democrats in passing a $1.2 trillion bipartisan bill. And on January 4, 2023, he posed for a photograph with Biden to announce a more than $2 billion project to repair the Brent Spence Bridge connecting Kentucky with Ohio.

Like Paisley's last-act conversion, this was a rare instance of the senator's cooperation. As Lindsay Wise reported in *The Wall Street Journal* (May 5, 2021), McConnell has objected to nearly everything the Biden administration has proposed, including stronger gun laws, the protection of voting rights and D.C. statehood, to name but three. Aware of this, early in his tenure, the president reminded Americans of a McConnell pronouncement from a decade earlier: "The single most important thing we want to achieve is for President Obama to be a one-term president." For these reasons, any announcement by McConnell of his willingness to work with Democrats if they meet Republicans "halfway" is usually little more than a cynical feint in the parties' ongoing fights. *This* Dr. No from Kentucky neither enables consideration of, nor fosters debate over, new legislation, which is why bills passed by a Democratic-controlled House throughout Trump's years in the White House gathered dust on the Majority Leader's desk. As Lisa Mascaro summarized in *AP News*, "Rarely has a political figure pinned his fortunes on accomplishing so little" (June 28, 2019). Moreover, whenever McConnell expressed hope that a bipartisan agreement over infrastructure might be reached, Greg Sargent in the *Washington Post* (June 2, 2021) detected his "pretend-optimism" while secretly "laughing in [our]faces." In other words, while the success of the Biden infrastructure bill, like Paisley's last-act conversion, suggests that McConnell's calcified negativism might be softening, don't count on it.

The pair, however, are hardly identical twins. As Senator Mitchell describes, Paisley was a large man over six feet three inches tall—some estimates place his height at six feet, five inches—with a "huge frame" and a "deep, booming voice" (52); at five feet, nine inches, McConnell is more than a half foot shorter with a slender frame. In the 1960s, Paisley vented his hatred of Northern Irish nationalists to anyone who would listen; the young McConnell, conversely, was more progressive, attending meetings of American civil rights groups and participating in the 1963 March on Washington. Paisley's emergence in 2007 as a leader willing to share political power with a former adversary *seems* to distinguish him from McConnell who, although muting his support for Donald Trump after the 2020 election, the attack on the Capitol on January 6 and the ninety-one indictments filed against him in 2023, has in no way embraced the commitments of his youth. His reversal of course on infrastructure, however, had more to do with the bill's estimated $5 billion earmarked for the improvement of Kentucky roads and bridges (plus $100 million for broadband expansion) than a sincere commitment to bipartisanship. Similarly, Paisley's cameo appearance as a peacemaker hardly merits comparison with St. Paul's conversion on the road to Damascus. In an interview with Robert Siegel, biographer Ed Moloney hints at a more selfish motive for the Big Man's "transformation," arguing that he "never dropped the political extremism. Even when he became the first minister in Northern Ireland, his unionism was untouched." His wife's ambitions for her husband, Moloney suggests, may have had more to do with his newly found equanimity than any Pauline epiphany (Siegel, "Ian Paisley").

Paisley and McConnell share other similarities, particularly where political ideology is concerned. It is hardly a coincidence, for example, that both received honorary degrees from two of America's most conservative educational institutions: Hillsdale College in McConnell's case, Bob Jones University (BJU) in Paisley's. The latter degree is the more important, as I suggested earlier in this book. The founding of Bob Jones College, now University, in 1927, was the product of Jones's dismay over what he bemoaned as the ascendant secularism of American colleges and his ambition to create a platform for Christian conservatism, including that of Bob Jones, Jr., president of the university when Paisley was awarded his Doctor of Divinity degree in 1966. Paisley served on BJU's Board of Trustees and, when he could secure a visa, attended meetings at its Greenville campus. Further, as Moloney describes, BJU helped him dampen his "very thick rural country accent" with the result that many American Baptists regarded him as one the best preachers they had ever heard.

The Northern Irish clergyman also shared many of the Jones's biases, anti-Catholicism for example. Asked about Al Smith's presidential candidacy in 1928, Bob Jones, Sr. (in)famously remarked that he "would rather see a saloon on every corner than a Catholic in the White House." Like Bob Jones, Jr., Paisley was opposed to the teaching of evolution; and, at present, the Bob Jones University Press is a leading publisher of textbooks used to homeschool children in a religious-centered science curriculum. According to its website, the BJU Press's "Emphasis on Truth" recalls Jones, Sr.'s interest in the 1925 Scopes Trial: "Much of modern scientific thought is influenced by an anti-God bias. We teach students to carefully analyze the theories they will encounter and to reject error in favor of *pure truth* and scientific *fact*. Every science textbook points out the infinite wisdom and designing hand of God" (my emphasis). Anti-Catholicism, anti-Darwinism, anti-science, an unwillingness to admit black students until 1971, a ban on interracial dating that wasn't lifted until the dawn of the twenty-first century —that's the "pure truth" about the institution that conferred an honorary degree on Dr. No.

So is its commitment to the corporal punishment of preschoolers at a campus daycare center. In a 2023 account of her enforced "parting of the ways" with BJU after seven years (2000–07) on the faculty, Camille Kaminski Lewis outlines the consequences of her refusal to allow its daycare staff to spank her two-year-old son. Her letter of termination specified that because she was unable to work at the university "without openly promoting it," her employment should end. It hardly came as a surprise, as her dismissal was preceded by meetings with older male administrators, one of whom, her academic dean, alleged that as a "young mom" of age 38 she lacked "enough life experience to know biblical parenting." In her rejoinder to the allegation, Lewis recalled a scene in the documentary *Shiny Happy People: Duggar Family Secrets* (Amazon Prime, 2023) in which a six-year-old boy is spanked by a pastor in front of a large, approving congregation, then compelled to embrace him. Lewis concludes, "Certain adults get grace; all children get hit" ("I Lost My Job"). That's another "pure truth" at BJU.

But what about resemblances between these demagogical Dr. No's and their namesake? As Umberto Eco observed some years ago, James Bond's adversaries are, in effect, monsters who possess characteristics of machines, animals or both. This bizarre congeries is often conveyed by physical grotesquerie or anomaly: Scaramanga in *The Man with the Golden Gun* (1965, published posthumously) has three nipples on his chest; Ernst Stavro Blofeld, Bond's nemesis in several novels, has attached earlobes and, as described in *Thunderball* (1961), eyes that resemble Mussolini's. Auric Goldfinger's body so weirdly lacks proportionality that it seems as if he had been assembled from the mismatched parts of other people's bodies. Among these gargoyles, Dr. No has perhaps the most complicated physiognomy of all. Introduced as a "bizarre, gliding figure," he "looked like a giant venomous worm wrapped in grey tin-foil"; his hands, replaced by steel prostheses, resembled the pincers of a praying mantis or the claw of a crab (156). More oddly, he is "the one man in a million who has his heart on the right side of his body" (164), an abnormality that once allowed him to survive an assassination attempt.

Neither Paisley nor McConnell displays such signs of monstrosity, although social media, as I have mentioned, has at times promoted the Grim Reaper's resemblance to a turtle (change.org once circulated a petition demanding that McConnell prove he is *not* a sea turtle). And, although neither so strange in appearance as Fleming's Dr. No nor so amphibian as the "Turtle Man," Paisley was often depicted in grotesque ways. As Cal McCrystal reported, "ghastly" wall murals of the DUP demagogue in some nationalist communities exaggerated his appearance ("Ian Paisley: 1926–2014"). On a trip to the library to see Marcella Morton in *Cal*, Bernard MacLaverty's young protagonist plucks a book off one of the shelves and discovers a small album of photographs of Protestant leaders past and present:

> There were pictures of Sir Edward Carson, Sir James Craig and the Reverend Ian Paisley, all on the one page. For sheer physical ugliness they were hard to beat. Three men with battering-ram blunt faces [who looked] like old boxers. (81)

However much he resembled an aging prizefighter, Paisley was seldom compared to machines, animals or insects, nor did he—unlike Donald Trump—alter his appearance through the application of facial "bronzer," strawberry blonde hair dye and an improbable coiffure. To avoid detection by his enemies, Fleming's Dr. No had all his hair torn out and underwent a prolonged spinal traction to make himself taller. Prior to this procedure, and like Trump, at one time Dr. No wore lifts in his shoes. In 2019, reporting for *Macleans*, Patricia Treble examines a portrait of G7 leaders where the supposed 6'3" Trump appears only slightly taller than his wife and shorter than Canadian Prime Minister Justin Trudeau, whose official height is listed as 6'2". As numerous reporters have noted, pictures of Trump standing next to the 6'1" Barack Obama suggest that they are basically the same height.

This self-fashioning—dyed hair and makeup, spinal traction and shoe lifts—all suggest the *performative* quality of both contemporary politics and fictional villainy. As David McKittrick and David McVea emphasize, Paisley began public life as a "hardline, young fundamentalist clergyman with a talent for self-publicity" before evolving "from a semi-comical and apparently insignificant pantomime demon into a formidable figure in Unionist politics" (30–31). And hardline politicians are not immune to criticism or caricature. In *Persecuting Zeal: A Portrait of Ian Paisley* (1996), Dennis Cooke considers this issue, beginning his biography with Paisley leading the congregation at Belfast's Martyrs' Memorial Presbyterian Church in a vituperative prayer two days after the signing of the Anglo-Irish Agreement in 1985:

> In the Name of Thy Blessed Self, Father, Son and Holy Ghost, we hand this woman Margaret Thatcher over to the Devil that she might learn not to blaspheme […]. And O God in wrath take vengeance upon this wicked, treacherous, lying woman. Take vengeance upon her, O Lord. (Cooke, 1)

Struggling to counterbalance the shrillness of this condemnation, Cooke cites passages from Rhonda Paisley's *Ian Paisley, My Father* (1988) that portray him as a "caring person" (Cooke, 5). Yet it is difficult to reconcile an "aggressive, judgmental, gratuitously insulting" bully with a "friendly, sympathetic and loving" father (8). As J. Bowyer Bell comments, the "old spectaculars, marches and murders" Paisley incited, like the "crude and cruel speeches" he delivered, cannot in the final analysis be ignored (290).

And they haven't been. More so than their physiognomies and antagonism to social progress, McConnell's and Paisley's view that politics is a zero sum game with winners and losers constitutes their greatest similarity to 007's adversaries. Eco explains that Fleming constructs his spy narratives from binary oppositions, renouncing "all psychology as the motive of narrative" by transferring "characters and situations to the level of an objective structural strategy" (146). In twenty-first-century America, "structural strategy" defines Moscow Mitch's "NO" in response to the "YES" of the Biden administration's more forward-looking agenda. After the Super Tuesday primary elections on March 5, 2024, as this book was being finalized for the printer, it also means that Dr. No from Kentucky is capable of affirmation when it is politically advantageous. For despite "years of acrimony" including Trump calling him "a 'piece of shit' and attacking his wife in racist terms"—and despite his deeming Trump "practically and morally responsible for the January 6 insurrection"—Dr. No commented that "it should come as no surprise" that "as [a] nominee, [Trump] will have my support" (Pengelly, "Top Senator"). This endorsement, however, hardly signals his magical transformation into "Dr. Yes." It means that the turtle man is reconciled to his role as a cog in the Republican machine—and that role is the automatic negation of, not dialogue with, his Democratic colleagues.

For Eco, the Fleming narrative machine begins with *Casino Royale* (1953), the novel that introduced James Bond to the reading public, and the encouragement of fellow agent René Mathis to surround himself with human beings but not to become "human" himself, for if he were to do so, "We would lose such a wonderful machine" (139). This machine performs fundamental moves in the conduct of the game, moves that overlay a Manichaean ideology reminiscent of fairy tales in which the world is made up of good and evil forces. With the rare exceptions of McConnell's belated support of COVID vaccines and the Bipartisan Infrastructure Bill, the ideologies of Northern Ireland's Dr. No and Kentucky's Dr. No are just as binary.

So, when Senator McConnell professed his antagonism to the Obama and Biden administrations and Reverend Paisley shouted "No. No. No. No" in decrying George Mitchell's leadership in brokering the Good Friday Agreement, they gave voice to a melodrama in which the forces of good and evil are forever in conflict. Troubles, both Northern Irish and American, originate in the loud denunciations of such demagogues for, as the speaker of William Butler Yeats's "The Second Coming" summarizes, "the worst" seem to have an inexhaustible supply of "passionate intensity."

Part Two: The Big Man and the Orange Man

> Hate crawls under the rocks, and, when given oxygen by any person in authority, it comes roaring back out.
> —Joe Biden, as quoted in Evan Osnos,
> *Joe Biden: The Life, the Run and What Matters Now* (2020)

I want to return to a topic with which this book began—the insurrection at the Capitol on January 6, 2021. As I mentioned in my preface, the more information became available about its plotting by Washington insiders, about meetings in parking garages between paramilitary groups and about obstruction in Congress to investigate such events, the more outraged—and disheartened—I became. More useful than my reactions, I hope, is the juxtaposition of the attack on the Capitol with an event during the Troubles in Northern Ireland: the July 1998 Orange parade at Drumcree near Portadown, County Armagh.

Admittedly, this analogy is imperfect. The insurrection at the Capitol occurred on one afternoon, while the chaos in Drumcree raged for days and was repeated. *Orange Parades: The Politics of Ritual Tradition and Control*, referenced so many pages ago, begins as Dominic Bryan stands on a hill near the Drumcree Church graveyard on July 10, 1995, watching Ian Paisley and David Trimble talk with policemen there to control the large crowd that had gathered. The police also planned to prevent the annual Orange Lodges' parade from marching through a Catholic estate, motivating thousands of Orangemen to protest this alteration of their marching route and to listen to Trimble and Paisley, the latter of whom warned that the new restrictions threatened "the very heart and foundation of our heritage" (qtd. in Bryan, 2). Eventually, the parade's traditional route was restored; and, as McKittrick and McVea note, this victory seemed to the most fervent of marchers momentous enough to memorialize through the striking of commemorative medallions (210). As in America, however, rhetoric like Paisley's that identifies a possible attack on a group's "heritage," foregrounds past heroism in guarding it or impugns others as threats to it serves both to divide people and rationalize the use of physical force. That's what Paisley did in Drumcree, and that's what such speakers as Mo Brooks and Rudy Giuliani did at the "Stop the Steal" rally in Washington on January 6. It might be added that Kimberly

Guilfoyle, paid $60,000 to introduce her fiancé, Donald Trump, Jr., proved again that not every political actor is a true believer (Ecarma, "It's a Grift").

Not surprisingly, during the Troubles figurative and *literal* demonizations of political opponents were hardly confined to just one political rally or event. In "Return to Drumcree," the final chapter of *Orange Parades*, Bryan summarizes Orange Lodge marches in 1996, 1997 and 1998, the last of which was held after the passing of the Public Processions (NI) Act and the founding of a Parades Commission. Although marchers were met by police, some attired in full riot gear, "Drumcree 1996" devolved into "one of the most destabilizing episodes of the troubles" as loyalists erected roadblocks and barricades across the country, "bringing life in whole areas to a standstill" (McKittrick and McVea, 210). Neighborhoods in Belfast were set ablaze and looted. The parade in 1997 similarly provoked "hand-to hand-fighting" and rioting. As a result, in July 1998—three months after the signing of the Good Friday Agreement—the Orange Order confronted a more formidable and well-prepared peacekeeping force (Bryan 174). In some ways, sadly, such measures didn't matter: ten Catholic churches were bombed in early July followed by retaliations against Orange Halls. After Unionist leaders "encouraged everyone to come to the protest," Bryan concludes, violent confrontations were "almost unavoidable" (175).

Other factors combine with the incitements of political leaders to cause violence. Urged to act by demagogues and their subordinates, individuals in mobs, as Gustave Le Bon diagnosed so many years ago in *The Crowd*, often behave in ways they later renounce or regret, as was the case both in Drumcree and Washington when rioters facing prison sentences accused politicians of manipulating them. "I am sorry I ever heard tell of that man Paisley or decided to follow him," a member of the Ulster Volunteer Force (UVF) convicted of a 1966 murder and attempted murder said (qtd. in Patterson, *Backstop*, 41). Similarly, a lawyer for an unnamed January 6 rioter explained that "Since his arrest [...] he now realizes he was duped into these mistaken beliefs [about the 2020 election]" (Billeaud and Tarm, "As prospect of jail looms"). As ABC News reported on February 9, 2021, over a dozen rioters awaiting trial claimed they were in Washington only "because President Trump said to come." One of them, Garrett Miller, believing he was following the president's instructions, not only participated in the melee at the Capitol but also called for the assassination of Representative Alexandria Ocasio-Cortez and the hanging of a Capitol policeman, threats his lawyer labeled "misguided effort[s] to show his support for former President Trump" (Rubin et al., "Because President Trump").

Further increasing the likelihood of violence, leaders in both Washington and Drumcree motivated a wide spectrum of groups to gather at their respective events: some were "inside" and controllable by event organizers, while others remained elusively "outside" their control and exploited the moment for their own ends (Bryan, 175). Such was the case in 1998 in Ballymoney, north of Belfast, when on July 12 a Catholic house in which the Quinn family resided was burned to the ground by a firebomb. Although a young mother, her boyfriend and another adult escaped, three children ages 7–10 could not be saved, and the attack was quickly condemned by political leaders on all sides (Clarity, "3 Catholic Brothers Killed"). This included the condemnation of the "Big Man." As the *Irish Times* reported on July 18, History "came and went" in Drumcree "leaving flotsam in its wake." The *Times* argued that it would be "wrong to think those who took part in the debacle during the latter days of the stand-off were typical of the Orangemen who had paraded there." Nor would it be accurate to infer that the murder of the Quinn children effectively destroyed the protest as "the crowds had begun to drop long before that." About 7,000 lodge members arrived in Drumcree "last Thursday week," one of the "first nights of bad violence." But the numbers steadily declined, so much so that by Saturday night the "scene was practically deserted." By then, the *Irish Times* concluded, it was apparent that "ordinary decent Orangemen and their families wanted nothing to do with violence and lawlessness [...]" ("The spirit of Drumcree evaporates"). But by then it was too late for three little boys.

Beyond the challenges of comparing a single day's event with those transpiring over years, my focus on political leaders in Portadown and Washington may also be criticized as unduly narrow. In *The Transformation of Ireland* (2005), Diarmaid Ferriter notes the relative paucity of studies of divisions within Northern Irish unionism in the 1970s and 1980s, while at the same time bristling at the excessive attention paid to figures like Paisley (646). My comparison does little to address this latter concern. But, at the same time, I want to insist that like the hijacking of unionism in Northern Ireland by Paisleyites, as they were commonly called, the hollowing out of the GOP by Trumpism—the naming of Lara Trump in February 2024 as cochair of the Republican Party and the later announcement that the party's headquarters would move to south Florida—was, and *is*, the major threat to social order and democracy in America.

Like similarities between Dr. No and the Grim Reaper, some parallels between the Big Man and Orange Man are glaringly evident. And, like my focus on Paisley, some may object to my use of the pejorative "Orange Man," laden as it is with baggage stemming from the "Orange Man bad" trope that once littered social media. For Isaac Schorr in the *National Review* (September 18, 2020), allusions to the "Orange Man bad" invariably signal cheekiness or intellectual laziness, "an easy, punchy way [...] to disregard any success had by the Trump administration." In addition, Schorr notes, the term "has meanings too divergent to different groups to be helpful"; its "only utility is to help pundits dunk on each other on Twitter."

The fact is, I'm too old to dunk on anyone—even if the basket is lowered a foot or two. But my impudence doesn't necessarily invalidate the comparison (and Trump in public *is* orange or, if you prefer, a shade of bronze). Both Paisley and Trump are and were big men, even if published estimates of the latter's height and weight are unreliable. Neither leader hesitated to launch uncivil attacks on opponents' appearance, ethics or intelligence. In his remarks to the crowd at Drumcree in July, 1995, for example, Paisley accused Catholicism of spiritual darkness, "superstition," "priestcraft" and "idolatry"; in various speeches, he actually challenged Catholicism as a Christian religion. Appealing to his audience's sense of identity in his address from an improvised dais at Drumcree, Paisley warned Catholic prelates to back off: "You may take on other people in your travels but you can't take on Ulster Protestants."

Trump's rhetoric is just as extreme. As Tim Miller contends in his opinion piece for *Bulwark* "Actually, the Orange Man Is Bad—and that's kind of the point" (May 8, 2020), the forty-fifth president's behavior was and continues to be "so far outside the realm of acceptable that even his supporters have been forced to concede it." For Miller, this conduct is epitomized by Trump's aspersions of rivals and critics: his tweeting that two cable television hosts are "murderers" and "dogs" (in this instance, he's referring to Joe Scarborough and Mika Brzezinski), and that a MAGA confederate's former spouse (George Conway) is a "moonfaced loser." These and similar slurs predate his disparagement of Special Counsel Jack Smith as a "thug" and a "deranged" Trump-hater. As I described earlier, Paisley's vilification of Prime Minister Margaret Thatcher as a "lying" and "treacherous" woman is but one of dozens of similar examples. The Big Man and the Orange Man traffic in incivility with the latter's invectives against immigrants, political opponents and the judicial system rivaling the former's efforts to deny the Christianity of Catholics. And then there are the issues of racism and racial division. A year after the January 6 insurrection Trump spoke at a rally in Arizona, warning the crowd that white patients in need of therapies or vaccines for COVID-19 are pushed "to the back of the line" behind patients of color (Colarossi, "Trump Claims"). This lie, one of the more outrageous and sinister of the thousands he has uttered, elicited angry howls from his supporters, adding yet another grievance to their already formidable list.

For both demagogues, there was and *is* no possibility of compromise or dialogue with losers, dogs, thugs, demons, deranged prosecutors or treacherous prime ministers. At the January 6 rally, Trump and his allies addressed a crowd estimated at 30,000 (not hundreds of thousands of supporters that the "fake news" decided not to show). Exemplifying Trumpism's deliberate perversion of terminology, and much as Paisley invoked history at Drumcree in lionizing his Protestant forefathers, Representative Mo Brooks told the MAGA crowd that the country—now in grave peril—was great "because our ancestors sacrificed" and "believed in moral principles." Trump's opponents, like priest-ridden papists, lack such principles. In his efforts to incite his listeners to action Brooks impugns Trump's political opponents as "socialists" a half-dozen times.

Almost as despicable as Catholics for Paisleyites and socialists for Trumpists are, for the former, "weak-kneed" Protestants willing to negotiate with papists and, for the latter, "cowardly, wimpy" Republicans (globalist RINOs) who talk to Democrats. The masculinist underpinnings of these accusations are obvious: only cowards and wimps seek compromise. Real men cannot be budged, one element of what Ruth Ben-Ghiat in *Strongmen: Mussolini to the Present* (2020) regards as Trump's cult of virility. In reviewing the cult's promotional work, Ben-Ghiat recalls an Infowars question from the early days of Trump's presidency—"During the Trump Era, will men finally start acting like men again?"—and the images displayed in pro-Trump advertising campaigns that replace his corporal flabbiness with the hard bodies of "male savior/figures" like John Wayne, Superman and Rambo (139). These *real* men don't need a pep talk from Mo Brooks to "kick ass and take names." And they never admit defeat or error. Just as Paisley before him had once promised that the Republic of Ireland would "never, never, never" be permitted to interfere with Northern Irish affairs, Trump assured his followers on January 6 that he would never accept the results of the 2020 presidential election. As NBC News predicted, trouble loomed ahead: "He's lost re-election," one of his allies said. "So, for somebody who has no sense of shame, there's no downside to him letting all the crazy out." On January 6, all the crazy came out; people died and many more were injured. The damage continues and so do the rantings of ideologues too often accepted as truth by today's version of Le Bon's mindless crowd.

What inferences might be derived from this comparison of the Big Man and the Orange Man? Here are two:

1. Both leaders' worldviews are defined by not only their demonization of those who hold opposite beliefs, but also their repudiation of those members of their own tribes who understand the importance of compromise and dialogue to effective governance. In a broader sense, President Kennedy's admonition in his inaugural address to "Let us never negotiate out of fear. But let us never fear to negotiate" has been replaced in America by a fierce tribalism and code of virility in which negotiation is regarded as weakness. Dennis Cooke similarly describes Paisley's disparagement of moderate Presbyterians as either apostates or ecumenists guilty of a "grave conspiracy [with Rome] to overthrow the Protestant Constitution of our land" (qtd. in Cooke, 77).

2. In twenty-first-century America, Trumpism, like Paisleyism before it, combines evangelicalism with political animus, gender surveillance and autocratic ambition; and both the Paisley–1975 and Trump–2024 subvariants have at least one additional viral "spike" in common: animosity toward multicultural modernity and "Others." These are non-Christian Others, as evident in Paisley's insinuation that Catholicism is not a Christian religion, and Trump's vow that, if he is reelected, only immigrants who adhere to "our religion" will be allowed to enter the country.

Religion is only one of the myriad discriminations Paisleyites and Trumpists espouse. As Glenn Patterson explains in *Backstop Land*, in Northern Ireland the denial of equal rights extends to women and gay citizens as well, and in October of 2023 MAGA Trumpists in Congress elected a Speaker of the House who in the past has voiced similar prejudices. Gay marriage was outlawed in Northern Ireland, but the law was amended allowing the first same sex marriage to occur in February of 2020.

That said, with the exceptions of deadly violence and often unimaginable cruelty, gender remains the most critical discrimination in societies torn by Troubles. At the time Patterson was writing his book, uniquely restrictive access to abortion in Northern Ireland drove women to seek medical attention elsewhere. In 2018, only sixteen abortions were performed there because the mother's health was endangered, while 1,053 women sought reproductive health assistance in England or Wales (13). Recent legislation in America restricting access to abortion—including that of a ten-year-old rape victim in the summer of 2022—thus returns the country to the inequities of the nation's past (in April 2024, the Arizona Supreme Court cited the precedent of an 1846 law banning abortion except in cases where the mother's life is endangered) and raises disturbing parallels with gender legislation during the Troubles.

The implications of such legislation extend well beyond issues of reproduction. Diarmaid Ferriter's summary of the experiences of young women in the IRA illuminates the sexism and policing of women's bodies inherent to paramilitarism. Female republicans, one woman confided, "were supposed to be a virgin on [their] death bed, with a rifle in one hand and rosary beads in the other." Given this view, the idea that "a republican woman would have an orgasm was blasphemy" (qtd. in *Transformation*, 632). In America, states like Texas, Alabama and Florida are intensifying their surveillance of women's bodies and of those who might provide them with medical care, devastating women's lives and destroying medical careers. In February 2023, for example, the South Carolina legislature debated a bill that criminalized participation in an abortion, making it in some cases a capital offense (Jenkins, "Proposed SC Bill"). And the most extreme partisan demagogues are seeking even more control over women (and men) by announcing goals to curb "recreational" sex and limit access to contraception. This became disturbingly clear when the Heritage Foundation—a group helping the Trump 2024 campaign draft policy—tweeted that "Conservatives have to lead the way in restoring sex to its true purpose and ending recreational sex and senseless use of birth control pills." The trajectory of such a position is abundantly clear as activist attorney and editorialist Jill Filipovic summarizes: "It's not about abortion; it's about pleasure and freedom" (Filipovic, "The Conservative War"). As Filipovic describes, Trumpism and the Heritage Foundation are "being increasingly honest about what sex is like in a conservative paradise: Definitely not for fun." The irony of this development is so thick that a jackhammer couldn't dent it.

For readers of modern and contemporary fiction, however, this mandate for joyless sexual intimacy possesses a familiar ring. As writers from Anne Devlin to Anna Burns have described, the Troubles provoked an assault not only on women, but on sexual freedom and desire itself, a repression conveyed in part by Burns's invocation in *Milkman* of George Orwell's *1984*. In addition to underscoring the state surveillance that enforces compliance, Burns recognizes the less technical, yet highly effective supplements to it that society imposes on young women: the pressure in working class neighborhoods for teenaged girls to begin thinking about motherhood, for instance. But this merely scratches the surface of evolving governmental control. Recall that in one chapter of *1984* the novel's lonely hero Winston Smith eludes the authorities' detection and ventures into a depressed section of the city to secure the services of a prostitute. After paying a poor woman for her attention, Smith reflects on the ruling party for which the "sexual act, successfully performed" was "rebellion"; desire itself, a "thoughtcrime" (82). Later in Orwell's novel, after recognizing the radical potential of sexual desire and its origin in a biological drive, Big Brother's ruling party endeavors to manage it more effectively or, better, quash it. While attempting to reprogram Winston, O'Brien, his party handler, informs him that neurologists are hard at work on the problem of sexual pleasure. "We shall abolish the orgasm," he predicts, and make procreation no more than an "annual" and joyless "formality" (307).

Although achieving this degree of invasion may exceed the power of Trumpism, the parallels are provocative. And, like the Newspeak designed to support Big Brother (Orwell's dictator is a larger-than-life figure like the Big Man and the Orange Man), demagogues invent antagonists like "woke" liberals and the "deep state" to malign. Worse, the most intimate aspects of human sexuality and desire itself are impugned as traitorous, and the pleasure of intimacy is replaced by an emotionally arid and passionless "consequential sex." In both Paisley's Belfast and Trump country, as in Orwell's Oceania, "Ignorance is Strength." When powerful demagogues speak, people listen and hatred is allowed to emerge from its dark corners into the light and oxygen of day.

Conclusion

VICTIMS AND MARTYRS, TROUBLES AND CIVIL WARS

A day after federal agents searched Donald Trump's Mar-a-Lago home [...] there were few signs that Republicans were ready to distance themselves from the former president. Instead, everyone from the Republican National Committee to potential 2024 presidential primary rivals [...] echoed Trump's assertion that the Justice Department's search was politically motivated, casting him as a political *martyr*.
—Mark Niquette and Gregory Korte, *Bloomberg* (August 9, 2022)

There was a horrible, 30-year conflict that brought death to thousands and varying degrees of misery to millions. There was terrible cruelty and abysmal atrocity. There were decades of despair in which it seemed impossible that a polity that had imploded could ever be rebuilt. *But the conflict never did rise to the level of civil war.* (my emphasis)
—Fintan O'Toole, "Beware Prophecies of Civil War," *The Atlantic,* December 16, 2021

Violence anticipated is already violence unleashed.
—Paul K. Saint-Amour, *Tense Future: Modernism, Total War, Encyclopedic Form* (2015)

A growing number of Americans fear that Trumpism may ignite a civil war and, as I have mentioned, for some the war has already begun. This grim thesis became more plausible after the FBI's August 8, 2022 recovery of classified documents from Donald Trump's Mar-a-Lago Club, which prompted many of his supporters to clamor for revenge. But they couldn't agree on what form the vengeance should take, or even what to call it. Apparently forgetting their disgust with the "Defund the Police" mantra heard during the Black Lives Matter demonstrations, some congressional Republicans embarked upon a "Defund the FBI" crusade. Ever entrepreneurial when it comes to funding opportunities, Trump's "Save America" PAC sought to extract more money from donors by sending some more than 100 email solicitations in the days after the search featuring such taglines as "THEY BROKE INTO MY HOME" and "They're coming after YOU" (Garcia, "Trump Supporters"). But in the contest over formulating indignant responses to the search of Mar-a-Lago, "civil war" seemed to garner the most attention, although in the dark corners of cyberspace sentiments like "Fuck a Civil War. Give them a REVOLUTION" attracted their share of support as well.

In Ohio, Ricky Shiffer posted some 374 messages on Truth Social, a platform of the Trump Media and Technology Group, exhorting readers to prepare for combat. On August 11, armed with an AR-15 rifle and a nail gun, he stormed a field office in Cincinnati, failing to breach its security and activating an alarm. Earlier, Shiffer had urged that FBI agents be "killed on sight," and that's apparently what he intended to do. Perhaps he was motivated by Congressman Paul Gosar's (R-AZ) call to arms the night before: "We must destroy the FBI," Gosar fumed. "We must save America." (A year later in September 2023, Gosar echoed Trump's disparagement of General Mark Milley, labeling him a "deviant" and miscasting him as a treasonous quisling.) Some six hours later, however, after a high-speed chase, standoff and shoot-out with police, Shiffer's body armor couldn't save him—and his attack on the Cincinnati field office didn't save America either.

In his tweet the night before, Gosar also fumed that "The FBI raid on Trump's home tells us one thing. Failure is not an option." Yet the episode and its aftermath tell us lots of other things, too. One is that the cyber village is a refuge for guys like Shiffer, a Navy veteran who had fallen off the grid of everyday life—what Colm Tóibín in *Brooklyn* calls "leftover" men pocked with resentments who discover a community of like-minded malcontents on social media. Many have the wherewithal to purchase long rifles, body armor and other tactical equipment, much as Stewart Rhodes of the Oath Keepers did before heading to Washington in the days before January 6 (Palmer, "Oath Keeper Stewart Rhodes"). More generally, MAGA outrage over the Mar-a-Lago search also exposes the shallowness of their claims to support law enforcement and the military. A few weeks earlier, it took both a public outcry *and* a shaming from comedian Jon Stewart to move the party of law and order to support the PACT Act, which provides medical benefits to veterans dying from exposure to burn pits in the theatres of war in which they served.

One other feature of this episode confirms a central tenet of Trumpism. In a 1975 lecture on political duplicity, a lecture of which Joe Biden later requested a copy, Hannah Arendt characterized lying as a "way of life" in countries under totalitarian rule. For this reason, she advised, "When the facts come home to roost let us try at least to make them welcome, let us not try to escape into some utopias—images, theories, or sheer follies" (qtd. in Osnos, 44). MAGA response to the FBI search of Trump's Florida club confirms Arendt's wisdom; wary of *facts*, Trumpism works tirelessly to invent theories and delusional follies. The list of such contrivances is endless: investigations of Russian involvement in the 2016 presidential election were a "witch hunt"; the COVID pandemic was a hoax; the 2020 election was stolen by voting machines owned by a deceased dictator's family, ballot-altering software or the corruption of local and state election officials. Many of these fabrications served as a preface to Trump's growing detachment from reality, as headlines across the country reported on September 3, 2022, after a MAGA rally in Pennsylvania: "Despite being out of office for a year and a half, Donald Trump said 'weirdo' Mark Zuckerberg joined him at the White House for dinner 'last week'"—and "kissed [his] ass." A year later in a speech at a Pray Vote Stand summit in Washington (September 15, 2023), Trump warned that a "cognitively impaired" Joe Biden will lead us into World War II. Such utterances transcend mere folly or duplicity.

Trumpism's numerous assaults on democracy and rational thought also feature strategies more subtle than blatant lying; one of the most reliable is the corruption of language. And here I am excluding such malapropisms as Marjorie Taylor Greene's "gazpacho police" and Lauren Boebert's rendering of "wanton killing" as "wonton killing." Joe Biden, whom Trump labeled an "enemy of the state" at his September 3, 2022, rally, is right when saying that the words of presidents, "even lousy ones," matter, as does the language of other elected officials and the media platforms that support them. Predictably, the January 6 insurrection and the search of Mar-a-Lago elicited tortured rhetoric from Trumpists. Gosar described January 6 rioters as "peaceful protestors," while Andrew Clyde (R–GA) issued this nonsensical synopsis of the day's events:

> Let me be clear, there was no insurrection [...]. You know, if you didn't know the TV footage was a video from January 6, you would actually think it was a normal tourist visit. (qtd. in Levin, "Republican Lawmakers Claim")

In the subtitle of her *Vanity Fair* evisceration of Clyde's partisan duplicity— or delusion— Bess Levin with tongue planted firmly in cheek proffered an equally risible hypothesis: the rioters were really "history buffs" studying a D.C. landmark. In a serious vein, she ponders a more disturbing possibility: in their indifference to the mob's assault of police officers and their deafness to chants of "Hang Mike Pence," Republicans seem "to have taken a stop at Delusionville on the way to 'What the Actual Fuck Are You Talking About Town.'" Mr. Clyde appears to be well on the way to the more lunatic of these destinations.

Like Trump's increasingly alarming symptoms of impaired thought, such flights of fantasy are becoming more portentous. As Peter Wehner argued in *The Atlantic* (August 11, 2022), Republican deflections of reality grew more sinister after the search of Mar-a-Lago—and more outlandish. Dinesh D'Souza maligned the FBI as "the most powerful organized crime syndicate in the world," and former Speaker of the House Newt Gingrich compared FBI agents to ravenous wolves who want "to eat you." Echoing Rand Paul's (R-KY) suspicion that government operatives planted incriminating evidence during their search of Trump's Florida club, Fox News host Jesse Watters added, "They've declared war on us, and now it's game on." In their efforts to smear officers executing a lawful search warrant at Mar-a-Lago, some Trump epigones impersonated historians. Former Senior Advisor Stephen Miller cast the FBI as avatars of the Praetorian Guard in ancient Rome, intimidating citizens and exercising their power ruthlessly. Lauren Boebert deemed the FBI's search "gestapo crap," while Marjorie Taylor Greene compared it to "the rogue behavior of communist countries [...] the type[s] of things that happen in countries during civil war." Greene called for an immediate investigation of the "enemies within," while former Trump advisor and television commentator Monica Crowley, in high melodramatic mode, called the search of Mar-a-Lago "a hill to die on" ("The Hill to Die On").

These unhinged broadsides from Delusionville are typically accompanied by both conspiracy theories and pervasive linguistic corruptions. The former includes MAGA's resuscitations of stalking horses from the 1980s and 1990s like "critical race theory" and "Deep State" to stoke the paranoid fires of the MAGA base. To be sure, these *are* significant strategies in contemporary demagoguery, but the distortion of common, everyday language is more odious and pervasive. Rationalizations of January 6 provide numerous examples. In September 2022, then Representative Louis Gohmert (R-TX) presented Simone Gold, founder of America's Frontline Doctors and notable anti-vaxxer, with a flag from the Capitol after she served her sentence for crimes committed on January 6, referring to her as a "political prisoner." Texas realtor Katherine Schwab, who took a private plane to Washington to help "stop the steal," was heard disparaging Capitol police as "traitors"; eighteen months later, she pleaded guilty to disorderly conduct in a restricted building or grounds (Volmert, "North Texas Real Estate Agent"). Like "traitor," "patriot" was totally evacuated of meaning when the January 6 rioters who beat police officers and committed numerous other felonies were convicted of crimes and sentenced to prison. During the 2024 presidential campaign, candidate Trump declared them to be "hostages" whom he intended to pardon should he win reelection.

Such lexical perversion is a common practice in America's culture wars. "Grooming," for example, a euphemism for a pedophile's preparation of a child to interact with an adult, has been co-opted by the ideological right to defame Disney and other entertainment providers that don't support their agendas (Ley, "Misuse and Use"). Small-town America is hardly immune from such lexical practices. As Danielle Paquette reported in the *Washington Post* (August 24, 2022), the term disrupted daily life in Jamestown, a Michigan farming town, when the Patmos Library was accused of grooming children and "promoting an LGBTQ ideology." Librarians resigned, and the library was defunded. When an old photograph emerged in February of 2023 that appeared to show a twenty-three-year-old Ron DeSantis drinking with high school students, Donald Trump shared this message on Truth Social: "Here is Ron DeSantimonious grooming high school girls with alcohol as a teacher" (Leonard, "Trump shares photos"). Librarians and teachers as groomers, police as traitors—these distortions continue to divide contemporary America. Culture wars precede civil wars and, as we shall see, Troubles as well. Like flags and parades, language is a formidable weapon in these conflicts.

Victims and Martyrs

Of all of these linguistic corruptions, one in particular may prove to be the most consequential: the miscasting of Donald Trump as a *martyr* suffering for a greater cause. That is to say, after the search, not "raid" or "siege," of Mar-a-Lago, Trump seemingly abandoned his role as low comic buffoon and assumed the more serious parts of innocent victim and figure of retribution. But a victim is not a martyr, and in campaign stops for his 2024 presidential campaign he shamelessly manipulated the discourse of martyrdom for his own purposes: "I don't mind being Nelson Mandela," he told an audience in Derry, New Hampshire, on October 23, 2023, "because I'm doing it for a reason [...]. We gotta save our country from these fascists, these lunatics." He's willing to suffer in pursuit of a greater good, or so he claims. Why is the distinction important? Because martyrdom is a venerated motif not only in Christian hagiography but also in the histories of nationalist movements. To be sure, victimization at times resembles martyrdom. Cyberspace is awash with tweets and chirps recounting the former president's serial victimizations, many of which have descended into Arendtian folly: "Trump as a victim of 9/11," "Trump as victim of coronavirus," "Trump as a victim of Democrats," "Trump as victim of liberal media" and so on. Accounts of the FBI search of Mar-a-Lago quickly detected the conceit: "Trump Claims He's a Victim of the Tactics He Once Deployed" (*New York Times*, August 10, 2022); "Trump Won't Turn Down the Heat—He Needs to Play the Victim" (*The Daily Beast*, August 16, 2022); and, as if such "abuse" possessed viral properties that infect others, "The Trump Raid's Newest Victim: The Texas GOP" (*Texas Monthly*, August 12, 2022). This focus on the former president's suffering is hardly surprising as, again, Trump, like Philoctetes in Seamus Heaney's *The Cure at Troy*, spends much of his time in public "Licking [his] wounds/And flashing them around like decorations," which in turn supports his disingenuous portrayal (Heaney, 2).

For some observers, however, the search of his Florida residence cast Trump in an even greater role, and in the days following the search, everyone from the former governor of Maryland to comedian Bill Maher referred to him as a "martyr." Reviewing Governor Larry Hogan's (R-MD) appearance on ABC's "This Week" on August 14, Breitbart featured a headline repeating the governor's belief that the "raid of Mar-a-Lago" was a "win" for Trump by providing him an occasion to be "martyred." On his talk show two days earlier, Maher, ventriloquizing Ron DeSantis, quipped, "I had [the 2024 Republican nomination] in the bag, and now I gotta run against President Martyr." Writing in *The Daily Beast*, Matt Lewis also speculated about the effect of the new impersonation: "Maybe the evidence seized was so valuable that the risk of turning Trump into *even more of a martyr* justified the raid. Otherwise, either the Feds obtained enough evidence to put him away, or they may have just put him in the White House" ("It's Time for Republicans"; my emphasis). Polling after the search suggested the latter possibility as Jack McCordick observed in *Vanity Fair* (June 25, 2023): "it happened yet again [...] after his 37-count federal indictment in early June on criminal charges of mishandling classified documents: Donald Trump's poll numbers got a bump" (Trump's Support Among Republicans").

As I have mentioned, the MAGA base rallied to condemn the actions of the FBI and Department of Justice, and many of their pejoratives were conveyed as threats. If, as Paul Saint-Amour explains, "violence anticipated is already violence unleashed," then Trump and Trumpism's inflammatory rhetoric is already violence unleashed. In this regard, Peter Wehner reminds us of the Orwellian dimension of Trumpism:

> This debasement of language comes at a considerable cost. George Orwell believed that political language mattered because politics mattered, and that the corruption of one leads to the corruption of the other. And in some cases, the misuse of words can lead to political violence. ("Now They're Calling for Violence")

He's right about this, of course. The repeated castigation of law enforcement—
and of prosecutors and special counsel like Jack Smith—as deranged "thugs,"
a pack of hungry wolves, the gestapo or the Corleone family is hardly innocent.
It's a call for violence. Neither is Trump's assumption of the role of a martyr an
instance of innocent role-playing. Unlike victims who are exploited or acted
upon, martyrs selflessly and intentionally pursue an at times fatal course of
action for a greater good. In his *Summa Theologica*, Thomas Aquinas posits
a martyr's chief motivation to be *caritas*, charity toward others; "of all
virtuous acts," he notes, martyrdom is "the greatest proof of the perfection of
charity" ("Question 124: Martyrdom"). In his reading of Aquinas by way of
Aristotle's *Nicomachean Ethics*, Patrick Clark emphasizes that a martyr's virtue
is realized in those acts "deliberately chosen for the sake of some rational
good." Such purposiveness constitutes a "paradigmatic act of courage,"
confirming a martyr's "excellence" in the face of great suffering or death
(143). In other words, martyrs act out of fortitude, intentionality and charity
toward others. By contrast, serving a larger ethical or moral good is not
among Donald Trump's most noble attributes, and neither does he possess
fortitude and charity in great abundance. And Trump as Nelson Mandela,
as the embodiment of selflessness? A figure who spent twenty-seven years
in prison for the sake of others? Preposterous.

Troubles and Civil Wars

While the denotations of "victim" and "martyr" are, for the most part,
unambiguous, those distinguishing Civil Wars from Troubles are more
porous. To be sure, violence in Northern Ireland was often characterized as
a civil war, or as evidence that one was imminent, suggesting the synonymy
of the terms. Yet, when Fintan O'Toole recalls his father's admonition
in the wake of Bloody Sunday in Derry that he and his brother should prepare
to fight, he implicitly draws a distinction between the Troubles and civil war.
By the end of January 1972, a "tipping point" had been reached, O'Toole
remembers, and his father was "calm and rueful, but also grimly certain" of
what lay ahead:

> Civil war was coming to Ireland, whether we wanted it or not. He and
> my brother, who was 16, and I, when I got older, would all be up in
> Northern Ireland with guns, fighting for the Catholics against the
> Protestants. ("Beware Prophecies of Civil War")

The elder O'Toole's prediction was completely understandable, as the "frenetic
levels of violence [...] convulsing Northern Ireland in 1972 and 1973"

accounted for over a quarter of all deaths from sectarian conflict between 1969 and 1990 (Bew et al., 190). The summer of 1971 was also especially unsettling, highlighted by the internment of nearly 350 civilians suspected of IRA involvement and a mass flight, mostly of Catholics, across the border into the Republic. Yet, however intensely the Troubles were exported to Ireland, England and America—from car bombings and assassinations to emigration—the O'Toole brothers were never required to take up arms and head North. The Troubles, he concludes, "never did rise to the level of a civil war" in which citizens on both sides of the partition were expected to fight.

An implicit hierarchy informs this assertion, implying that a civil war is a more destructive, all-encompassing level of conflict, something to which the Troubles might have risen. But the disruptions of daily life, the terror created by kidnappings and murder, and the maimed bodies of bomb victims strewn across sidewalks like so many pieces of "cheap fruit" as referenced in Robert McLiam Wilson's *Eureka Street*—these scenes hardly need to rise to any higher level of horror. Further, the violence of the Troubles persisted for decades, a fact to which Marc Mulholland alluded in the title of his book *The Longest War: Northern Ireland's Troubled History* (2002). Albeit muted, it still continues. Not unlike Trumpism—which, as many commentators including O'Toole and Stephen Marche have observed, gave a name to a malignancy long metastasizing in the American body politic—the Troubles began centuries earlier, as Mulholland usefully delineates. But even without considering these origins, sectarian conflict in Northern Ireland claimed innocent lives longer than any civil war—in Vietnam or nineteenth-century America—the United States has ever experienced. Moreover, the spread of Trumpism is hardly so geographically bounded as conflicts in North and South Vietnam, North and South Korea, Northern Ireland and the Republic, the Union and the Confederacy. No partition, Mason-Dixon line or 38th parallel divides anyone from the total war and "tense future" of the Troubles.

This is as much to say that civil wars and Troubles are different. This is more than a semantic quibble, but rather a prediction akin to that made by O'Toole's father of what may lie ahead. The protracted length of the Troubles and the unrelenting terror it introduced in daily life are only a few of the differences that obtain between it and most civil wars. But even this assertion fails to capture the extent of Troubles in the twenty-first century. In the age of social media and since 2016, how many days have Americans been spared headlines and news focusing on Trumpism or its effects? How many bipartisan bills, judicial confirmations and military promotions have been stalled or scuttled all together because of the vast moat dividing and isolating Congressional aisles? How have the repeated manifestations of "Trump time" denatured our experience of temporal sequencing and damaged Americans' collective memory? Is this where America is heading? Will fear insinuate itself into the most mundane of daily activities, shopping at the market or enjoying a coffee with a friend?

To return briefly to the topic of martyrdom, perhaps the most dangerous of its ramifications is the creation of what Patrick Radden Keefe terms a "cult of martyrdom" and a cult, he adds, is a "dangerous thing" (12). In an American context, both "cult" and "martyrdom" possess powerful resonances. Trumpism—in its blind devotion to a leader, its ability to unite aggrieved followers in a political movement, and its casting of law enforcement and government agencies as enemies—bears strong resemblances to a cult. Recall that in the months prior to the 1993 Waco massacre, Branch Davidian leader David Koresh prepared for what he foresaw as an inevitable battle with many of the same governmental opponents. Fortunately, Donald Trump has not yet been beatified as a martyr, for martyrdom is capable of creating a congregation of disciples wedded to a violent project akin to that with which Trump incited his loyalists on January 6: "You've got to fight like hell or you won't have a country left." The Troubles had a similar provenance, which in turn became symbolized by epiphenomena (flags and parades, for instance) that shaped Northern subcultures just as "Make America Great" caps and flags identify MAGA believers. As Jeff Sharlet described in a profanely entitled article "'F—k Your Feelings': In Trump's American the Partisan Battle Flag is the New Stars and Stripes" (*Vanity Fair*, 2020), "Trump flags aren't so much about his campaign as they are about identity." And, within that identity, a toxic mixture of Christian nationalism, American exceptionalism, authoritarian populism and blind devotion to a victim, not a nation, festers a violent potential that is impossible to ignore; it will grow more uncontrollable and destructive if the victim becomes a martyr.

The Troubles in Northern Ireland, to state the matter slightly differently, were sustained by both a belief system and cultural practices in which, on both sides of the ideological divide, martyrdom occupied a privileged place. Dolours and Marian Price, whom I have mentioned in an earlier chapter, grew up with an emblem of blood sacrifice for Irish nationalism living just up the stairs: their aunt Bridie, who lost her hands when an incendiary device she was holding exploded. Convicted in 1973 of setting explosives in an IRA bombing campaign in London, the Price sisters were given life sentences and remanded to Brixton Prison. But even before their incarceration they announced their intention to go on hunger strike, and in doing so they advanced a powerful "philosophy of self-sacrifice that would help define the emerging traditions of Irish republican martyrdom" (Keefe, 149). After 167 days of striking and forced feeding, the Price sisters used the philosophy of self-sacrifice to win the status of political prisoners and transfer to Northern Ireland.

Because martyrdom for the imagined community of a nation often resembles religious sacrifice, novelists, poets and playwrights frequently braid the two together. Yeats's poem "Easter 1916" commemorates the sacrifice of Irish nationalists who rose up against British rule, were captured and later executed. "Wherever green is worn," the poem's narrator observes, these men will be remembered forever. Such is the case with Padraic Pearse, who in 1913 wrote that "Bloodshed is a cleansing and sanctifying thing," a Messianic thesis undercut by Sean O'Casey in *The Plough and the Stars* (1926). In one scene in *Cal*, Bernard MacLaverty's protagonist attends mass on Sunday and hears a sermon about Matt Talbot, a reformed alcoholic whose waist was discovered after his death to have been "lapped in chains" so "tightly tied about him that it was almost impossible to remove them [...]" (39). This account of a man "willing to put himself through such suffering for the love of Jesus" moved Cal to prayer before his mind drifted to a "rebel song" his mother had taught him recalling the sacrifice of a nationalist hero (40). The line between religious martyrdom and nationalist sacrifice begins to blur.

The narrative of Irish nationalism comprises a secular hagiography of martyrs who sacrificed themselves for the cause, and in this history 1798, 1867 and 1916 occupy places of privilege. But so, too, as discussed so many pages ago, does 1981, when ten men led by Bobby Sands emulated Terence MacSwiney's protest in 1920 by going on a hunger strike. Jez Butterworth's *The Ferryman* (2017) is set in a rural farmhouse in County Armagh as Sands's and other strikers' health declined, a topic heard frequently on radio newscasts and woven tightly into daily conversation. The opening scene of Anne Devlin's *Ourselves Alone* (1985) is set in a West Belfast club where the "*traditional prominence of [Padraic] Pearse and [John] Connolly has given way to the faces in black and white*" of Sands and the hunger strikers, now gone. The play's dialogue begins with a female vocalist singing a Republican ballad and complaining bitterly that she is "fed up with songs where the women are doormats" (Devlin, 13). The singer, Frieda, recognizes that the history of the Troubles is a *gendered* chronicle and its epiphenomena—songs, banners, posters, wall murals—inflect daily life and subjective experience.

Frieda's commitment to a feminist Sinn Féin ("we ourselves" or "ourselves alone"), to women's self-determination and freedom, will also need to replicated and nurtured in contemporary America. By the end of the summer of 2022, when residents of Jackson, Mississippi could not access clean drinking water, and when a ten-year-old rape victim in Ohio was forced to travel to Indiana for medical attention, and when the school year began in several states without enough teachers in classrooms, Trumpists could take comfort, however cold, in their cultural victories. Libraries were being defunded because of objectionable titles on their shelves, and a poor sixteen-year-old Florida girl—ten weeks pregnant, working to complete her GED and lacking legal guardians to sign necessary forms—was judged *not* to be "mature enough" to receive an abortion but old enough to raise a child on her own. However different in other respects, civil wars and Troubles share one thing in common: they are always gender struggles that create real victims.

Northern Ireland and America

Other parallels exist between contemporary America and Northern Ireland during the Troubles. And, although some of these have been mentioned earlier, their inherent dangers deserve one last look:

- *The suppression of voting rights.* As many historians emphasize, gerrymandering in Northern Ireland assured Catholics' second-class status by constraining their vote which, in turn, energized the civil rights movement of the 1960s. As the *Cameron Report* concluded in 1969, voting rights also exerted other social effects; in particular, housing projects and developments were delayed or abandoned in instances where a perceived "electoral disadvantage" might be created. Such tactics, including the "rate payers franchise" that afforded voting rights only to property owners and a plural voting system that awarded an additional vote to business owners and university graduates, allowed Unionists to win a majority of seats in a Derry/Londonderry Borough in which 62% of the voting population was Catholic. In the wake of NICRA's 1967 campaign "One Man One Vote," the Electoral Law Act of 1968 abolished the plural system (Gráinséir, "Irish Legal Heritage").

    Similar strategies of voter suppression have been implemented across America to allow a minoritarian party to dominate a majority. And such strategies must be opposed. Ronald Reagan knew this in 1947 when, as the President of the Screen Actors Guild, he was called to testify in front of the House Committee on Un-American Activities (HUAC). When asked about steps that might be taken to rid Hollywood of communist influence, Reagan offered a reply that strikes an uncannily relevant chord: "I can certainly testify that in the case of the Screen Actors Guild, we have been eminently successful in preventing [communists] from, with their usual tactics, trying to run a majority of an organization with a well-organized minority." How was this achieved? "In opposing these people the best thing to do is make democracy work [...] by insuring [sic] everyone a vote and by keeping everyone informed" (qtd. in Matthews, 88).

- *Town and Country.* Demographical data describing voting patterns in the 2020 American presidential election are revealing in at least two respects. One is that while Donald Trump won 95 of America's 100 *smallest* counties by population, Joe Biden won 91 of America's 100 *largest* counties. The second is that Trump won 65 of the 100 counties whose population decreased the most according to the last census (Wilson, "Trump's Electoral Gain"). In other words, Trump carried small-town America, sometimes hubristically promoted as "real" America, where populations are in decline. Such factors are familiar to students of postwar Ireland. "One of the attractions of a rural and agrarian society," Mary E. Daly argues in *The Slow Failure: Population Decline and Independent Ireland, 1920–1973* (2006), "was the belief that it was synonymous with stability, whereas an urban and industrial society was associated with change" (50). Yet, rural Ireland was hardly a "timeless place" with generations of the same family living on the land of their ancestors. In twentieth-century Ireland, "the myth of a stable prelapsarian rural society exercised a strong influence on people's minds, and on social policy" (51).

  A similarly potent myth is central to Trumpism. Rural counties support a Republican party taken over by zealots and conspiracy theorists that aspire to return America to a largely white, prelapsarian utopia before multiculturalism existed and the Respect for Marriage Act was signed into law by President Biden at the end of 2022, before transgenderism had a name, before the Voting Rights and Civil Rights Acts of the 1960s and before *Roe v. Wade.* American conservatives and their evangelical supporters cling desperately to a mythology of when America was "great," not recognizing or caring that it was hardly great for everyone.

- *Guns and Decommissioning.* Until 2011, John de Chastelain, Chairman of the Independent International Commission on Decommissioning, was charged with enforcing terms of the 1998 Belfast Agreement related to weapons. On September 25, 2005, he announced that "The decommissioning of the arms of the IRA is now an accomplished fact." The list of arms included ammunition, rifles, machine guns, mortars, grenades and explosives, among other weapons. In June 2009, the leader of the Progressive Unionist Party in the North, along with Protestant paramilitaries including the UVF and the Red Hand Commando, announced the decommissioning of their weapons with the UDA doing likewise the following January (Kelly, "UDA and Red Hand Commando"). Although the exact number of weapons put "beyond use" is difficult to calculate, one source speculates that, in the earlier decommissioning, the IRA destroyed some 1,000 rifles. An American arms procurer who funneled guns to the PIRA explained this cache most likely included "any kind of assault rifle, Armalites especially, AR-15s, M16s, AR-18s, but almost any kind of high-powered, self-loading weapons" (Blake, "The American Connection"). Paramilitaries prefer them.

So, it seems, do many Americans. In *The Next Civil War*, Stephen Marche estimates that seventeen million Americans purchased guns in 2020 alone, contributing to the larger tabulation of 400 million guns in circulation (50). What kinds of guns? The AR-15 in particular, in part because "you can buy one for as little as $349," making it "easily the most popular gun in the United States" even though it is "useless for hunting and useless for home defense" (58). No matter. They will provide protection "for when the government fails them, and protection from the government" itself (59).

The search at Mar-a-Lago melds perfectly with what is, finally, this paranoid rationale for acquiring weapons of war. Nurturing "vicious monsters" within its institutions—Trump's term of disparagement for the FBI and the Department of Justice—the US government shamelessly invaded the home of a former president who needs well-armed patriots to protect him. Sooner or later, the (il)logic goes, these monsters will be coming for you.

Coda: Troubles, Total War and Martyrs

Troubles and Civil Wars: again, how might they be distinguished? Marche provides a useful starting point: "Civil wars are *total wars* laced with atrocities, fought not between professional soldiers but between populations" (11; my emphasis). This definition seems reasonable enough as far as it goes, as civil wars engender conflicts in which non-combatant civilians inevitably become "collateral damage" and actual combatants, even if previously trained for a military or police force, do not qualify as professional soldiers. But one question begs another: what is a *total* war? Marche never quite explains this, but meditations about the concept have informed literary and culture criticism for some time. Paul Saint-Amour, for example, provides a nuanced unpacking of the concept that also confirms the acuity of Jan Kott's insight about the writing of both history *and* cultural criticism illuminating the times in which we live—and, perhaps, those to come as well. Total war produces collective anxiety with no clearly defined terminus, a violent temporality within which anticipation is weaponized as the relationship between warfare and futurity grows more intertwined (Saint-Amour, 7).

Primarily interested in modernist writing between the World Wars and the lived experience during World War Two of residents of such urban targets as London, Hamburg and Hiroshima, Saint-Amour catalogs the psychical effects of nightly air raid sirens, sudden explosions, evacuations from homes and the devastation of a city's built environment. In its expansion beyond the battlefield, in its ubiquity, total war dominates "a nation's every political, economic, and cultural domain" (7). It is inescapable and so all-encompassing that it revises modern understandings of the relationship between time and trauma. Trauma, as such writers as Sigmund Freud in *Beyond the Pleasure Principle* (1920) and Virginia Woolf in *Mrs. Dalloway* (1925) underscore, is typically tethered to the past. A case in point, Woolf's shellshocked soldier Septimus Smith living in post-WWI London continually relives an event from the battlefield that claimed the life of a comrade, a symptom of what Freud termed "traumatic war neurosis" and what today is termed PTSD (post-traumatic stress disorder).

By contrast, total war "weaponizes anticipation" by focusing a population's attention not on a prior devastation, but on the next war, thereby producing a "future conditional anxiety," not a haunting from the past or a return of the repressed. Total war "always designates a war to come, an asymptote that the *next* war—which is often imagined now as the *final* next war—will approach more nearly" (Saint-Amour, 57). Donald Trump's warning to the crowd assembled at the Ellipse on January 6, "Fight like hell, or you won't have a country left," possesses such an air of finality, implying that a battle must be waged *now*, the last chance to set things right. Through their unrelenting cascades of outrages, Troubles time and Trump time, as I argued earlier, affect our experience of lived time, inevitably confounding our memory and our ability to construct coherent narratives from a series of individual events. In his exegesis of total war, Saint-Amour thus adds a crucial dimension to our understanding of time and Trumpism: namely, the omnipresence of a tense future.

And like this dilation of the relationship between *time* and anxiety, the *space* of our American Troubles can be equally challenging to map. That is, in contemporary America the binary qualities of disputants and spaces from past civil wars—Cavaliers and Roundheads, nationalist and loyalists; Union and Confederacy, North and South—have fragmented into a jagged cartography of battleground states: Florida and Pennsylvania, Arizona and Ohio, Nevada and Wisconsin. On such a map, there is no partition, no border to install towers equipped with searchlights or position heavily armed guards, and no demilitarized zone serving as a respite from armed conflict. Unless states secede from the nation, a possibility Marche considers, what lies ahead may be better described as Troubles.

For the sake of connotational accuracy, then, "a destructive force able to catalyze a total war like the Troubles in Northern Ireland" might be added to definitions of Trumpism. And sectarian martyrs and divisive demagogues described earlier in this book like "Dr. No" and "The Grim Reaper," "The "Big Man" and "The Orange Man," will help stoke the fires of total war. Speaking to the American Enterprise Institute on September 19, 2022, Liz Cheney recalled an ironic moment in the House cloakroom before the January 6 insurrection. As she paints the scene, printed statements had been posted requiring signatures, and many of her Republican colleagues were busy signing them, thus confirming their intention to protest the certification of the 2020 presidential election. After doing so, one of her colleagues was overheard mumbling under his breath, "Oh, the things we do for the Orange Jesus." Perhaps a better question is this: What will Trumpists *not* do for their deeply wronged victim-leader? What might his canonization as a martyr do to make our future even more tense?

Intimations of his transformation from victim to martyr surfaced on Truth Social at the end of 2023 with his announcement that a new series of forty-seven Trump Digital Cards would be accompanied—for an additional charge, of course—by a small swatch of fabric from the business suit he wore when being processed at the Fulton County Jail. The first 200 people to buy 100 cards with cryptocurrency could also attend a reception with Trump before enjoying a gala dinner at Mar-a-Lago. After all, he announced, "America needs a superhero," one reason his images on the cards depict him as a svelte, absurdly muscled action figure (Roush, "Donald Trump Releases 'Mugshot Edition'"). But beneath the hucksterism and nonsense of an impossibly muscled senior citizen, the remnant of his business suit and promise of a trip to Florida recall the traditional context of martyrdom, in which everything from a martyr's bones to splinters from crosses and stitchwork on garments become venerated relics. True believers also make pilgrimages to sites associated with martyrs' lives while treasuring small shards of their person or property in gold-trimmed reliquaries that, in turn, become precious possessions to bequeath to heirs. Once Trump transcends victimization to martyrdom, total war and Troubles will almost surely follow—if they haven't already started.

REFERENCES

Abbas, Mo, Matt Bradley, and Matthew Symington. "Biden Becomes a Divisive Figure in Northern Ireland as Post–Brexit Tensions Simmer." *NBC News*, July 18, 2021. https://www.nbcnews.com/news/world/biden-becomes-divisive-figure-northern-ireland-post-brexit-tensions-simmer-n1274308.

Abramsky, Sasha. "McConnell-Led Opposition to Infrastructure Plan May Haunt GOP in Next Elections." *Truthout*, April 8, 2021. https://truthout.org/articles/mcconnell-led-opposition-to-infrastructure-plan-may-haunt-gop-in-next-elections/.

Adams, Gerry. "Gerry Adams remembers 'extraordinary' Jean Kennedy Smith." *IrishCentral*, June 19, 2020. https://www.irishcentral.com/news/gerry-adams-jean-kennedy-smith.

——— "A Republican in the Civil Rights Campaign." In *Twenty Years On*, edited by Michael Farrell, 39–53. Dingle, County Kerry, Ireland: Brandon Books, 1988.

"After 27 Years, U.S. Airlines Get the Right to Land at Dublin." *New York Times*, June 12, 1973. https://www.nytimes.com/1973/06/12/archives/irish-planes-to-be-barred-here-unless-us-jets-can-use-dublin-irish.html.

Alberta, Tim. *The Kingdom, the Power, and the Glory: American Evangelicals in an Age of Extremism*. New York: Harper, 2023.

Aldous, Richard. *Reagan & Thatcher: The Difficult Relationship*. New York: Arrow Books, 2012.

Alexander, Ella. "Ian Paisley's Most Caustic Quotes: 'Catholics Breed Like Rabbits and Multiply Like Vermin'." *Independent*, September 12, 2014. https://www.independent.co.uk/news/people/ian-paisley-s-most-caustic-quotes-catholics-breed-like-rabbits-and-multiply-like-vermin-9729672.html.

Alonso, Johanna. "Chaos at New College of Florida." *Inside Higher Education*, August 16, 2023. https://www.insidehighered.com/news/students/academics/2023/08/16/chaos-reigns-new-college-florida-fall-semester-nears.

"Ambassador in Times of Crisis Had Irish Roots." *Irish Times*, January 11, 2000. https://www.irishtimes.com/news/ambassador-in-time-of-crisis-had-irish-roots-1.232734.

Anbinder, Tyler. "Moving Beyond 'Rags to Riches': New York's Irish Famine Immigrants and Their Surprising Savings Accounts." *Journal of American History* 99 (December 2012): 741–70.

Anderson, Benedict. *Imagined Communities: Reflections on the Origin and Spread of Nationalism*. Revised edition. London: Verso, 2006.

Apple, Jr., R. W. "Galway's Mood for Reagan Subdued." *New York Times*, June 3, 1984. https://www.nytimes.com/1984/06/03/world/galway-s-mood-for-reagan-subdued.html.

Applebaum, Anne. "Coexistence Is the Only Option." *The Atlantic*, 20 January 2021. https://www.theatlantic.com/ideas/archive/2021/01/seditionists-need-path-back-society/617746/.

Armus, Teo. "Make Hope and History Rhyme: Why Joe Biden Loves to Quote a Passage from Irish Poet Seamus Heaney." *Washington Post*, August 21, 2020. www.washingtonpost.com/nation/2020/08/21/seamus-heaney-biden-dnc-speech/.

Auden, W. H. *Collected Poems*, edited by Edward Mendelson. New York: Vintage International, 1991.

Austerlitz, Saul. *Just a Shot Away: Peace, Love, and Tragedy with the Rolling Stones at Altamont.* New York: St. Martin's, 2018.

Baker, Peter. "Bush Intervened in Northern Ireland Dispute." *New York Times*, March 10, 2010. https://www.nytimes.com/2010/03/11/world/europe/11bush.html.

Balz, Dan, and Clara Ence Morse. "American Democracy is Cracking. These Forces Help Explain Why." *Washington Post*, August 18, 2023. https://www.washingtonpost.com/politics/2023/08/18/american-democracy-political-system-failures/.

Barry, Aoife. "Thousands of Northern Refugees Streamed Over the Border in the 1970s—Some were Called 'ungrateful'." *Thejournal.ie*, December 27, 2014. https://www.thejournal.ie/northern-refugees-ireland-state-papers-1820942-Dec2014/.

Behan, Brendan. *Brendan Behan's New York*. Boston: Little Brown, 1964.

——— "Note to President Kennedy," July 15, 1961. John F. Kennedy's Presidential Papers. President's Office Files. Special Correspondence. John F. Kennedy Presidential Library.

Bell, J. Bowyer. *The Gun in Politics: An Analysis of Irish Political Conflict, 1916–1986.* New Brunswick, NJ, and Oxford: Transaction Books, 1987.

Ben-Ghiat, Ruth. *Strongmen: Mussolini to the Present.* New York: Norton, 2020.

Beresford, David. *Ten Men Dead: The Story of the 1981 Irish Hunger Strike.* New York: Atlantic Monthly Press, 1987.

Berry, Wendell. *November Twenty Six Nineteen Hundred Sixty Three.* New York: George Braziller, 1964.

Bew, Paul, Peter Gibbon and Henry Patterson. *Northern Ireland 1921–1996: Political Forces and Social Classes.* Revised and Updated New Edition. London: Serif, 1995.

Biden, Joseph R. *Promise Me, Dad: A Year of Hope, Hardship, and Purpose.* New York: Flatiron Books, 2017.

——— *Promises to Keep: On Life and Politics.* New York: Random House, 2007.

——— "Remarks by President Biden to the Houses of the Oireachtas." April 11, 2023. https://www.whitehouse.gov/briefing-room/speeches-remarks/2023/04/13/remarks-by-president-biden-to-the-houses-of-the-oireachtas/.

Billeaud, Jacques, and Michael Tarm. "As Prospect of Jail Looms, Capitol Riot Suspects Express Regret." *Christian Science Monitor*, March 31, 2021. https://www.csmonitor.com/USA/Politics/2021/0331/As-prospect-of-jail-looms-Capitol-riot-suspects-express-regret.

Binder, David. "Kennedys' Tardiness Annoys Germans." *New York Times*, April 22, 1971. https://www.nytimes.com/2021/04/23/world/europe/ted-kennedy-germany-diplomats.html.

Bixby, Ashleigh Larissa. "Conflicted Tourism: Heritage Narratives, Sectarian Schism, and Economic Growth in Northern Ireland." 2015. *Electronic Theses and Dissertations.* Paper 2300. https://doi.org/10.18297/etd/2300.

Blake, Andrew. "The American Connection: Running Guns to the IRA." *Washington Post*, September 4, 1979. https://www.washingtonpost.com/archive/politics/1979/09/04/the-american-connection-running-guns-to-the-ira/cc17f812-fc79-4b3c-8b7e-4d42815fed9a/.

REFERENCES

Bleaney, Michael. "Conservative Economic Strategy." In *The Politics of Thatcherism*, edited by Stuart Hall and Martin Jacques, 132–47. London: Lawrence and Wishart, 1983.

Blight, David W. *Frederick Douglass: Prophet of Freedom*. New York: Simon & Schuster, 2018.

Bloch, Ernst. *The Principle of Hope, Volume 1*, 1954. Translated by Neville Plaice, Stephen Plaice and Paul Knight. Cambridge: The MIT Press, 1995.

Bloody Sunday, 1972: Lord Widgery's Report of Events in Londonderry, Northern Ireland, on 30 January 1972. London: The Stationery Office, 2001.

Boland, Eavan. "The Famine Road." In *New Collected Poems*, 42–43. New York: Norton, 2008.

Bolger, Dermot. *Tanglewood*. Dublin: New Island Books, 2015.

Booth, Cathy. "More than 1000 anti-Reagan Protesters Including Roman Catholic Nuns [...]". *UPI Archives*, June 2, 1984a. https://www.upi.com/Archives/1984/06/02/More-than-1000-anti-Reagan-protesters-including-Roman-Catholic-nuns/5441454996800/.

——— "Reagan Booed en route to doctorate." *UPI Archives*, June 2, 1984b. https://www.upi.com/Archives/1984/06/02/Reagan-booed-en-route-to-doctorate/4294454996800/.

Bornstein, George. *The Colors of Zion: Blacks, Jews, and Irish from 1845 to 1945*. Cambridge, MA: Harvard University Press, 2011.

——— "Irish, Jewish, or Both: Hybrid Identities of David Marcus, Stanley Price, and Myself." In *Irish Questions and Jewish Questions*, edited by Aidan Beatty and Dan O'Brien, 127–39. Syracuse: Syracuse University Press, 2018.

Bradley, John. "Changing the Rules: Why the Failures of the 1950s Forced a Transition in Economic Policy-Making." In *The Lost Decade*, eds. Keogh, et al. 105–17. Cork: Mercier Press, 2004.

Brearton, Fran. "'Wounds,' Michael Longley." *Irish University Review*, 39. 2 (2009): 231–38.

Breen, Suzanne. "Unionist MPs demand Mowlam's resignation." *Irish Times*, August 27, 1999. https://www.irishtimes.com/news/unionist-mps-demand-mowlam-s-resignation-1.220760.

Bremmer, Ian. *Us vs. Them: The Failure of Globalism*. New York: Portfolio/Penguin, 2018.

"Brown Welcomes Weapons Disposal." UTV, February 8, 2010.

Bryan, Dominic. *Orange Parades: The Politics of Ritual, Tradition and Control*. London: Pluto Press, 2000.

Bryant, Nick. *When America Stopped Being Great: A History of the Present*. London: Bloomsbury Continuum, 2021.

Bulik, Mark. "1854: No Irish Need Apply." *New York Times*, September 8, 2015. https://www.nytimes.com/2015/09/08/insider/1854-no-irish-need-apply.html.

Bump, Philip. "Trump Pledges to Turn Away Those Who Don't Like 'our religion'." *Washington Post*, October 24, 2023. https://www.msn.com/en-us/news/politics/trump-pledges-to-turn-away-those-who-dont-like-our-religion/ar-AA1iLz3A.

Burns, Anna. *Milkman: A Novel*. Minneapolis: Graywolf Press, 2018.

——— *No Bones: A Novel*. New York/London: W.W. Norton, 2001.

"Bush phones Adams over NI talks." *BBC.com*, November 30, 2004. http://news.bbc.co.uk/2/hi/uk_news/northern_ireland/4050343.stm.

Butterworth, Jez. *The Ferryman*. London: Nick Hern Books, 2017.

Byrne, Cormac, and Ferghal Blaney. "Donald Trump Ireland visit 2019: Live updates as US President's sons arrive in Doonbeg, Co Clare." *Irish Mirror*, June 6, 2019. https://www.irishmirror.ie/news/irish-news/politics/donald-trump-ireland-visit-2019-16254664.

Cameron Commission. *Disturbances in Northern Ireland*. Belfast: Her Majesty's Stationery Office, 1969.

Carroll, Rory. "Irish Police Chief Warns of Further Disruptions after Dublin riot." *Guardian*, November 24, 2023. https://www.theguardian.com/world/2023/nov/24/dublin-rioters-could-face-jail-helen-mcentee-justice-minister-says?ref=upstract.com.

——— "'It's Still Shocking': Site of Mountbatten's Killing Braces for 40th Anniversary." *Guardian*, August 26, 2019. https://www.theguardian.com/world/2019/aug/26/its-still-shocking-site-of-mountbattens-killing-braces-for-40th-anniversary.

——— *Killing Thatcher: The IRA, the Manhunt and the Long War on the Crown*. London: Mudlark, 2023.

Caruth, Cathy. *Unclaimed Experience: Trauma, Narrative, and History*. Baltimore: Johns Hopkins University Press, 1995.

Chaffin, Tom. *Giant's Causeway: Frederick Douglass's Irish Odyssey and the Making of an American Visionary*. Charlottesville: University of Virginia Press, 2014.

Chan, Sewell, and Eric Neugeboren. "Texas Republican Convention Calls Biden Win Illegitimate and Rebukes Cornyn Over Gun Talks." *Texas Tribune*, June 18, 2022. https://www.texastribune.org/2022/06/18/republican-party-texas-convention-cornyn/.

Chaudhuri, Una. *Staging Place: The Geography of Modern Drama*. Ann Arbor: University of Michigan Press, 1995.

Cillizza, Chris. *Power Players: Sports, Politics, and the American Presidency*. New York: Twelve, 2023.

Clancy, Mary Alice C. "The United States and Post-Agreement Northern Ireland, 2001–6." *Irish Studies in International Affairs*, 18 (2007): 155–73.

Clarity, James F. "I.R.A. Bombing Kills 9 in a Shopping Area of Belfast." *New York Times*, October 24, 1993. https://www.nytimes.com/1993/10/24/world/ira-bombing-kills-9-in-a-shopping-area-of-belfast.html.

——— "3 Catholic Brothers Killed in Fire, Stunning Ulster and Raising Fears." *New York Times*, July 13, 1998. https://www.nytimes.com/1998/07/13/world/3-catholic-brothers-killed-in-fire-stunning-ulster-and-raising-fears.html.

Clark, Dennis. *The Irish in Philadelphia: Ten Generations of Urban Experience*. Philadelphia: Temple University Press, 1973.

Clark, Patrick. "Is Martyrdom Virtuous? An Occasion for Rethinking the Relation of Christ and Virtue in Aquinas." *Journal of the Society of Christian Ethics*, 30.1 (Spring/Summer 2010): 141–59.

Clinton, Bill. "Belfast City Hall Tree Lighting Ceremony." In *"Days Like This": President Clinton's Diplomacy in Northern Ireland*, November 30, 1995. William Jefferson Clinton Presidential Museum and Library.

——— "Mackie Plant Keynote Speech." In *"Days Like This": President Clinton's Diplomacy in Northern Ireland*, November 30, 1995. William Jefferson Clinton Presidential Museum and Library.

——— *My Life*. New York: Alfred E. Knopf, 2004.

Cohen, Zachary. "Kimberly Guilfoyle was Paid $60,000 Speaking Fee for Ellipse Rally Intro, Jan. 6 committee member says." CNN Politics, June 14, 2022. https://www.cnn.com/2022/06/13/politics/kimberly-guilfoyle-paid-60000-speaking-fee-ellipse-january-6/index.html.

Colarossi, Natalie. "Trump Claims White People 'at the Back of the Line' for Covid Vaccines, Treatments." *Newsweek*, January 16, 2022. https://www.newsweek.com/trump-claims-white-people-back-line-covid-vaccines-treatments-1669884.

Collins, Robert. *Noraid and the Northern Ireland Troubles, 1970–1994*. Dublin: Four Courts Press, 2022.

Coogan, Tim Pat. *The Famine Plot: England's Role in Ireland's Greatest Tragedy*. New York: Palgrave Macmillan, 2012.
Cooke, Dennis. *Persecuting Zeal: A Portrait of Ian Paisley*. Dingle, County Kerry, Ireland: Brandon Books, 1996.
Cooper, James. "'The Situation Over There Really Bothers Me': Ronald Reagan and the Northern Ireland Conflict." *Irish Historical Studies*, 41.159 (May 2017): 97–116.
Corcoran, Paul. "Heaney's *The Cure at Troy* and the Christian Virtue of Hope." *Studies: An Irish Quarterly Review*, 109 (Winter 2020/2021): 435–47.
Cranley, Ellen. "Here's How Trump Reportedly Spent $3.6 Million On His 'convenient' Two–Day Trip to Ireland." *Business Insider*, June 8, 2019. https://www.businessinsider.com/trump-travel-costs-ireland-trip-2019-6.
Crowley, Monica. "The Hill to Die On." *The Monica Crowley Podcast*, June 12, 2023. https://podcasts.apple.com/us/podcast/the-hill-to-die-on/id1614718499?i=1000616710047.
Cupp, S. E. "How I Felt Watching Trump Hug Our flag." *CNN Opinion* +, March 4, 2019. https://www.cnn.com/2019/03/04/opinions/watching-donald-trump-hug-american-flag-se-cupp/index.html.
Cusack, George. "A Cold Eye Cast Inward: Seamus Heaney's 'Field Work'." *New Hibernia Review*, 6 (Autumn 2002): 53–72.
Dallison, Paul. "The Fall and Fall of Trump Groupies Farage and Giuliani." *Politico*, May 21, 2021. https://www.politico.eu/article/donald-trump-nigel-farage-rudi-giuliani-fall/.
Daly, Augustin. *A Flash of Lightning*. New York: Printed for the Author, 1885.
Daly, Mary E. *The Slow Failure: Population Decline and Independent Ireland, 1920–1973*. Madison: University of Wisconsin Press, 2006.
"Darkley, Armagh: Shootings." *HL Deb* 445 (November 21, 1983). https://api.parliament.uk/historic-hansard/lords/1983/nov/21/darkley-armagh-shootings.
Dáte, Shirish V. "Trump Finally Arrives in Ireland for Tax-Payer Funded Visit to His Golf Resort." *Huffington Post*, June 5, 2019. https://www.huffpost.com/entry/trump-ireland-golf_n_5cf82efde4b0e3e3df14abab.
Davis, Mike. *Buda's Wagon: A Brief History of the Car Bomb*. London: Verso, 2007.
"Death of Liam McCloskey," April 9, 2022. Bobby Sands Trust. https://www.bobbysandstrust.com/death-of-liam-mccloskey/.
De Bréadún, Deáglan. "Carter's Staff Did Not Take North 'Seriously'." *Irish Times*, December 31, 2009. https://www.irishtimes.com/news/carter-s-staff-did-not-take-north-seriously-1.796527.
——— "Falklands a Ridiculous War, Said Haughey." *Irish Times*, December 28, 2012. https://www.irishtimes.com/news/falklands-a-ridiculous-war-said-haughey-1.5149.
Deignan, Tom. "When Northern Irish Civil Rights Activist Bernadette Devlin Came to America." *Irish Central*, October 8, 2012. https://www.irishcentral.com/opinion/others/when-northern-irish-civil-rights-activist-bernadette-devlin-came-to-america-video-174753481-238154541.
Delaney, Enda. "The Vanishing Irish? The Exodus from Ireland in the 1950s." In *The Lost Decade*, eds. Keogh, et al., 80–86. Cork: Mercier Press, 2005.
Dempsey, Branagh. "The Forgotten Visit." *"Famous Faces at Dublin Castle" Exhibition*, January 6–February 22, 2022. https://www.dublincastle.ie/the-forgotten-visit/.
Dessem, Matthew. "Here Are All the Books Donald Trump Recommended in 2019." *Slate*, December 29, 2019. https://slate.com/culture/2019/12/donald-trump-book-recommendations-2019-plus-ray-donovan-for-some-reason.html.

De Valera, Éamon. Recorded Interview with Joseph E. O'Connor, September 15, 1966. John F. Kennedy Library Oral History Program, Kennedy Presidential Library.

Devlin, Anne. *Ourselves Alone*. London: Faber and Faber, 1986.

Devlin (McAliskey), Bernadette. "A Peasant in the Halls of the Great." In *Twenty Years On*, edited by Michael Farrell, 77–88. Dingle, County Kerry, Ireland: Brandon Books, 1988.

——— *The Price of My Soul*. New York: Knopf, 1969.

Dickens, Charles. *Hard Times*. London: Bradbury and Evans, 1854.

Dinnerstein, Leonard, and David M. Reimers. *Ethnic Americans: A History of Immigration*, 5th ed. New York: Columbia University Press, 2009.

"Disarmament: Northern Ireland Good Friday Agreement." University of Notre Dame Peace Accords Matrix. Kroc Institute for International Peace Studies. https://peaceaccords.nd.edu/provision/disarmament-northern-ireland-good-friday-agreement.

"Divisive 'Dr No' turned peacemaker." *Belfast Telegraph*, September 12, 2014. https://www.belfasttelegraph.co.uk/news/northern-ireland/divisive-dr-no-turned-peacemaker-30582304.html.

Dixon, Paul. "Performing the Northern Ireland Peace Process on the World Stage." *Political Science Quarterly*, 121 (Spring, 2006): 61–91.

Donlon, Seán. "Hume Has Place in Pantheon of Irish Nationalist Leaders." *Irish Times*, August 8, 2020, 3.

"Don't Let Clothes Make the Martyr." *New York Times*, November 27, 1980. https://www.nytimes.com/1980/11/27/archives/dont-let-clothes-make-the-martyr.html.

Douglass, Frederick. *Narrative of the Life of Frederick Douglass*. New York: New American Library, 1968. First published 1848.

Dowd, Maureen. "D.C. and Joyce—Both Incomprehensible." *New York Times*, February 12, 2022. https://www.nytimes.com/2022/02/12/opinion/ulysses-joyce-trump.html.

Downing, John. "Haughey, Thatcher, and the Falklands That Led to Low–Point in Irish–British Relations." *Independent.ie*, June 13, 2022. https://www.independent.ie/opinion/haughey-thatcher-and-the-falklands-stance-that-led-to-low-point-in-irish-british-relations/41749634.html.

Doyle, Roddy. *The Barrytown Trilogy: The Commitments, The Snapper, The Van*. New York: Penguin, 1995.

"Dublin Protest Over Reagan Visit." *New York Times*, May 27, 1984. https://www.nytimes.com/1984/05/27/world/dublin-protest-over-reagan-visit.html.

Dumbrell, John. "The New American Connection: President George W. Bush and Northern Ireland." In *A Farewell to Arms? Beyond the Good Friday Agreement*, 2nd edition, edited by Michael Cox, Adrian Guelke and Fiona Stephen, 357–66. Manchester: Manchester University Press, 2006.

——— "The United States and the Northern Irish Conflict, 1969–94: From Indifference to Intervention." *Irish Studies in International Affairs*, 6 (1995): 107–25.

Earle, Geoff. "Trump ups his attack on 'MAGA hating Globalist RINO' Rupert Murdoch and calls Fox news hosts who 'endorsed' election fraud lies 'brave and patriotic'." *Daily Mail*. March 1, 2023. https://www.dailymail.co.uk/news/article-11807939/Trump-ups-attacks-MAGA-Hating-Globalist-RINO-Rupert-Murdoch.html.

Ecarma, Caleb. "'It's a Grift': Kimberly Guilfoyle Made $60,000 for Her Jan. 6 Rally Speech." *Vanity Fair*, June 14, 2022. https://www.vanityfair.com/news/2022/06/kimberly-guilfoyle-jan-6-speech.

REFERENCES

Eco, Umberto. *The Role of the Reader: Explorations in the Semiotics of Texts.* Bloomington: Indiana University Press, 1984.

Edgington, Tom, and Chris Morris. "Brexit: What's the Northern Ireland Protocol?" *BBC News*, updated July 21, 2021. www.bbc.com.

Editorial Board. "Anatomy of a Biden Tax Hike." *Wall Street Jounal*, April 5, 2021. https://www.wsj.com/articles/anatomy-of-a-biden-tax-hike-11617662273.

——— "Ireland's Tax Lessons for Biden." *Wall Street Journal*, May 27, 2021. https://www.wsj.com/articles/irelands-tax-lesson-for-biden-11622154655.

Edwards, Elaine. "Anglo–Irish Agreement 'a great shock' to Unionists, FitzGerald told Reagan." *Irish Times*, December 30, 2016. https://www.irishtimes.com/news/ireland/irish-news/anglo-irish-agreement-a-great-shock-to-unionists-fitzgerald-told-reagan-1.2907108.

Egan, Timothy. *The Immortal Irishman: The Irish Revolutionary Who Became an American Hero.* Boston: Houghton Mifflin, 2016.

Ellmann, Maud. *The Hunger Artists: Starving, Writing, and Imprisonment.* Cambridge: Harvard University Press, 1993.

el Moncef, Salah. *Benghazi.* Paris/Los Angeles: Penelope Books, 2023.

Evans, Melanie, et al. "U.S. Covid-19 Hospitalizations Approach a Peak as Delta Variant Spreads." Wall Street Journal, August 28, 2021. https://www.wsj.com/articles/u-s-covid-19-hospitalizations-approach-a-peak-as-delta-variant-spreads-11630155627.

"Fact Sheet–President Trump's Historic Deregulation Is Benefiting All Americans." October 21, 2019. American Presidency Project, University of California Santa Barbara https://www.presidency.ucsb.edu/documents/fact-sheet-president-trumps-historic-deregulation-benefitting-all-americans.

Fanning, Charles. "James T. Farrell's O'Neill–O'Flaherty Novels: An Introduction." In *The World I Never Made*, by James T. Farrell, v–lvii. 1936. Urbana: University of Illinois Press, 2007.

Farrell, Michael, ed. *Twenty Years On.* Dingle, County Kerry, Ireland: Brandon Books, 1988.

Federal Reserve of St. Louis. "The American Economy of 1964." *Survey of Current Business*, 45.1 (January 1965): 1–3. https://fraser.stlouisfed.org/title/survey-current-business-46/january-1965-9713.

Fenton, Laurence. *Frederick Douglass in Ireland: The Black O'Connell.* Leicester: Ulverscroft, 2014.

Ferriter, Diarmaid. *The Border: The Legacy of a Century of Anglo-Irish Politics.* London: Profile Books, 2019.

——— *The Transformation of Ireland.* Woodstock, NY: The Overlook Press, 2005.

Filipovic, Jill. "The Conservative War on Sex." *Substack*, February 28, 2024. https://jill.substack.com/p/the-conservative-war-on-sex.

Fitsanakis, Joseph. "U.S. Gave N. Ireland Police Weapons, Spy Equipment Despite Congress Ban." *IntelNews.org*, January 4, 2012. https://intelnews.org/2012/01/04/01-901/.

Fitzgerald, Maurice. "Ireland and the US in the Post–War Period." In *The Lost Decade*, edited by Keogh, et al. 187–205. Cork: Mercier Press, 2005.

——— *John Hume in America: From Derry to DC.* South Bend: University of Notre Dame Press, 2019.

Flanagan, Eimear. "Stormont Without NI Leadership for Third of Its Lifespan." *BBC News*, February 12, 2022. https://www.bbc.com/news/uk-northern-ireland-60249249.

Fleming, Ian. *Casino Royale.* New York: Penguin Books, 2002. First published 1953.

——— *Doctor No.* New York: Penguin Books, 2002. First published 1958.

Ford, Gerald R. "Remarks of Welcome to Prime Minister Liam M. Cosgrave of Ireland," March 17, 1976. The American Presidency Project, University of California Santa Barbara. https://www.presidency.ucsb.edu/documents/remarks-welcome-prime-minister-liam-m-cosgrave-ireland.

Fowler, Glenn. "John D.J. Moore, an Executive and a Former Envoy, Dies at 77." *New York Times*, September 13, 1988. https://www.nytimes.com/1988/09/13/obituaries/john-d-j-moore-an-executive-and-a-former-envoy-dies-at-77.html.

Franco, Jean. "The Nation as Imagined Community." In *Dangerous Liaisons: Gender, Nation, and Postcolonial Perspectives*, edited by Anne McClintock, Aamir Mufi and Ella Shohat, 130–37. Minneapolis: University of Minnesota Press, 1997.

Frank, Jeffrey. "Extreme Conventions: San Francisco, 1964, and Cleveland, 2016." *New Yorker*, June 21, 2016. https://www.newyorker.com/news/daily-comment/extreme-conventions-san-francisco-1964-and-cleveland-2016.

Freud, Sigmund. *Beyond the Pleasure Principle*. In *The Standard Edition of the Complete Psychological Works of Sigmund Freud*, vol. 18, edited by James Strachey, 24 vols. London: The Hogarth Press and the Institute of Psycho-Analysis, 1955.

——— *Group Psychology and the Analysis of the Ego*. In *The Standard Edition of the Complete Psychological Works of Sigmund Freud*, vol. 18, edited by James Strachey, 24 vols. London: The Hogarth Press and the Institute of Psycho-Analysis, 1955.

——— *The Interpretation of Dreams*. In *The Standard Edition of the Complete Psychological Works of Sigmund Freud*, vol. 5, edited by James Strachey, 24 vols. London: The Hogarth Press and the Institute of Psycho-Analysis, 1955.

Freyne, Patrick, and Ula Mullaly. "Before I Would Have Held My Husband's Hand Walking Around the Streets. But Now I Wouldn't." *Irish Times*, March 4, 2023. https://www.irishtimes.com/life-style/people/2023/03/04/many-lgbtq-people-increasingly-feel-they-have-to-be-cautious-holding-their-partners-hand-in-public/.

Friel, Brian. *Crystal and Fox and The Mundy Scheme*. New York: Farrar, Straus and Giroux, 1969.

——— *Philadelphia, Here I Come!* In *Brian Friel: Plays 1*, 23–99. London: Faber and Faber, 1996.

——— *Translations*. In *Brian Friel: Plays 1*, 377–447. London: Faber and Faber, 1996.

Furay, Julia, and Redmond O'Hanlon, eds. *Critical Moments: Fintan O'Toole on Modern Irish Theatre*. Dublin: Carysfort Press, 2003.

Furlong, Irene. *Irish Tourism 1880–1980*. Dublin: Irish Academic Press, 2009.

——— "Tourism and the Irish State in the 1950s." In *The Lost Decade: Ireland in the 1950s*, edited by Keogh et al. 164–86. Cork: Mercier Press, 2005.

Gaffikin, Frank, and Mike Morrissey. *Northern Ireland: The Thatcher Years*. London: Zed Books, 1990.

Garcia, Catherine. "Trump Supporters Have Received More than 100 Fundraising emails Since Mar-a-Lago Search." *The Week*, August 17, 2022. https://theweek.com/donald-trump/1015989/trump-supporters-have-received-more-than-100-fundraising-emails-since-mar-a.

Gold, Hadas. "Michael Medved Suffers for His Anti-Trump Stance." *Politico*, November 6, 2016. https://www.politico.com/story/2016/11/michael-medved-salem-radio-donald-trump-23081.

Goldberg, Robert Alan. *Barry Goldwater*. New Haven: Yale University Press, 1995.

"Goldwater Opposes GOP on Abortion." *Los Angeles Times*, August 7, 1992. https://www.latimes.com/archives/la-xpm-1992-08-07-mn-4874-story.html.

Goodall, David. "The Making of the Anglo-Irish Agreement of 1985 (The Hillsborough Agreement): A Personal Account." In *The Making of the Anglo-Irish Agreement of 1985*, edited by Frank Sheridan. 3–131. Dublin: National University of Ireland, 2021.

Goodall, Morwenna. "Introduction." In *The Making of the Anglo-Irish Agreement of 1985*, edited by Frank Sheridan. xii–xiv. Dublin: National University of Ireland, 2021.

Goodfriend, Marvin, and Robert G. King. "The Incredible Volcker Disinflation." *NBER Working Paper Series*, no. 11562 (August 2005): 1–49. Rpt. *Journal of Monetary Economics* 52 (2005): 981–1015.

Goodwin, Doris Kearns. *The Fitzgeralds and the Kennedys: An American Saga*. New York: St. Martin's Press, 1987.

Goshko, John M. "Reagan Asks $250 Million Aid to Ulster." *Washington Post*, March 6, 1986. https://wapo.st/4cIQUkf.

Gough, Ian. "Thatcherism and the Welfare State." In *The Politics of Thatcherism*, edited by Hall and Jacques, 148–68. 1983.

Government of Ireland. *Programme for Economic Expansion*. 1958. https://opac.oireachtas.ie.

——— Second Programme for Economic Expansion. 1963. https://opac.oireachtas.ie.

Graham, David A. "Donald Trump's Narrative of the Life of Frederick Douglass." *The Atlantic*, February 1, 2017. https://www.theatlantic.com/politics/archive/2017/02/frederick-douglass-trump/515292/.

——— "The New Lost Cause." *The Atlantic*, October 18, 2021. https://www.theatlantic.com/ideas/archive/2021/10/donald-trumps-new-lost-cause-centers-january-6/620407/.

Gráinséir, Seosamh. "Irish Legal Heritage: One Man, One Vote." *Irish Legal News*, October 12, 2018. https://www.irishlegal.com/articles/irish-legal-heritage-one-man-one-vote.

Greenhouse, Linda. "What We Lost When We Lost Sandra Day O'Connor." *New York Times*, September 23, 2021. https://www.nytimes.com/2021/09/23/opinion/sandra-day-oconnor-supreme-court.html.

Guardian Staff. "Barack Obama Releases List of His 19 Favorite Books from 2019." *Guardian*, December 29, 2019. https://www.theguardian.com/us-news/2019/dec/29/barack-obama-favorite-books-list-2019.

Haass, Richard N. "Fatal Distraction: Bill Clinton's Foreign Policy." *Foreign Policy* 108 (Autumn 1997): 112–23.

——— "The Squandered Presidency: Demanding More from the Commander–in–Chief." *Foreign Affairs*, 79 (May-June 2000): 136–41.

——— "What Northern Ireland Teaches Us About Ending the Ukraine War." *Project Syndicate*, April 21, 2023. https://www.project-syndicate.org/commentary/northern-ireland-lessons-for-ending-ukraine-war-by-richard-haass-2023-04.

Hagen, Lisa. "Antisemitism Is On the Rise, and It's Not Just About Ye." *NPR: All Things Considered*, December 1, 2022. https://www.npr.org/2022/11/30/*1139971241*/antisemitism-is-on-the-rise-and-not-just-among-high-profile-figures.

Hall, Stuart. "The Great Moving Right Show." In *The Politics of Thatcherism*, edited by Hall and Jacques, 19–39. 1983.

Hall, Stuart, and Martin Jacques, eds. *The Politics of Thatcherism*. London: Lawrence and Wishart, 1983.

Hamilton, Wilborn. "THEATER REVIEW; Greek Drama Unfolds, Also Moves and Shakes." *New York Times*, December 15, 1997. https://www.nytimes.com/1997/12/15/theater/theater-review-greek-drama-unfolds-also-moves-and-shakes.html.

Harrington, John P. *The Irish Play on the New York Stage, 1874–1966*. Lexington: The University Press of Kentucky, 1997.
Haughey, Charles J. "Ireland's Corner on US Business." *Christian Science Monitor*, May 24, 1982. https://www.csmonitor.com/1982/0524/052428.html.
Healy, Alison, and Dan Keenan. "Obama's Irish Ancestry Highlighted during First Family's Trip to Trinity." *Irish Times*, June 17, 2013. https://www.irishtimes.com/news/obama-s-irish-ancestry-highlighted-during-first-family-s-visit-to-trinity-1.1431607.
Heaney, Seamus. *The Cure at Troy*. New York: Farrar, Straus and Giroux, 1990.
——— *Death of a Naturalist*. London: Faber and Faber, 1966.
——— *Field Work*. London: Faber and Faber, 1979.
——— "From Feeling into Words." In *Finders Keepers: Selected Prose 1971–2001*, 15–27. New York: Farrar, Straus and Giroux, 2002.
——— *North*. London: Faber and Faber, 1975.
——— "Place and Displacement: Recent Poetry from Northern Ireland." *Finders Keepers: Selected Prose 1971–2001*, 122–45.
Heneghan, Philip. "The Tourist Industry in Ireland–1960 to 1975." *Studies: An Irish Quarterly Review*, 65 (Autumn, 1976): 225–34.
Hennessey, Thomas. *The Evolution of the Troubles 1970–72*. Dublin/Portland, OR: Irish Academic Press, 2007.
Higgins, Michael D. *New and Selected Poems*. Dublin: Liberties Press, 2011.
——— "Speech at the First International Shaw Conference, Dublin." In *Shaw and the Making of Modern Ireland*, edited by Audrey McNamara and Nelson O'Ceallaigh Ritschel, 11–18. London: Palgrave Macmillan, 2020.
Hillman, G. Robert. "UI Steers Clear of Firebombs." *Daily Illini*, December 2, 1970. https://idnc.library.illinois.edu/?a=d&d=DIL19701202.2.5&e=-.
Holland, Steve, and Conor Humphries. "Biden Arrives in Northern Ireland to Mark Peace Deal Anniversary." *Reuters*, April 11, 2023. https://www.reuters.com/world/biden-heads-northern-ireland-delicate-political-juncture-2023-04-11/.
"How Much Aid for Ireland?" *Chicago Tribune*, January 22, 1986. https://www.chicagotribune.com/news/ct-xpm-1986-01-22-8601060253-story.html.
Hulse, Carl. "'Moscow Mitch' Tag Enrages McConnell and Squeezes G.O.P. on Election Security." *New York Times*, July 30, 2019. https://www.nytimes.com/2019/07/30/us/politics/moscow-mitch-mcconnell.html.
Hume, John. "The Irish Question in a Changed World." *Irish Times*, August 14, 1989.
——— "A Northern Catholic Writes ... Hume in 1964." Reprint of "The Northern Catholic" in Special Tribute Supplement, "John Hume, 1937–2020." *Irish Times*, August 8, 2020: 7.
Hutchins, Robert M. *The University of Utopia*, 2nd edition. Chicago: University of Chicago Press, 1964.
Ignatiev, Noel. *How the Irish Became White*. New York: Routledge, 1995.
Ireland, David. *Cyprus Avenue*. London: Bloomsbury Methuen Drama, 2016.
"Ireland's Friends." *New York Times*, March 17, 1981. https://www.nytimes.com/1981/03/17/opinion/ireland-s-friends.html.
Ireland-U.S. Council. www.irelanduscouncil.com. Accessed: December 7, 2022.
Irish Central Staff. "Where to Protest Donald Trump During His Visit to Ireland." *IrishCentral*, June 4, 2019. https://www.irishcentral.com/news/politics/trump-protests-ireland.

REFERENCES

"Irish to Protest Reagan's Visit." *New York Times*, May 22, 1984. https://www.nytimes.com/1984/05/22/world/irish-to-protest-reagan-s-visit.html.

Italie, Hillel. "Does Trump Read? If So, What? Fiery 2005 Letter Shines Light on His Relationship with Books." *Chicago Tribune*, February 15, 2018. https://www.chicagotribune.com/2018/02/15/does-trump-read-if-so-what-fiery-2005-letter-shines-light-on-his-relationship-with-books/.

Jeffs, Rae. *Brendan Behan: Man and Showman*. Cleveland: World Publishing, 1968.

Jenkins, S. E. "Proposed SC Bill Could Make Abortion a Death Penalty Eligible Offense." WMBF News, February 22, 2023. https://www.wmbfnews.com/2023/02/22/proposed-sc-bill-could-make-abortion-death-penalty-eligible-offense/.

"John Hume, 1937–2020: The Man Who Built the Peace." Special Tribute Supplement. *Irish Times*, August 8, 2020. 1–8.

Johnson, Steven. "The Fall, and Rise, of Reading." *Chronicle of Higher Education*, April 21, 2019. www.chronicle.com/article/the-fall-and-rise-of-reading.

Jones, Jonathan. "Joe Biden's Love for Seamus Heaney Reveals a Soul You Can Trust." *Guardian*, November 9, 2020. https://www.theguardian.com/books/booksblog/2020/nov/09/joe-biden-love-for-seamus-heaney-poetry.

Jordan, Richard L. "The 'Prophet' of Interposition: The Reverend Ian Paisley and American Segregation." *New Hibernia Review*, 15.2 (2011): 40–63.

Joyce, James. "Ireland, Island of Saints and Sages." In *The Critical Writings of James Joyce*, edited by Ellsworth Mason and Richard Ellmann, 153–74. Ithaca: Cornell University Press, 1989.

——— "James Clarence Mangan." In *The Critical Writings of James Joyce*, 175–86. Ithaca: Cornell University Press, 1989.

——— *A Portrait of the Artist as a Young Man*. New York: Penguin, 2003. First published 1916.

——— *Ulysses: The Corrected Text*. New York: Vintage Books, 1986.

Kagan, Robert. "Opinion: Our Constitutional Crisis is Already Here." *Washington Post*, September 23, 2021. https://www.washingtonpost.com/opinions/2021/09/23/robert-kagan-constitutional-crisis/.

Keating, Dan, Adrian Blanco and Clara Ence Morse. "Trump's Biggest Iowa Gains are in Evangelical Areas, Smallest Wins in Cities." *Washington Post*, January 16, 2024. https://www.washingtonpost.com/politics/2024/01/16/trump-iowa-evangelical-vote/.

Keefe, Patrick Radden. *Say Nothing: A True Story of Murder and Memory in Northern Ireland*. New York: Doubleday, 2019.

Keeley, Theresa. "Reagan's Real Catholics vs. Tip O'Neill's Maryknoll Nuns: Gender, Intra-Catholic Conflict, and the Contras." *Diplomatic History*, 40.3 (2016): 530–58.

Kelly, Antoinette. "UDA and Red Hand Commando Decommission Weapons." *Irish Central*, June 27, 2009. https://www.irishcentral.com/news/uda-and-red-hand-commando-decommissions-weapons-49342282-237648731.

Kelly, Stephen. *'A Failed Political Entity': Charles Haughey and the Northern Ireland Question 1945–1992*. Newbridge, County Kildare, Ireland: Merrion Press, 2016.

——— "Love/Hate: The Haughey/Thatcher Relationship Revisited." *Irish Times*, December 24, 2014. https://www.irishtimes.com/opinion/love-hate-the-haughey-thatcher-relationship-revisited-1.2047899.

Kenen, Joanne. "Vaccine-skeptical Trump Country Poses Challenge to Immunization Push." *Politico*, March 8, 2021. https://www.politico.com/news/2021/03/08/coronavirus-vaccine-rural-america-473940.

Kennedy, John F. "Address to the Greater Houston Ministerial Association," September 12, 1960. Papers of John F. Kennedy, President's Office. Files. Speech. John F. Kennedy Presidential Library.

——— "Eamon De Valera Seeks to Unite All Ireland." *New York Journal American*, July 29, 1945. L–10:1,2. John F. Kennedy Presidential Library.

——— Memo to Dean Rusk. National Security Action Memorandum No. 83. Papers of John F. Kennedy, President's Office, August 28, 1961. John F. Kennedy Presidential Library.

——— "Remarks of the President to a Joint Session of the Dáil and Seanad Éireann, Leinster House, Dublin Ireland." Papers of John F. Kennedy, President's Office. Files. Speech. Address to Irish Parliament, Dublin, June 28, 1963. John F. Kennedy Presidential Library.

——— "Remarks at Shannon Airport upon Leaving Ireland, June 29, 1963." John F. Kennedy Presidential Library.

Kennedy, Leslie. "The IRA Assassination of Lord Mountbatten: Facts and Fallout." *History*, September 23, 2022. https://www.history.com/news/mountbatten-assassination-ira-thatcher.

Kennedy, Louise. *Trespasses*. New York: Riverhead Books, 2022.

Keogh, Dermot. *Jews in Twentieth Century Ireland: Refugees, Anti-Semitism and the Holocaust* Cork: Cork University Press, 1998.

Keogh, Dermot, Finbarr O'Shea and Carmel Quinlan, eds. *The Lost Decade: Ireland in the 1950s*. Cork: Mercier Press, 2004.

Kiberd, Declan. *Irish Classics*. Cambridge: Harvard University Press, 2000.

——— *The Irish Writer and the World*. Cambridge: Cambridge University Press, 2005.

Kilpatrick, Chris. "Shankill Bomb: The Nine Innocent Victims Who Perished in IRA attack." *Belfast Telegraph*, October 23, 2013. https://www.belfasttelegraph.co.uk/news/northern-ireland/shankill-bomb-the-nine-innocent-victims-who-perished-in-ira-attack/29687669.html.

Kirschenbaum, Julia, and Michael Li. "Gerrymandering Explained." Brennan Center for Justice, August 10, 2021; updated June 9, 2023. https://www.brennancenter.org/our-work/research-reports/gerrymandering-explained.

Kristol, Bill [@BillKristol]. Tweet on Trumpism. *Twitter*, June 9, 2022. https://twitter.com/BillKristol/status/1534578835248795651.

Lee, Bandy X., ed. *The Dangerous Case of Donald Trump: 37 Psychiatrists and Mental Health Experts Assess a President*. Expanded edition. New York: Thomas Dunne, 2019.

Lee, Jesse. "President Obama in Dublin: 'Never Has a Nation So Small Inspired So Much in Another." Obama White House Archives, May 23, 2011. https://obamawhitehouse.archives.gov/blog/2011/05/23/president-obama-dublin-never-has-nation-so-small-inspired-so-much-another.

Lehner, Stefanie. "Nation: Reconciliation and the Politics of Friendship in Post-Troubles Literature." In *The New Irish Studies*, edited by Paige Reynolds, 47–62. Cambridge: Cambridge University Press, 2020.

Leonard, Kimberly. "Trump Shares Photos of DeSantis Alleging He Partied and Drank with High School Girls When He Was a Teacher." *Insider*, February 7, 2023. https://www.businessinsider.com/trump-shares-photos-of-desantis-alleging-partied-with-high-schoolers-2023-2.

Leonnig, Carol, and Philip Rucker. *I Alone Can Fix It: Donald J. Trump's Catastrophic Final Year*. New York: Penguin Press, 2021.

REFERENCES

Levin, Aaron. "Goldwater Rule," 2016. Rpt. by American Psychological Association. https://www.psychiatry.org/news-room/goldwater-rule.

Levin, Bess. "Of Course Eric and Don Jr. Descended on Irish Village Like Frat Boys on Spring Break." *Vanity Fair*, June 7, 2019. https://www.vanityfair.com/news/2019/06/don-jr-eric-trump-ireland-pub-crawl.

——— "Republican Lawmakers Claim January 6 Rioters Were Just Friendly Guys and Gals Taking a Tourist Trip Through the Capitol." *Vanity Fair*, May 12, 2021. https://www.vanityfair.com/news/2021/05/capitol-attack-tourist-visit.

Lewis, Anthony. "Weary, Fearful Refugees from Ulster Crowd into Ireland." *New York Times*, August 13, 1971. https://www.nytimes.com/1971/08/13/archives/weary-fearful-refugees-from-ulster-crowd-into-ireland.html.

Lewis, Camille Kaminski. "I Lost My Job Because I Wouldn't Let My Employer Hit My Toddler." *Huffpost*, June 15, 2023. https://news.yahoo.com/lost-job-because-wouldn-t-123001525.html?fr=yhssrp_catchall.

Lewis, Matt. "It's Time for Republicans to Go Nuclear and Dump Trump." *Daily Beast*, August 14, 2022. https://www.thedailybeast.com/its-time-for-republicans-to-go-nuclear-and-dump-trump?ref=author.

Ley, David J. "Misuse and Abuse of the Term 'Grooming' Hurts Victims." *Psychology Today*, April 10, 2022. https://www.psychologytoday.com/us/blog/women-who-stray/202204/misuse-and-abuse-the-term-grooming-hurts-victims.

Lifton, Robert Jay. "Foreword to the First Edition: Our Witness to Malignant Normality." In *The Dangerous Case of Donald Trump*, edited by Bandy X. Lee, Expanded Edition, xlvii–lii. New York: Thomas Dunne, 2019.

Light, Paul C. "The Crisis Last Time: Social Security Reform." *Brookings*, March 5, 2005. https://www.brookings.edu/opinions/the-crisis-last-time-social-security-reform/.

Lillis, Michael. "John Hume's Legacy." *Studies: An Irish Quarterly Review*, 109 (Winter 2020/2021): 371–85.

Limón, Elvia. "Gov. Greg Abbott Signs Off on Texas' New Political Maps, Which Protect GOP Majorities While Diluting Voices of Voters of Color." *Texas Tribune*, October 25, 2021. https://www.texastribune.org/2021/10/25/2021-texas-redistricting-explained/.

Lloyd, David. *Anomalous States: Irish Writing and the Post-Colonial Moment*. Durham, NC: Duke University Press, 1993.

Lloyd, Whitney. "Resolution Proposes Separating Chicago from Illinois to Create 51st State." *ABC News*, April 15, 2019. https://abcnews.go.com/US/resolution-proposes-separating-chicago-illinois-create-51st-state/story?id=62405752.

Loftus, Paul. "The Politics of Cordiality: Continuity and Change in Irish–American Diplomacy during the Johnson Presidency, 1963–9." *Irish Studies in International Affairs*, 20 (2009): 143–66.

Lohr, Steve. "Push on Hiring Bias in Ulster." *New York Times*, September 4, 1986. https://www.nytimes.com/1986/09/04/business/push-on-hiring-bias-in-ulster.html.

Longley, Michael. *An Exploded View: Poems, 1968–1972*. London: Victor Gollancz, 1973.

Lozada, Carlos. "Think You Can Remember Every Outrage of the Trump Presidency So Far? A New Book Will Test You." *Washington Post*, March 16, 2018. https://www.washingtonpost.com/news/book-party/wp/2018/03/16/think-you-remember-every-outrage-of-the-trump-presidency-so-far-a-new-book-will-test-you/.

——— *What Were We Thinking: A Brief Intellectual History of the Trump Era*. New York: Simon & Schuster, 2020.

Luce, Edward, "Joe Biden's Long Good Friday." *Financial Times*, April 12, 2023. https://www.ft.com/content/b371438a-dbdc-4d17-8fca-1efc1ba51895.

Lydon, Christopher. "Irish Planes to be Barred Here Unless U.S. Jets Can Use Dublin." *New York Times*, August 19, 1971. https://www.nytimes.com/1971/08/19/archives/irish-planes-to-be-barred-here-unless-us-jets-can-use-dublin-irish.html.

Lynch, Suzanne. "Trump in Ireland: President Looking Forward to Visiting 'a Great Place'." *Irish Times*, May 30, 2019. https://www.irishtimes.com/news/world/us/trump-in-ireland-president-looking-forward-to-visiting-a-great-place-1.3909855.

MacBride, Seán. "Introduction" to *Bobby Sands, Writings from Prison*, 13–22. Dublin: Mercier Press, 1998.

MacLaverty, Bernard. *Cal*. London: Jonathan Cape, 1983.

——— *Grace Notes*. New York: Norton, 1997.

Maher, Bill. *Real Time with Bill Maher*. HBO, Season 20, August 12, 2022.

——— "Sub-literate America." *Real Time with Bill Maher*. HBO, Season 16, February 19, 2018.

Mahon, Derek. *The Yellow Book*. Winston-Salem, NC: Wake Forest University Press, 1998.

Mallon, Séamus. "I Saw John Hume's Raw Courage as He Faced Troop of Bloodthirsty Paras." *Irish Times*, August 8, 2020, 3.

Manchester, Julia. "Tensions with Evangelicals Threaten Trump White House Bid." *The Hill*, January 21, 2023. https://thehill.com/homenews/campaign/3821714-tensions-with-evangelicals-threaten-trump-white-house-bid/.

Marche, Stephen. *The Next Civil War: Dispatches from the American Future*. New York: Avid Reader Press, 2022.

Mascaro, Lisa. "Senate GOP Leader Relishes Role as 'Grim Reaper'." *AP News*, June 28, 2019. https://apnews.com/article/c842a0bcecc840628a991092da3e7ce3.

Matthews, Chris. *Tip and the Gipper: When Politics Worked*. New York: Simon and Schuster, 2013.

Mayer, Jane. "Donald Trump's Ghostwriter Tells All." *The New Yorker*, July 18, 2016. www.newyorker.com/magazine/2016/07/25/donald-trumps-ghostwriter-tells-all.

McCann, Colum. *TransAtlantic*. New York: Random House, 2014.

McCarthy, Niall. "How Often Has President Trump Played Golf Since He Took Office?" *Forbes*, November 11, 2020. https://www.forbes.com/sites/niallmccarthy/2020/11/11/how-often-has-president-trump-played-golf-since-he-took-office-infographic.

McClements, Freya. "Europa Hotel: From 'most bombed' to a Belfast Beacon of Change." *Irish Times*, September 11, 2021a. https://www.irishtimes.com/news/ireland/irish-news/europa-hotel-from-most-bombed-to-a-belfast-beacon-of-change-1.4670710.

——— "Northern Ireland's Refugees 50 Years On: 'I Can Still See Him Standing there Waving'." *Irish Times*, August 7, 2021b. https://www.irishtimes.com/life-and-style/northern-ireland-s-refugees-50-years-on-i-can-still-see-him-standing-there-waving-1.4632825.

McClintock, Anne. "'No Longer in a Future Heaven': Gender, Race, and Nationalism." In *Dangerous Liaisons: Gender, Nation, and Postcolonial Perspectives*, edited by McClintock, Aamir Murfi and Ella Shohat, 89–112. Minneapolis: University of Minnesota Press, 1997.

McCordick, Jack. "Trump's Support Among Republicans Increased After Criminal Indictments: Poll." *Vanity Fair*, June 25, 2023. https://www.vanityfair.com/news/2023/06/trump-poll-increases-after-indictments.

McCourt, Frank. *Angela's Ashes*. New York: Scribner's, 1996.

McCracken, Niall. "Doonbeg: Welcome to 'Trump Town'." *BBC News*, June 5, 2019a. https://www.bbc.com/news/world.

———. "President Trump Ireland Visit: Border Blip and the Blimp." *BBC News*, June 8, 2019b. https://www.bbc.com/news/world-europe-48542473.

McCrudden, Christopher. "Human Rights Codes for Transnational Corporations: What Can the Sullivan and MacBride Principles Tell Us?" *Oxford Journal of Legal Studies*, 19.2 (1999): 167–201.

McCrystal, Cal. "Ian Paisley, 1926–2014: The 'Big Man' vs. the Pope." *New Statesman*, September 12, 2014. https://www.newstatesman.com/politics/2014/09/ian-paisley-1926-2014-big-man-vs-pope.

McDonagh, Martin, dir. *The Banshees of Inisherin*. London: Blueprint Pictures, 2022.

McDonald, Henry. "Ian Paisley, the Dr No of Ulster Politics, Dies Aged 88." *Guardian*, September 12, 2014. https://www.theguardian.com/politics/2014/sep/12/ian-paisley-dies-aged-88-northern-ireland.

———. "Northern Ireland Talks Collapse as Main Unionist Parties Reject Haass Proposals." *Guardian*, December 31, 2013. https://www.theguardian.com/uk-news/2013/dec/31/northern-ireland-talks-collapse-as-main-unionist-parties-reject-haass-proposals.

———. "700 US Companies Now Located in Ireland as Direct Investment Soars." *Guardian*, March 5, 2015. https://www.theguardian.com/world/2015/mar/05/ireland-attracts-soaring-level-of-us-investment.

McGuinness, Frank. *Observe the Sons of Ulster Marching Towards the Somme*. London: Faber, 1985.

McKinney, Seamus. "New Video to Mark 50th Anniversary of IRA Members' Deaths." *Irish News*, June 26, 2020. https://www.irishnews.com/news/northernirelandnews/2020/06/26/news/new-video-to-mark-50th-anniversary-of-ira-members-deaths-1985818/.

McKittrick, David, and David McVea. *Making Sense of the Troubles: The Story of the Conflict in Northern Ireland*. Chicago: New Amsterdam Books, 2002.

McLemore, Morris. "It's a Big Night for Mr. Stockdale." *Miami Daily News*, March 20, 1961. Presidential Papers. John F. Kennedy Presidential Library.

McLoughlin, P. J., and Alison Meagher. "The 1977 'Carter Initiative' on Northern Ireland." *Diplomatic History*, 43 (September 2019): 671–98.

McNally, Frank. "An Irishman's Diary." *Irish Times*, May 22, 2004. https://www.irishtimes.com/opinion/an-irishman-s-diary-1.1141579.

Meacham, Jon. *American Lion: Andrew Jackson in the White House*. New York: Random House, 2008.

Meyers, David. "U.S. Remains a 'Flawed Democracy' in Annual Ratings." *The Fulcrum*, February 14, 2022. https://thefulcrum.us/big-picture/Leveraging-big-ideas/flawed-democracy.

Miller, Amanda. "May 1970 Student Antiwar Strikes." *Mapping American Social Movements Through the 20th Century*. Date Retrieved: April 10, 2023. https://depts.washington.edu/moves/antiwar_may1970.shtml.

Miller, Judith. "Goldwater Vows to Fight Tactics of 'New Right'." *New York Times*, September 16, 1981. https://www.nytimes.com/1981/09/16/us/goldwater-vows-to-fight-tactics-of-new-right.html.

Miller, Kerby A. *Emigrants and Exiles: Ireland and the Irish Exodus to North America*. Oxford: Oxford University Press, 1988.

———. *Ireland and Irish America: Culture, Class, and Transatlantic Migration*. Dublin: Field Day, 2008.

Miller, Marissa. "Donald Trump's Ties Are Produced in Chinese Factories Under Horrific Conditions, According to a New Report." *Teen Vogue*, October 6, 2016. https://www.teenvogue.com/story/donald-trump-ties-chinese-factory-horrific-conditions-racked-report.

Miller, Tim. "Actually, the Orange Man Is Bad." *The Bulwark*, May 8, 2020. https://thebulwark.com/actually-the-orange-man-is-bad/.

Mitchell, George J. "John Hume: Founding Father." Foreword to Maurice Fitzpatrick, *John Hume in America: From Derry to DC*, ix–xi. South Bend: University of Notre Dame Press, 2019.

——— *Making Peace*. Updated edition. Berkeley: University of California Press, 2000.

Moore, Charles. *Margaret Thatcher: The Authorized Biography—From Grantham to the Falklands*. New York: Vintage, 2013.

Morton, Robin. "US Firms Who Love Ulster." *Belfast Telegraph*, July 8, 2008. https://www.belfasttelegraph.co.uk/Migrated_Articles/us-firms-who-love-ulster-28388350.html.

Muldoon, Paul. *Rising to the Rising*. Loughcrew: The Gallery Press, 2016.

Mulholland, Marc. *The Longest War: Northern Ireland's Troubled History*. Oxford: Oxford University Press, 2002.

Mulqueen, John. "On This Day in 1968: Richard Nixon Elected President of the United States." *IrishCentral.com*, November 5, 2022. https://www.irishcentral.com/opinion/others/richard-nixon-ireland-1970.

Murray, Mimi. "Irish Firms are Flying High in the US." *Irish Times*, November 22, 2018. https://www.irishtimes.com/special-reports/american-thanksgiving/irish-firms-are-flying-high-in-the-us-1.3702948.

Muzzio, Douglas. "When Boz Came to Town: Remembering Charles Dickens's First Visit to New York." *City Journal* (Autumn 2018). https://www.city-journal.org/charles-dickens-first-visit-to-new-york.

Nath, Saume Saptparna. "Democracy Index 2023: Understanding the Global Scenarios." *TGP: The Geopolitics*, February 25, 2023. https://thegeopolitics.com/democracy-index-2023-understanding-the-global-scenarios/.

National Advisory Commission on Civil Disorders. *The Kerner Report*. 1968. Princeton: Princeton University Press, 2016.

Neely, Bill, and Adela Suliman. "Joe Biden's Irish Ancestral Hometown, Ballina, Revels in Win as London Grows Uneasy Over Brexit." *NBC News*, November 18, 2020. https://www.nbcnews.com/news/world/joe-biden-s-irish-ancestral-hometown-ballina-revels-win-london-n1248080.

Neeson, Conor. "Clinton, Bush and Obama: US President Visits That Brought NI to a Standstill." *BBC News*, March 14, 2023. https://www.bbc.com/news/uk-northern-ireland-64949360.

Nelson, Sophia A. "Hell No, We Can't 'co-exist' with White Terrorists." *TheGrio*, January 29, 2021. www.thegrio.com.2021/01/29.no-we-can't-co-exist-white-terrorists.

Neveau, James. "27 Counties in Illinois Have Passed Referendums to Explore Seceding from the State. Here's Where." *NBC Chicago*, November 11, 2022. https://www.nbcchicago.com/news/local/chicago-politics/27-counties-in-illinois-have-passed-referendums-to-explore-seceding-from-state-heres-where/2993937/.

Nicholson, Robert. "'Irish Times' from the Archive." Letter to *The Irish Times*, June 6, 2009. https://www.irishtimes.com/opinion/letters/irish-times-from-the-archive-1.778475.

Nietzel, Michael T. "New Bill Latest Assault in Florida's War on Higher Education." *Forbes*, February 26, 2023. https://www.forbes.com/sites/michaeltnietzel/2023/02/25/new-bill-latest-assault-in-floridas-war-on-higher-education/?sh=1a0bbbe46583.

Niquette, Mark, and Gregory Korte. "GOP Casts Trump as Victim, Attacks FBI in Midterm Rally Cry." *Bloomberg*, August 9, 2022. https://www.bloomberg.com/news/articles/2022-08-09/gop-casts-trump-as-victim-attacks-fbi-in-midterm-rallying-cry.

Nixon, Richard M. "Remarks on Arrival at Shannon Airport, Ireland." October 3, 1970. The American Presidency Project, University of California Santa Barbara. https://www.presidency.ucsb.edu/documents/remarks-arrival-shannon-airport-ireland.

Nordheimer, Jon. "5 Killed in London as Bomb Explodes Outside Harrods." *New York Times*, December 18, 1983. https://www.nytimes.com/1983/12/18/world/5-killed-in-london-as-bomb-explodes-outside-harrods.html.

"Northern Ireland: Richard Haass talks end without deal." *BBC News*, December 31, 2013. https://www.bbc.com/news/uk-northern-ireland-25556714.

Obert, Julia C. *The Making and Unmaking of Colonial Cities: Urban Planning, Imperial Power, and the Improvisational Itineraries of the Poor*. New York: Oxford University Press, 2023.

——— "Troubles Literature and the End of the Troubles." In *Irish Literature in Transition, 1980–2020*, edited by Eric Falci and Paige Reynolds, 65–80. Cambridge: Cambridge University Press, 2020.

O'Brien, Matthew J. "Irish America, Race, and Bernadette Devlin's 1969 American Tour." *New Hibernia Review*, 14.2 (2010): 84–101.

O'Brien, Shane. "JFK's 1945 Article on De Valera and Reuniting Ireland." *IrishCentral*, July 29, 2020. https://www.irishcentral.com/roots/history/jfk-1945-article-de-valera-ireland.

O'Casey, Sean. *The Complete Plays of Sean O'Casey*. 5 vols. London: Macmillan, 1984.

O'Clery, Conor. *Daring Diplomacy: Clinton's Secret Search for Peace in Ireland*. Boulder, CO: Roberts Rinehart, 1997.

——— "Haass to Be Made Bush's Envoy to Northern Ireland." *Irish Times*, June 12, 2003. https://www.irishtimes.com/news/haass-to-be-made-bush-s-envoy-to-northern-ireland-1.362244.

——— "Reagan in the White House Leaned on Thatcher to Reach Historic Agreement." *Irish Times*, November 6, 2015. https://www.irishtimes.com/news/politics/reagan-in-the-white-house-leaned-on-thatcher-to-reach-historic-agreement-1.2429317.

O Connor, Fionnuala. "Leader of SDLP Who Fought for Peace." Special Tribute Supplement. *Irish Times*, August 8, 2020, 6.

O'Connor, Thomas H. *Boston Catholics: A History of the Church and Its People*. Boston: Northeastern University Press, 1998.

O'Donovan, Brian. "Forty Years of 'Friends of Ireland' on Capitol Hill." RTÉ, March 14, 2021. https://www.rte.ie/news/analysis-and-comment/2021/0314/1203853-ireland-friends-capitol/.

O'Dowd, Niall. "Carter and Thatcher Clashed Strongly Over US Ban on Guns to RUC." *IrishCentral*, February 22, 2023. https://www.irishcentral.com/opinion/niallodowd/jimmy-carter-margaret-thatcher.

——— *Lincoln and the Irish: The Untold Story of How the Irish Helped Abraham Lincoln Save the Union*. New York: Skyhorse, 2018.

——— "On This Day: Bill Clinton's Historic Visit to Northern Ireland." *IrishCentral*, November 30, 2015. https://www.irishcentral.com/opinion/niallodowd/the-peacemaker-bill-clintons-historic-visit-ireland.

——— "A Staggering Blow for Ireland." *IrishCentral*, August 26, 2009. https://www.irishcentral.com/news/loss-of-irreplacable-kennedy-a-staggering-blow-for-ireland-55075617-2376566.

O'Driscoll, Dennis. *Stepping Stones: Interviews with Seamus Heaney.* New York: Farrar, Straus and Giroux, 2008.

Ó Faoleán, Gearóid. "The Ulster Defence Regiment and the Question of Catholic Recruitment, 1970–1972." *Terrorism and Political Violence*, 27.5 (2015): 838–56. Pub. online 2014.

O'Hearn, Denis. *Bobby Sands: Nothing but an Unfinished Song.* London/Dublin: Pluto, 2010.

O'Loughlin, Ed. "Ireland Readies a Warm Welcome for Biden, the 'Most Irish' President Since J.F.K." *New York Times*, April 9, 2023. https://www.nytimes.com/2023/04/09/world/europe/biden-ireland-visit.html.

Onkey, Lauren. *Blackness and Transatlantic Irish Identity: Irish Soul Brothers.* New York: Routledge, 2010.

O'Rawe, Richard. *Blanketmen: An untold story of the H–Block hunger strike.* Dublin: New Island, 2005.

Orwell, George. *1984.* New York: RosettaBooks, 2002. First published 1949.

Osnos, Evan. *Joe Biden: The Life, the Run, and What Matters Now.* New York: Scribner, 2020.

O'Toole, Fintan. "Beware Prophecies of Civil War." *The Atlantic*, December 16, 2021. https://www.theatlantic.com/magazine/archive/2022/01/america-civil-war-prophecies/620850/.

———. "Donald Trump Has Destroyed the Country He Promised to Make Great Again." *Irish Times*, April 25, 2020. https://johnmenadue.com/fintan-otoole-donald-trump-has-destroyed.

———. "The Trump Inheritance." *New York Review*, February 25, 2021. https://www.nybooks.com/articles/2021/02/25/trump-inheritance/.

———. *We Don't Know Ourselves: A Personal History of Modern Ireland.* New York: Liveright, 2021.

Palmer, Ewan. "Oath Keeper Stewart Rhodes Spent $33K on Guns, Equipment while Plotting Sedition: DOJ." *Newsweek*, January 14, 2022. https://www.newsweek.com/oath-keeper-stewart-rhodes-sedition-jan-6-doj-capitol-riots-1669367.

Paquette, Danielle. "A Mich. Library Refused to Remove an LGBTQ Book. The Town Defunded It." *Washington Post*, August 24, 2022. https://www.washingtonpost.com/nation/2022/08/24/michigan-library-defunded-gender-queer/.

Patterson, Glenn. *Backstop Land.* London: Head of Zeus, 2019.

———. *Here's Me Here: Further Reflections of a Lapsed Protestant.* Dublin: New Island Books, 2015.

Paybarah, Azi. "Trump Calling Opponents 'vermin' Draws Rebukes from White House, Some in GOP." *Washington Post*, November 13, 2023. https://www.washingtonpost.com/politics/2023/11/13/white-house-biden-trump-vermin/.

Pellish, Aaron, and Marshall Cohen. "Republican Congressman Presents Convicted January 6 Rioter with Flag Flown Over US Capitol after Her Release from Prison." *CNN.com*, September 11, 2022. https://www.cnn.com/2022/09/10/politics/louie-gohmert-january-6-simone-gold/index.html.

Pengelly, Martin. "Florida Schools Plan to Use Only Excerpts from Shakespeare to Avoid 'Raunchiness'." *Guardian*, August 8, 2023. https://www.theguardian.com/us-news/2023/aug/08/florida-schools-shakespeare-sexual-material.

———. "Top Senator Mitch McConnell Endorses Trump for President Despite Acrimony." *Guardian*, March 6, 2024. https://www.theguardian.com/us-news/2024/mar/06/mitch-mcconnell-endorses-trump.

Perlstein, Rick. "How the 1964 Republican Convention Sparked a Revolution from the Right." *Smithsonian Magazine,* August 2008. https://www.smithsonianmag.com/history/1964-republican-convention-revolution-from-the-right-915921/.

Phoenix, Éamon. "State Papers: Last-ditch Effort to Stop Adams' US Visa Revealed." *BBC News,* December 28, 2018. https://www.bbc.com/news/uk-northern-ireland-46621642.

Pogatchnik, Shawn. "Police Outnumber Fans as Donald Trump Lands in Ireland." *Politico,* May 4, 2023. https://www.politico.eu/article/joe-biden-donald-trump-us-police-outnumber-fans-ireland/.

"President Trump's Historic Deregulation Is Benefitting All Americans," *White House Archives,* October 21, 2019. https://trumpwhitehouse.archives.gov/briefings-statements/president-trumps-historic-deregulation-benefitting-americans/.

"Prince Charles Denounces IRA Bombing." *UPI Archives,* December 19, 1983. https://www.upi.com/Archives/1983/12/19/Prince-Charles-denounces-IRA-bombing/8509440658000/.

"Reagan feared Irish roots would damage his career." *Independent.ie.* October 24, 2004. https://www.independent.ie/irish-news/reagan-feared-irish-roots-would-damage-his-career-26225824.html.

Reagan, Ronald. "Address at Commencement Exercise at the University of Notre Dame." May 17, 1981. Ronald Reagan Presidential Library.

——— "Address Before a Joint Session of the Irish National Parliament, Dublin, Ireland." June 4, 1984. Ronald Reagan Presidential Library.

——— "President Reagan in Ballyporeen, Ireland, on June 3, 1984." June 3, 1984. Ronald Reagan Presidential Library.

——— "President Reagan's Remarks at a Dinner Honoring Speaker of the House Tip O'Neill." March 17, 1986. Ronald Reagan Presidential Library.

——— "Remarks on St. Patrick's Day at the Irish Embassy." March 17, 1983. Ronald Reagan Presidential Library.

——— "Remarks on the United Kingdom-Ireland Agreement Concerning Northern Ireland." November 15, 1985. Ronald Reagan Presidential Library.

Reimann, Nicholas. "Here are the Groups Who Don't Want a Vaccine—and Trump Supporters are Near Top." *Forbes,* March 11, 2021. https://www.forbes.com/sites/nicholasreimann/2021/03/11/here-are-the-groups-who-dont-want-a-vaccine-and-trump-voters-are-near-top/.

Renfro, Paul M. "War Has Been the Governing Metaphor for Decades of American Life. This Pandemic Exposes Its Weakness." *Time,* April 15, 2020. https://time.com/5821430/history-war-language/.

Reynolds, Paige, *Modernism, Drama, and the Audience for Irish Spectacle.* Cambridge: Cambridge University Press, 2007.

——— ed. *The New Irish Studies.* Cambridge: Cambridge University Press, 2020.

Rich, Spencer. "Irish Protestant Militant Granted U.S. Visa." *Washington Post,* July 17, 1983. https://www.washingtonpost.com/archive/politics/1983/07/17/irish-protestant-militant-granted-us-visa/81278f0d-7b32-4e0d-83cc-684695a9060d/.

Richards, Shaun. "'A Solution to the Present Crisis'? Seamus Heaney's *The Cure at Troy.*" *Études Irlandaises,* 20. 2 (1995): 77–85.

Richtarik, Marilynn. *Getting to Good Friday: Literature and the Peace Process in Northern Ireland.* Oxford: Oxford University Press, 2023.

——— "Hume, Heaney, Harvard—and Peace in Northern Ireland." *Harvard Magazine,* April 3, 2023. https://www.harvardmagazine.com/2023/04/hume-heaney-harvard-and-peace-in-northern-ireland.

Ricoeur, Paul. *Memory, History, Forgetting*. Translated by Kathleen Blamey and David Pellauer. Chicago: University of Chicago Press, 2004.

"Rise in number of US companies operating in Ireland." RTÉ, March 7, 2022. https://www.rte.ie/news/business/2022/0307/1284917-rise-in-number-of-us-companies-operating-in-ireland/.

Rivers, Caryl. "POV: Comparing Trump to Hitler Misses the Point." *BU Today*, February 16, 2016. https://www.bu.edu/articles/2016/comparing-donald-trump-to-hitler.

Ross, Jamie. "Brexit Brits Freak Out at 'Senile' Biden After He Wades Into Boris Johnson's Sausage War." *Daily Beast*, June 10, 2021. https://www.thedailybeast.com/brexit-brits-freak-out-at-senile-biden-after-he-wades-into-boris-johnsons-sausage-war.

Roush, Ty. "Donald Trump Releases 'Mugshot Edition' Digital Trading Cards—Offers Pieces of Suits From Fulton County Arrest." *Forbes*, December 12, 2023. https://www.msn.com/en-us/money/news/donald-trump-releases-mugshot-edition-digital-trading-cards-offers-pieces-of-suit-from-fulton-county-arrest/ar-AA1loKZV.

Rovere, Richard H. "John F. Kennedy's Ambiguous Victory." *The New Yorker*, November 11, 1960. https://www.newyorker.com/magazine/1960/11/19/letter-from-washington-john-f-kennedys-ambiguous-victory.

Rowland, Neil, Duncan McVicar and Ian Shuttleworth. "The Evolution of Catholic/Protestant Unemployment Inequality in Northern Ireland, 1983–2016." *Population, Space and Place*, 28.4 (2021): 1–16.

Rozsa, Matthew. 'Malignant normality: The psychological theory that explains naked emperors, narcissists and Nazis." *Salon*, August 12, 2021. https://www.salon.com/2021/08/12/malignant-normality-the-psychological-theory-that-explains-naked-emperors-narcissists-and-nazis/.

Rubin, Olivia, Alexander Mallin and Alex Hosenball. "'Because President Trump Said to': Over a Dozen Capitol Rioters Say They were Following Trump's Guidance." *ABC News*, February 9, 2021. https://abcnews.go.com/US/president-trump-dozen-capitol-rioters-trumps-guidance/story?id=75757601.

Russell, Richard Rankin. *Poetry and Peace: Michael Longley, Seamus Heaney, and Northern Ireland*. South Bend and London: University of Notre Dame Press, 2010.

Sablik, Tim. "Recession of 1981–82." *Federal Reserve History*, November 22, 2013. https://www.federalreservehistory.org/essays/recession-of-1981-82.

Sachs, Jeffrey D. "Blood in the Sand." *Project Syndicate*, August 17, 2021. https://www.jeffsachs.org/newspaper-articles/93p6b2pk77y2fdfcgxtsd6p5k9xdfs.

Saint-Amour, Paul K. *Tense Future: Modernism, Total War, Encyclopedic Form*. New York: Oxford University Press, 2015.

Samuel, Raphael. "Mrs. Thatcher's Return to Victorian Values." Special issue on Victorian Values. *Proceedings of the British Academy*, 78 (1992): 9–29.

Sanders, Andrew. "Landing Rights in Dublin: Relations between Ireland and the United States 1945–72." *Irish Studies in International Affairs*, 28 (2017): 147–71.

———. *The Long Peace Process: The United States of America and Northern Ireland, 1960–2008*. Liverpool: Liverpool University Press, 2019.

Sands, Bobby. *Writings from Prison*. Dublin: Mercier Press, 1998. First published 1983.

Santucci, Jeanine. "Donald Trump Mispronounces 'Yosemite' at White House Event." *USA Today*, August 4, 2020. https://www.usatoday.com/story/news/politics/2020/08/04/trump-mispronounces-yosemite-white-house-event/3289122001/.

REFERENCES

Sargent, Greg. "Mitch McConnell Is Laughing in Your Faces." *Washington Post*, June 2, 2021. https://www.washingtonpost.com/opinions/2021/06/02/mitch-mcconnell-is-laughing-your-face/.

Schatzman, G. K. "Review: *The Cure at Troy* at Quintessence Theater." *Broadway World*, February 6, 2022. https://www.broadwayworld.com/philadelphia/article/Review-The-Cure-at-Troy-at-Quintessence-Theater-20220206.

Schlesinger, Jr., Arthur M. *A Thousand Days: John F. Kennedy in the White House*. 1965. Boston: Houghton Mifflin, 2002.

Schorr, Isaac. "Enough of 'Orange Man Bad'." *National Review*, September 18, 2020. https://www.nationalreview.com/2020/09/enough-of-orange-man-bad/.

Scull, Maggie. "Timeline of 1981 Hunger Strike." *Irish Times*, March 1, 2016. https://www.irishtimes.com/culture/books/timeline-of-1981-hunger-strike-1.2555682.

Sennott, Charles M. "Northern Ireland's Troubled Peace." *The Atlantic*, May 6, 2023. https://www.theatlantic.com/international/archive/2023/05/northern-ireland-unrest-paramilitary-ira-good-friday-agreement/673969/.

Shannon, Jennifer Bray. "'Very Pleasant' Donald Trump Plans to Return to Ireland, Breen Says." *Irish Times*, June 5, 2019. https://www.irishtimes.com/news/ireland/irish-news/very-pleasant-donald-trump-plans-to-return-to-ireland-breen-says-1.3915949.

Sharkey, Jim. "What Can Ireland Expect from Joe Biden?" *Irish Times*, January 20, 2021. https://www.irishtimes.com/opinion/what-can-ireland-expect-from-joe-biden-1.4462417.

Shaw, Bernard. *Complete Plays with Prefaces [CPP]*. 6 vols. New York: Dodd, Mead, 1963.

——— *Sixteen Self Sketches*. London: Constable, 1949.

Shesol, Jeff. "'Reagan: The Life,' by H.W. Brands." *New York Times*, June 1, 2015. https://www.nytimes.com/2015/06/07/books/review/reagan-the-life-by-h-w-brands.html.

Siegel, Robert. "Ian Paisley Was 'Powerful in the Pulpit' and On Political Platforms." *All Things Considered*, NPR, September 12, 2014. https://www.npr.org/2014/09/12/348010233/ian-paisley-was-powerful-in-the-pulpit-and-on-political-platforms.

Siemaszko, Corky. "Florida Court Says Teen is Not 'Mature' Enough to Have An Abortion." *NBC News.com*, August 16, 2022. https://www.nbcnews.com/news/us-news/florida-court-says-teen-not-mature-enough-abortion-rcna43344.

Smith, Eoghan and Simon Workman. "Introduction: The rise of the phoenix: restoration and renaissance in contemporary Irish writing." *Irish Studies Review* 31.3 (August 2023): 325–330.

Smyth, Patrick. "Bush Stresses the Need for Decommissioning." *Irish Times*, August 3, 2001. https://www.irishtimes.com/news/bush-stresses-the-need-for-decommissioning-1.320866.

Sophocles. *Philoctetes*. In *Electra and Other Plays*. Translated and edited by David Raeburn, 191–256. London: Penguin, 2008.

Spector, Jesse. "Horrible Turtle Man Mitch McConnell Has Never Done a Damn Thing Worth Being Proud of." *Deadspin*, October 27, 2020. https://deadspin.com/horrible-turtle-man-mitch-mcconnell-has-never-done-a-da-1845496265.

"The Spirit of Drumcree Evaporates and History Leaves Paisley Behind." *Irish Times*, July 18, 1998. https://www.irishtimes.com/news/the-spirit-of-drumcree-evaporates-and-history-leaves-paisley-behind-1.174466.

Staines, Michael. "'Always Back the People Who Back You'—Doonbeg Residents Voice Trump support." *Newstalk*, November 3, 2020. https://www.newstalk.com/news/doonbeg-donald-trump-support-1100108.

Stockdale, Grant. Letters to Evelyn Lincoln. John F. Kennedy's Presidential Papers. President's Office Files. Special Correspondence. Stockdale, Grant, February 1959–June 1963. John F. Kennedy Presidential Library.

Suliman, Adela, and Timothy Bella. "GOP Rep. Boebert: 'I'm Tired of This Separation of Church and State Junk'." *Washington Post*, June 28, 2022. https://www.washingtonpost.com/politics/2022/06/28/lauren-boebert-church-state-colorado/.

Svirnovskly, Gregory. "Gosar, GOP Allies Call for Abolishing the FBI in Response to Mar–a–Lago Search." *Arizona Republic*, August 9, 2022. https://news.yahoo.com/gosar-gop-allies-call-abolishing-001718891.html?fr=yhssrp_catchall.

Synge, John Millington. *The Aran Islands*. London: Penguin, 1992. First published 1901.

Tangalakis-Lippert, Katherine. "Despite Being Out of Office for a Year and a Half, Donald Trump Said 'weirdo' Mark Zuckerberg Joined Him at the White House for Dinner 'last week'." *Business Insider Africa*, September 3, 2022. https://africa.businessinsider.com/politics/despite-being-out-of-office-for-a-year-and-a-half-donald-trump-said-weirdo mark/tgb2mhz.

Taylor, Miles. *Blowback: A Warning to Save Democracy from the Next Trump*. New York: Atria Books, 2023.

Taylor, Paul. "Bob Jones Jr. Calls Haig a 'Monster'." *Washington Post*, April 3, 1982. https://www.washingtonpost.com/archive/lifestyle/1982/04/03/bob-jones-jr-calls-haig-a-monster/47372abc-c4c8-437f-9e9b-7bb0515c867a/.

Taylor, Tess. "We are Going to Have a President Who Quotes Poetry." *CNN Opinion*, November 11, 2020. www.cnn.com/2020/11/11/opinions/joe-biden-values-poetry-taylor/index.html.

Thatcher, Margaret. *The Downing Street Years*. New York: HarperCollins, 1993.

Thompson, Neal. *The First Kennedys: The Humble Roots of an American Dynasty*. Boston/New York: Mariner Books, 2022.

Thorndike, Joseph J. "Reagan's Tax Cuts Just Turned 40—And It's Still The Most Important Tax Reform Since World War II." *Forbes*, September 3, 2021. https://www.forbes.com/sites/taxnotes/2021/09/03/reagans-tax-cut-just-turned-40-and-its-still-the-most-important-tax-reform-since-world-war-ii/?sh=40e7809c5d14.

Tóibín, Colm. *Brooklyn*. New York: Scribner, 2009.

"Tony Blair warned Northern Ireland Peace Talks Would 'lose all credibility' Without Progress." *itvNews*, December 30, 2022. https://www.itv.com/news/utv/2022-12-30/blair-warned-peace-talks-would-lose-all-credibility-without-progress.

"Tourist Traffic Bill, 1970: Second Stage." Seanad Éireann debate—Thursday, July 30, 1970. Tithe an Oireachtais/Houses of the Oireachtas. https://www.oireachtas.ie/en/debates/debate/seanad/1970-07-30/6/.

Treble, Patricia. "The G7 Group Shot, Where Donald Trump Can't Hide from His Height." *Macleans*, August 26, 2019. https://www.macleans.ca/news/world/the-g7-group-shot-where-donald-trump-cant-hide-from-his-height/.

Trevithick, Joseph. "'Air Force One' 747s Now Cost $177K an Hour to Fly." *The War Zone*, April 5, 2022. https://www.twz.com/45066/here-is-what-the-vc-25a-air-force-one-jets-now-cost-per-hour-to-fly.

Tubridy, Ryan. *JFK in Ireland: Four Days that Changed a President*. Guilford: Lyons, 2010.

United States Bureau of Economic Analysis [St. Louis Federal Reserve]. "The American Economy in 1964," January 1965. https://fraser.stlouisfed.org/files/docs/publications/SCB/pages/1965-1969/8106_1965-1969.

Updegrove, Mark K. *Incomparable Grace: JFK in the Presidency*. New York: Dutton, 2022.

"U.S. Cancels Visa of Ulster Activist." *New York Times*, December 22, 1981. https://www.nytimes.com/1981/12/22/world/us-cancels-visa-of-ulster-activist.html.

REFERENCES

"US Envoy in Early 1990s Whose Nomination Caused Controversy." *Irish Times*, January 14, 2006. https://www.irishtimes.com/news/us-envoy-in-early-1990s-whose-nomination-caused-controversy-1.1001948.

Vendler, Helen. *The Music of What Happens: Poems, Poets, Critics*. Cambridge: Harvard University Press, 1988.

——— "A Nobel for the North." *The New Yorker*, October 23, 1995. 84–89.

——— *Seamus Heaney*. Cambridge: Harvard University Press, 1998.

Volmert, Isabella. "North Texas Real Estate Agent Pleads Guilty to Federal Charge in Capitol Riot." *Dallas Morning News*, August 19, 2022. https://www.dallasnews.com/news/courts/2022/08/19/north-texas-real-estate-agent-pleads-guilty-to-federal-charge-in-capitol-riot/.

Wade, Peter. "Trump's Ireland Golf Course Visit Cost Taxpayers $3.6 Million." *Rolling Stone*, June 8, 2019. https://www.rollingstone.com/politics/politics-news/trumps-ireland-golf-course-3-6-million-846009/.

Wald, Matthew L. "U.S. Suspends Deportation in I.R.A. Cases." *New York Times*, September 10, 1997. https://www.nytimes.com/1997/09/10/nyregion/us-suspends-deportation-in-ira-cases.html.

Wall, Martin. "Ireland and the United States 1973–5: New Dynamics in the Transatlantic Relationship." *Irish Studies in International Affairs*, 21 (2010): 123–47.

Washington, Michaela Kufner. "U.S. Creates New Antisemitism Task Force." *DW*, March 2, 2023. https://www.dw.com/en/us-creates-new-antisemitism-task-force/a-64863454.

Watt, Stephen. *"Something Dreadful and Grand": American Literature and the Irish-Jewish Unconscious*. New York: Oxford University Press, 2015.

Weaver, Amy E. "The Ronald Reagan Pub Comes to America." *American Heritage*, 57.1 (February/March 2006). https://www.americanheritage.com/ronald-reagan-pub-comes-america.

Webb, James. *Born Fighting: How the Scots-Irish Shaped America*. New York: Broadway Books, 2004.

Wehner, Peter. "Now They're Calling for Violence." *The Atlantic*, August 11, 2022. https://www.scribd.com/article/586525601/Now-They-re-Calling-For-Violence.

Weiner, Jennifer. "'What's Your Favorite Book?' Is Not a Trick Question." *New York Times*, April 11, 2019. www.nytimes.com/2019/04/11/opinion/favorite-books-romance-politics.html.

Weinraub, Bernard. "Belfast Soured and Exhausted by Constant Violence." *New York Times*, October 14, 1972. https://www.nytimes.com/1972/10/14/archives/belfast-soured-and-exhausted-by-constant-violence.html.

——— "Catholic Protesters Flock to March in Tense Newry." *New York Times*, February 6, 1972. https://www.nytimes.com/1972/02/06/archives/catholic-protesters-flock-to-march-in-tense-newry-catholics-flock.html.

——— "More than 1,500 Killed in the Last Seven Years." *New York Times*, July 25, 1976. https://www.nytimes.com/1976/07/25/archives/more-than-1500-killed-in-the-last-seven-years-the-violence-in.html.

——— "30 Held in North Ireland as Parades Stir Violence." *New York Times*, March 30, 1970. https://www.nytimes.com/1970/03/30/archives/30-held-in-north-ireland-as-parades-stir-violence.html.

Westenfeld, Adrienne. "Lord Louis Mountbatten's Assassination Shaped Prince Charles's Life and the Future of The Crown." *Esquire*, November 15, 2020. https://www.esquire.com/entertainment/tv/a34659147/lord-mountbatten-assassination-death-the-crown-season-4-true-story/.

Wheatley, Leesa, and Florian Krobb, eds. "Introduction" to Richard Arnold Bermann, *Ireland [1913]*, 1–24. Cork: Cork University Press, 2021.

Whelan, Gerard, with Carolyn Swift. *Spiked: Church-State Intrigue and The Rose Tattoo.* Dublin: New Island, 2002.

"Why America is a 'flawed democracy'." *Economist*, March 21, 2024. https://www.economist.com/graphic-detail/2024/03/21/why-america-is-a-flawed-democracy.

Willman, Skip. "The Kennedys, Fleming, and Cuba: Bond's Foreign Policy." In *Ian Fleming and James Bond: The Cultural Politics of 007*, edited by Edward P. Comentale, Stephen Watt and Willman, 178–201. Bloomington: Indiana University Press, 2005.

Wilson, Andrew J. "'Doing the Business': Aspects of the Clinton Administration's Economic Support for the Northern Ireland Peace Process, 1994–2000." *The Journal of Conflict Studies* 23.1 (2003): 155–76.

——— *Irish America and the Ulster Conflict, 1968–1995*. Washington, D.C./Galway: The Catholic University of America Press/Blackstaff, 1995.

Wilson, Reid. "Trump's 2020 Gains in Rural America Offset by Biden's Urban Dominance." *The Hill*, September 14, 2021. https://thehill.com/homenews/state-watch/571792-trumps-2020-gains-in-rural-america-offset-by-bidens-urban-dominance/.

Wilson, Robert McLiam. *Eureka Street*. New York: Ballantine Books, 1996.

Wise, Lindsay. "McConnell Says '100%' of His Focus Is on Blocking Biden Agenda." *The Wall Street Journal*, May 5, 2021. https://www.marketwatch.com/story/mitch-mcconnell-says-100-of-my-focus-is-standing-up-to-the-biden-administration-11620306510.

Witcover, Jules. *Joe Biden: A Life of Trial and Redemption*. New York: HarperCollins, 2010.

Woolf, Virginia. *Mrs. Dalloway*. Orlando, FL: Harcourt, 2005. First published 1925.

Young, James S. "Interview with John Hume." The Miller Center Foundation and the Edward M. Kennedy Institute for the United States Senate, 2016. https://www.emkinstitute.org/resources/john-hume.

Zuelow, Eric G. E. "'Ingredients for Cooperation': Irish Tourism in North–South Relations, 1924–1998." *New Hibernia Review*, 10 (Spring 2006): 17–39.

INDEX

Adams, Gerry 36, 52, 58, 113, 115–18, 122, 162
African Americans and Northern Irish Catholics, comparisons between 10–12, 51, 52–53
Ahern, Bertie 115
Air travel, disputes over 74–75
Alberta, Tim 32, 45
Aldous, Richard 20, 21, 25, 30n13
Alexander, Ella 69, 82n14
American and multinational investment in Ireland 68, 76–78, 89
American Committee for Ulster Justice (ACUJ) 70
American Congress for Irish Freedom (ACIF) 70
Anbinder, Tyler 8, 30n8
Anderson, Benedict 127, 129, 130
Anglo-Irish Agreement 78, 103, 106–9, 166
Apple, R.W., Jr. 18, 77
Applebaum, Anne 142, 152
Aquinas, Thomas 45, 181
Arendt, Hannah 177, 179
Armstrong, Robert 107, 108
Armus, Teo 159n11
Atkins, Humphrey 108
Auden, W.H. 140, 149
  "Another Time" 140
  "As I Walked Out One Evening" 139–140, 151
Austerlitz, Saul 68
authoritarian populism 40–44, 94, 135, 183

Baker, Jim 20
Baker, Susan 20
Balz, Dan, and Clara Ence Morse 136, 159n6
Battersby, Eileen 139
Behan, Brendan 12, 21, 23, 30n14, 101
Belfast (Good Friday) Agreement 2, 35, 57–58, 80, 85, 91, 114–19, 145, 155, 158, 161–63, 167, 169, 186
Bell, J. Bowyer 167
Ben-Ghiat, Ruth 172
Beresford, David 80, 102, 104, 105
Bergson, Henri 142
Berry, Wendell 47
Bew, Paul, et al. 82n21, 94, 96, 97, 182
Biaggi, Mario 106
Biden, Jill 136
Biden, Joseph "Beau" 154
Biden, Joseph R. xvi, xviii, 2, 3, 32, 45, 50, 56, 76, 83, 88, 110, 113, 123, 124n6, 130, 135–37, 153, 155–58, 163, 167, 168, 176, 177, 186
  and Brexit 84, 85, 111
  and the Friends of Ireland 111, 158
  and Irish identity xviii, 138, 154, 157–58
  and Northern Ireland 84–85, 158
  and reading xviii, 136, 138
Bixby, Ashleigh 63, 81n10
Blair, Tony 114, 115, 121
Bleaney, Michael 41, 44
Blight, David W. 12, 14, 52
Bloch, Ernst 140
"Bloody Sunday" (Derry) 38, 39, 54, 81, 99, 181

"Bloody Sunday" (Selma) 69
Bob Jones University (*see* Christian colleges and universities)
Bob Jones University Press (*see* Christian colleges and universities)
Boebert, Lauren 33, 41, 46, 177, 178
Boland, Eavan (*see* "Famine Road" (Boland))
Bolger, Dermot (*see Tanglewood* (Bolger))
bombs 40, 71–73, 98–99, 106–07, 116–117
Bongino, Dan 134
Booth, Cathy 18, 84
Bornstein, George 5, 6
Brabourne, Lady Doreen 98
Bradley, John 61
Brady, James 21
Breen, Pat 86, 115
Brexit and Northern Ireland Protocol 84, 157
Brezhnev, Leonid 113
Brooklyn (Tóibín) 4, 176
Brooks, Morris "Mo" 168, 172
Brown, Ron 114
Bruton, John 113
Bryan, Dominic xiv, 168–70
Bryant, Nick xiv, xvii, 128
Brzezinski, Mika 171
Buckley, William F. 66–67
Bulik, Mark 10
Burns, Anna xiv, 144, 174
  Milkman xiv, 143, 144, 153, 155, 174
  No Bones 131, 132
Bush, George H.W. 55, 120, 121
Bush, George W. 58, 111, 112, 118–20, 122, 123, 136, 162
Butterworth, Jez 184
Buttigieg, Pete 137, 138
Byrne, Gabriel 86, 133, 134, 158n1

Callaghan, Jim 79
Cameron Report, the 185
Campaign for Social Justice (Northern Ireland) 51
Campos-Duffy, Rachel 159n3
Carey, Hugh 21, 70
Carroll, Rory 57, 82n16, 94, 99, 128
Carson, Sir Edward 96, 166
Carter, Jimmy xviii, 2, 20, 45, 47, 57, 73, 78–80, 95, 113, 118
  the Carter Doctrine 82n19
  the Carter Initiative 79–80
  the Moral Majority's opposition to 45
Caruth, Cathy 142
Chaffetz, Jason 134
Chaffin, Tom 13, 14, 30n12
Cheney, Liz 36, 149, 189
Christian colleges and universities
  Bob Jones University 45, 104–5, 164–65
  Bob Jones University Press 164
  Hillsdale College 164
  Liberty University 45
  Regent University 42
Christopher, Warren 117
Cillizza, Chris 124n5
Clancy, Mary Alice C. 107, 120, 121
Clarity, James F. 116, 124n9, 170
Clark, Dennis 9, 10, 30n8
Clark, Patrick 181
climatic censorship 35–40, 149
Clinton, Bill xiv, xviii, 2, 26, 50, 58, 76, 81n5, 83, 85, 110, 111–14, 117–23, 141, 153, 158
Clinton, Hillary 3, 50, 123
Clyde, Andrew 177, 178
Cochrane, Feargal 55
Coles, John 108
Collins, Robert 51, 70, 81n7, 97
Commitments, The (Doyle) 53
Conway, George 171
Coogan, Tim Pat 12
Cooke, Dennis 166, 167, 172
Cooper, James 67, 78, 97, 104, 110, 111
Corcoran, Paul 135, 140
Corcoran, Richard 42
Cornyn, John 32, 33, 36
Cosgrave, Liam 67
Costello, John A. 55
Cranley, Ellen 86, 87
Crenshaw, Dan 32, 33, 36
Crowd, The (Le Bon) 22, 169
Crowley, Monica 178

INDEX

Cupp, S.E. xiv
Cyprus Avenue (Ireland) 141

Dahlberg, Edward 30n7
Daley, Richard 67
Dallek, Robert 18, 22, 26–28
Dallison, Paul 157
Daly, Augustin 6–8
   A Flash of Lightning 1, 3–4, 6–7, 8, 15, 22, 29n3, 29n4
   Leah, the Forsaken 6, 29n4
   Under the Gaslight 6
Daly, Mary E. 59–61, 186
Dáte, S. V. 86, 87
Davis, Angela 67
Davis, Mike 71–73
De Bréadún, Deaglán 79, 124n3
de Burca, Máirín 74
de Chastelain, John 186
de Valera, Éamon 17, 25–27, 29, 57, 81n9
De Vos, Betsy 88
Deaver, Michael 103
Deignan, Tom 67
Delaney, Enda 59
Democratic Unionist Party (DUP) 25, 104, 108, 119, 124n1, 161, 166
   and obstruction of the Belfast Agreement 85, 114, 162
   and violence 162
Dempsey, Branagh 82n18
DeSantis, Ron 41, 159n9, 179, 180
Dessem, Matthew 134, 159n3
Devlin, Anne 174
   Ourselves Alone 184
Devlin, Bernadette 54, 58, 62, 67, 69, 71, 81n4, 82n13, 82n15
   appearances on American television 66–67
   "A Peasant in the Halls of the Great" 81n4
   The Price of My Soul 69, 82n12
   tours of America 69
Dickens, Charles 9, 43, 94
Dinkins, David 116
Dinnerstein, Leonard, and David M. Reimers xvi, 29n1

Dixon, Paul 122
Dodd, Chris 177
Doherty, Kieran 103, 104
Donlon, Seán 20, 79, 103
Donoghue, Denis 144
Dooley, Brian 51, 52
Douglass, Frederick 11, 13–15, 19, 52, 88
   and the civil war 12
   and the "Irish Analogy" 14, 15
   trip to Ireland 14
Dowd, Maureen 44–46
Downing, John 103
Doyle, Roddy (*see Commitments, The* (Doyle))
D'Souza, Dinesh 178
Dumbrell, John 53, 54, 81n5, 119, 123

Eagleton, Terry 149
Easter 1916 and historical memory 128, 143, 184
Eco, Umberto 165, 167
Egan, Timothy 2, 9, 10, 30n5
Engels, Friedrich 43
Eisenhower, Dwight D. 26, 57
Eisenhower, Milton 48
Emmer, Tom 33
emigration and immigration, during the Irish Famine 2, 3, 5–8, 10, 29n1, 30n8, 157 (*see also* Famine-era immigrants)
   in postwar Ireland 59, 89
empathy 133, 135, 136, 138
Engels, Friedrich 43
Evans, Gwynfor (*see* hunger strikes)

Falwell, Jerry, Jr. 45
Falwell, Jerry, Sr. 45, 46, 50, 81n2
Famine-era immigrants 2, 4, 5, 8, 29n1, 30n8
   discrimination against 10, 12, 13
   hazardous work and squalid tenements of 4, 8, 10
   riots against in Philadelphia and Louisville 10
"The Famine Road" (Boland) 13
Fanning, Charles 30n7

Farage, Nigel 157, 158
Farrell, James T. 8, 30n7
Farrell, Michael 52, 68, 82n13
Faulkner, Brian 70
Faulks, Sebastian 161
Fenton, Laurence 13, 30n12
Ferriter, Diarmaid 154, 170, 173
Ferryman, The (Butterworth) 184
Field Day Theatre Company 145
Filipovic, Jill 174
Fitsanakis, Joseph 95
FitzGerald, Garret 58, 103, 104, 106
Fitzgerald, Maurice 55
Fitzgerald, Thomas (Rose Kennedy's grandfather) 4, 7
FitzGerald, William H.G. 55
flags and banners xiii–xiv, 34, 119, 143, 184
Flanagan, Eimear 85
flawed democracy and gerrymandering in America 136, 159n5, 186
  rule of the minority 136
Fleming, Ian 138, 159n10, 161, 167
  Casino Royale 167
  Dr. No 161–68, 170, 189
  From Russia with Love 23, 138
  Goldfinger 165
  The Man with the Golden Gun 165
  Thunderball 165
Foot, Michael 100
Ford, David 119
Ford, Gerald xviii, 45, 67
"Four Horsemen," the 21, 78, 79, 106
  (*see also* Kennedy, Edward)
Fox, Bernard (*see* hunger strikes)
Frank, Jeffrey 47–49
Franklin, Benjamin 16
Freud, Sigmund xi, xii, 96, 127, 141, 152, 188
Freyne, Patrick, and Ula Mullaly 34
Friedersdorf, Max 20
Friedersdorf, Priscilla 20
Friel, Brian 64, 145
  The Mundy Scheme 64, 66
  Philadelphia, Here I Come! 61
  Translations 154
Friends of Ireland, the 98, 106, 111, 158
Furlong, Irene 61, 74, 75

Gaffikin, Frank, and Mike Morrissey 42, 91, 94, 95, 97
Gardner, John 161
Gergen, David 30n13
Gillespie, Patrick 145, 160n18
Gingrich, Newt 178
Giuliani, Rudy 168
globalism and globalization 32, 33–34, 77–78, 120
Gold, Simone 178
Goldberg, Robert Alan 49–51, 81n3
Goldwater, Barry 47–51, 81n2, 81n3
  friendship with JFK and other democratic rivals 50–51
  on psychoanalysis and the "Goldwater Rule," 49
  on the separation of church and state 50, 51
Goodall, David 107, 108
Goodall, Morwenna 107
Goodfriend, Marvin, and Robert King 91, 92
Goodwin, Doris Kearns 1, 4, 8, 28, 30n4, 30n8
Gosar, Paul 176, 177
Goshko, John M. 109
Gough, Ian 94
"Gramm-Rudman" Act 109
Graves, Robert 136
Greenblatt, Jonathan xix
Greene, Marjorie Taylor 45, 177, 178
Greenhouse, Linda 81n2
Greenwood, Lee 46
Gregory, Lady Augusta 127
Guilfoyle, Kimberly 168–69

Haass, Richard N. 112, 119, 120, 124
Haig, Alexander 73, 104
Hall, Stuart 40, 41, 43
Hanson, Victor Davis 134
Harris, Drew 34, 155
Harris, Kamala 136
Haughey, Charles J. 58, 68, 103, 124n3
Heaney, Seamus ix, 2, 135, 136, 138, 140, 141, 143, 147–50
  "Bogland" 144

INDEX

The Cure at Troy xviii, 133, 136–40, 141–43, 145–53, 160n12, 180
"From Feeling into Words" 146
"The Grauballe Man" 144
"Place and Displacement: Recent Poetry from Northern Ireland" 144
"Punishment" 144, 145, 160n16, 160n17
Heath, Edward 54, 66, 70
Heneghan, Philip 63
Hennessey, Thomas 40, 69
Heritage Foundation, The 174
Hess, Jonathan M. 29n4
Hibernian Anti-Slavery Society (*see* Webb, Richard)
Hickerson, John D. 56
Higgins, Michael D. xviii, 84, 133–35, 138, 159n2
Higgins, Sabina 84
Hillery, Patrick 73
Hillsdale College (*see* Christian colleges and universities)
Hogan, Larry 180
Hogan, Patrick 15
hope, theories of xii, 3, 16, 24, 109, 123, 126, 135, 136, 139, 142, 147, 149, 152, 157, 163, 168
Horowitz, Anthony 161
Howe, Irving 30n4
Hughes, Frank (*see* hunger strikes)
Hughes, John 10
Hughes, Langston 136
Hume, John 35–38, 44, 47, 58, 71, 78, 97, 105, 109, 113, 116, 149
Humphrey, Hubert 27, 50, 108
hunger strikes 21, 96, 98–111, 124n4, 132, 146, 147, 158, 183, 184
  of Bernard Fox and Liam McCluskey 105
  of Bobby Sands, 21, 58, 69, 96, 98, 100, 104, 105, 146, 184
  Frank Hughes and colleagues 105
  of Gwynfor Evans 101
  of Martin Meehan 102
  of the Price sisters 183
  of Terence MacSwiney 101, 184
Hunter, Meredith 48, 68
Hunter, Robert 78, 79
Hutchins, Robert Maynard 137

Ignatiev, Noel 1, 7, 8, 10, 30n8
inmate protests (Northern Ireland)
  blanket protest 100
  dirty protest 101
  No Wash protest 101
internment 35, 36, 54, 70, 71, 80, 97, 182
Ireland, David (*see Cyprus Avenue* (Ireland))
Ireland-United States Council (*see* Moore, John)
Irish Brigade (*see* Kennedy, John F., "Remarks to the Dáil"; Meagher, Thomas Francis)
Irish National Liberation Army (INLA) 100, 106, 115
Irish Northern Aid Committee (Noraid) 70
Irish People, The ix, 53
Irish tourism 63, 64
Irish Voice, The, 118
Irvine, David 113

Jackson, Andrew xvi, 3, 7
Jackson, Jesse 67, 178
Jefferson, Thomas 33, 41
Jeffress, Robert 31
Jeffrey, Keith 47, 128
Jeffs, Rae 30n14
Johansen, John M. 56
Johnson, Boris 156
Johnson, Lyndon B. 27, 47, 48
Johnson, Steven 138
Jordan, Richard L. 104
Joyce, James xviii, 5, 6, 23, 24, 134, 138
  "James Clarence Mangan" 30n10
  A Portrait of An Artist as a Young Man 5
  Ulysses 44, 45, 55, 88, 125, 137

Kagan, Robert 132
Keefe, Patrick Radden 137, 160n14, 183
Kelly, Stephen 97, 103, 186
Kennedy, Bridget Murphy (JFK's great-grandmother) 4, 30n6
Kennedy, Edward 21, 79, 106
  and the Friends of Ireland 98, 109–110, 158
  the "Kennedy Resolution" 70–71
Kennedy, John F., x, xii, xviii, 1–3, 6, 14–20, 23–29, 30n14, 33, 35, 53, 55–58, 65, 71, 83, 85, 88, 138, 153, 154
  address in West Berlin 22
  "Address to the Greater Houston Ministerial Association" 25–26, 28–29
  and misquotations of Joyce and Shaw 23–24, 88
  presidential campaign 26, 50
  "Remarks to the Dáil" 15–16, 23–24
  trip to Ireland xviii, 15–17, 54–55
Kennedy, Joseph, Sr. 22
Kennedy, Leslie 99
Kennedy, Louise (*see Trespasses* (Kennedy))
Kennedy, Patrick (JFK's great-grandfather) 4, 17
Kennedy, Robert F xii
Kennedy, Rose Fitzgerald 4
Kenny, Enda 84, 153
Kerner, Otto (*see* National Advisory Commission on Civil Disorders)
Kerry, John 7, 117
Kiberd, Declan xvi, xviii
Kiernan, Thomas J. 47, 55
Kiker, Douglas 66
Kilpatrick, Chris 116
King, Martin Luther, Jr. xii, 48, 68, 82n13, 104
Kinzinger, Adam 36, 149
Kirschenbaum, Julia, and Michael Li 136
Kissinger, Henry 71
Knatchbull, John 98
Knatchbull, Patricia 98
Knightley, Phillip 105

Know-Nothing party 10–12
Knox, Robert 5, 6
Koresh, David, 183
Kott, Jan xi, xvii, 123, 187

Lake, Tony 116, 117, 187
Lange, Jessica 133, 134, 158
Le Bon, Gustav 22, 169, 172
Lee, Bandy X., 49
Lee, Robert E. 16
Lemass, Seán 15, 59, 62, 74, 75
Lenihan, Brian, Sr. 62–64
Leonnig, Carol, and Philip Rucker 130, 131
Levin, Bess 49, 86, 177
Levitsky, Steven, and Daniel Ziblatt 136
Lewis, Camille Kaminski 165
Lewis, Matt 180
Liberty University (*see* Christian colleges and universities)
Light, Paul C. 93
Lillis, Michael 78, 82n19, 108
Limón, Elvia 38
Lincoln, Abraham 1, 11, 12, 14, 15, 23, 30n10, 43, 48
Lincoln, Evelyn 56
Lloyd, David 141, 154
Long, Naomi 119
Longley, Michael 142–143, 144, 145
  (*see also* "Wounds" (Longley))
Lord Mountjoy 16
Loyalist Volunteer Force (LVF) 115
Lozada, Carlos xviii, 130, 131
Luce, Edward 85
Lugar, Richard 110
Lynch, Jack 66, 71, 79, 86, 102

MacBride, Seán 100
Macdonald, Torby 26, 27
MacLaverty, Bernard
  Cal 53, 125, 127–129, 166, 184
  Grace Notes 125–127
  Walking the Dog xviii
MacSwiney, Terence (*see* hunger strikes)
Maddow, Rachel 83, 87
Magee, Patrick 57
Maginnis, Ken 115
Magruder, Jeb Stuart 49

INDEX

Maher, Bill 137, 180
Mahon, Derek 58, 144
Mailer, Norman 23
Major, John 113, 114, 116, 162
Marche, Stephen xix, 182, 187, 188
Marquand, David 95
Mascaro, Lisa 163
Matthews, Chris 20, 92, 94, 111, 185
McCain, John 33
McCann, Colum (*see Transatlantic* (McCann))
McCarthy, Colman 105
McCarthy, Kevin 33, 45
McCarthy, Tim (*see* Reagan, Ronald, attempted assassination of)
McCartney, Robert 115, 162
McClements, Freya 70, 82n15, 97
McCloskey, Liam (*see* hunger strikes)
McCluskey, Conn 51
McCluskey, Patricia 51, 81n4
McConnell, Mitch 161, 163–64, 167
McCordick, Jack 180
McCourt, Frank xvii, 8
McDaniel, Ronna 31
McDonagh, Martin xvii
McDonald, Henry 119
McDonald, Mark 76, 107
McEnaney, Kayleigh 31
McGuinness, Frank (*see Observe the Sons of Ulster Marching Towards the Somme* (McGuinness))
McGuinness, Martin 162
McKenna, Sean 102
McKinney, Seamus 71
McKittrick, David 54, 70, 166, 168, 169
McLoughlin, P.J., and Alison Meagher 54, 55, 80
McLemore, Morris 56
McMichael, Gary 113
Meagher, Thomas Francis 9, 10
  and the Irish Brigade 9, 12, 14, 15
Medved, Michael 31, 32
Melber, Ari 38
Meredith, James 48
Meyers, David 136
Miami Showband, The 71, 97
Michener, James 23

Miller, Amanda 72
Miller, Garrett 169
Miller, Judith 50
Miller, Kerby xvi, 2, 10, 59
Miller, Marissa 33
Miller, Stephen 178
Miller, Tim 171
Milley, Mark 176
Miranda, Lin-Manuel 153
Mitchell, George 35, 58, 124, 167
  Making Peace 57, 84, 114, 115, 161, 162
Moloney, Ed 65, 71, 164
Molyneaux, Jim 108, 109
Mondale, Walter 19
Moore, Charles 94, 98, 99, 102, 103, 118
Moore, John 75, 118
  ambassadorship 58, 73, 74
  founding of Ireland-United State Council 76
Morrison, Toni 136
Mountbatten, Lord Louis 98, 99, 102
Mowlam, Marjorie "Mo" 115
Moynihan, Daniel Patrick 21, 78, 154
Muldoon, Paul 127–29, 144
Mulhall, Daniel 111
Mulqueen, John 74
Murdoch, Rupert 33
Murray, Mimi 76
Muskie, Edmund 113
Muzzio, Douglas 9

National Advisory Commission on Civil Disorders 66
National Association of Irish Freedom (NAIF) 73
National Association for Irish Justice (NAIJ) 73
Navarro, Peter 130, 131
Neal, Richard 106
Neave, Airey 99
Nelson, Sophia A. 142
New College (Florida) 42
New IRA 155
Nicholson, Robert 23
Niquette, Mark, and Gregory Korte 175
Nixon, Patricia (Pat) 73, 74

Nixon, Richard xviii, 2, 17, 66, 67, 71, 72, 84, 153
  appointment of John Moore as ambassador 73
  policy toward Ireland 53, 55
  visit to Ireland 73–80
Nordheimer, Jon 106, 107
Northern Irish employment data 96
Nugent, Kieran 100

O Connor, Fionnuala 38, 39
Obama, Barack xii, xvi, 17, 45, 137, 166
Obama, Michelle 17, 85, 116, 153
Obert, Julia 96
O'Brien, Matthew J. 12, 67
Observe the Sons of Ulster Marching Towards the Somme (McGuinness) 152
O'Casey, Sean 184
Ocasio-Cortez, Alexandria 169
O'Clery, Conor 55, 107, 110, 116, 118
O'Connor, Sandra Day 50, 81n2
O'Donnell, Kirk 78
O'Donovan, Brian 106, 111
O'Dowd, Niall, 12, 21, 30n10, 95, 113, 118, 124n7
  on Abraham Lincoln 30n10
  on Bill Clinton 11
  on Ronald Reagan 21
O'Driscoll, Dennis 146, 149
Ó Faoleán, Gearóid 81n6
Ó Fiaich, Tomás 102
O'Hearn, Denis 69, 96, 98, 100, 124n1
O'Kelly, Seán T. 57
Okker, Patricia 41–42 (*see also* New College (Florida))
O'Neill, Eugene 133
O'Neill, Millie 20
O'Neill, Terence 57
O'Neill, Thomas P. "Tip" 20, 21, 92, 109, 111, 158
Onkey, Lauren 52
Orange lodge marches xiv, 84, 119, 125, 168, 169
O'Rawe, Richard 99, 101
O'Reilly, Bill xiii
Orwell, George 174, 180
Osnos, Evan 135, 159n11, 168, 177
O'Sullivan, Meghan 119

O'Toole, Fintan xv–xvi, xvii, xix, 3, 76, 122, 175, 181, 182
  "Donald Trump has Destroyed the Country," xv–xvii, xix
  on the effects of multinational investment in Ireland 77, 89
  We Don't Know Ourselves and critique of Clinton's interest in Northern Ireland 77, 121–22

Paisley, Ian 25, 28, 58, 68, 69, 104, 105, 108, 109, 111, 112, 114, 115, 124n1, 161–74 (*see also* Democratic Unionist Party (DUP))
  and Bill Clinton 112
  and Bob Jones University 104, 164
  and Fleming villains 161
  fomentation of violence 54
  slurs of Catholics 69, 104, 162
  vilification of Margaret Thatcher 171
  visa problems 104–105
Paisley, Rhonda 167
Paquette, Danielle 179
Parnell, Charles Stewart 16
Parr, Jerry (*see* Reagan, Ronald, attempted assassination of)
Patterson, Glenn 51, 70, 82n21, 85, 134, 155, 162, 169
  Backstop Land 51, 155, 158, 162, 173
  Here's Me Here 133
Paul, Rand 134, 178
Pearse, Padraic 127, 184
Pelosi, Nancy 45
Pence, Michael 32
Pengelly, Martin 159n9, 167
Perlstein, Rick 48
Philoctetes (Sophocles) 145, 148–50
Phoenix, Éamon 117
Pirro, Jeanine 134
Polk, Major General James 23
Pompeo, Mike 31
Pope John Paul II 25, 162
Powers, Dave 17, 22, 54, 110
Price, Dolours 101, 183 (*see also* hunger strikes)
Price, Marian 101, 183 (*see also* hunger strikes)
Prince Charles (King Charles III) 99, 107
Prior, Jim 105, 106, 108

INDEX 223

Pritzker, J. B. 130, 131
protests 18, 48, 54, 59, 74, 83, 100–2, 104, 123, 129, 147, 168–70, 184, 189 (*see also* hunger strikes; inmate protests (Northern Ireland))
   civil rights protests in America 10, 26, 51–52, 71–72, 89–90
   civil rights protests in Northern Ireland 48
   on college and university campuses against the Vietnam war ix, 71
Provisional IRA (PIRA) 57, 69–71, 79, 98, 100, 106, 117, 146, 160n14, 186

Reagan, Nancy 18, 21, 124n5
Reagan, Ronald xviii, 2, 14, 17, 19, 21, 22, 25, 45, 50, 58, 84, 93, 110, 153, 156, 158, 185
   attempted assassination of 21
   collaborations with Tip O'Neill and Congressional Democrats 20, 21, 111
   protests over his visit to Ireland 17–19, 110
   relationship with Margaret Thatcher 3, 23, 25, 58, 94, 156, 158
   visit to Ballyporeen 18, 19, 110
Reaganomics 92
   budget-cutting, deregulation, Economic Recovery Tax Act (ERTA) 92–93
Red Hand Commando (RHC) 186
Rees, Merlyn 79
Regent University (*see* Christian colleges and universities)
Renfro, Paul F. xiii
Reynolds, Albert 113
Reynolds, Paige ix, 101
Rhodes, Stewart 176
Ribicoff, Abraham 70
Richtarik, Marilynn 81n5, 139, 145–146, 149, 151, 160n18
Ricouer, Paul 142
rioting in Ireland and Northern Ireland
   Battle of the Bogside 66, 71
   at Burntollet Bridge 35, 69
   in Dublin 34
Robinson, Marian 18, 19
Robinson, Mary 133
Rockefeller, Nelson 48
rolling devolution 108

Rooney, Sally 137
Ross, Jamie 157
Rovere, Richard H. 3
Rowland, Neil, et al 96
Royal Ulster Constabulary (RUC) 66, 80, 95, 106
Russell, Richard Rankin ix, xviii, 144, 160n16
Russert, Tim 78

Sablik, Tim 91, 92
Saint-Amour, Paul K. 175, 180, 187–88
Salvesen, Kenneth 107
Samuel, Raphael 42, 43
Sands, Bobby 58, 69, 96, 98, 104, 105, 146, 184
   hunger strike 21, 105, 184
   upbringing and employment 96
   Writings from Prison 100
Sargent, Greg 163
Scarborough, Joe 171
Schatzman, G.K. and Carson 159n12
Schlesinger, Arthur, Jr. 3, 22, 23
Schmidt, Helmut 113
Schorr, Isaac 170
Schwab, Katherine 178
Schwartz, Tony 159n8
Scranton, William 48
Seitz, Ray 117
Sennott, Charles M. 158
Shakespeare, William 6, 125, 137, 159n9
Shankill bombing 116, 117
Sharkey, Jim 158
Shaw, Bernard 6, 23, 24, 69, 83, 88, 89, 138, 159n2
   Back to Methuselah 24, 88
   John Bull's Other Island 83, 89, 159n2
   Major Barbara 69, 134
   Mrs. Warren's Profession 134
   as "public man" 134, 135
   Widowers' Houses 134
Shesol, Jeff 124n5
Shiffer, Ricky 176
Shiny Happy People: Duggar Family Secrets 165
Siskind, Amy 131
Smathers, George 26
Smith, Al 25, 164

Smith, Eoghan xv
Smith, Jack 171, 181
Smith, Jean Kennedy 56, 58, 117, 118
Social Democratic and Labour Party
    (SDLP) 35, 109, 119
Soderberg, Nancy 114, 118
Sophocles (*see Philoctetes* (Sophocles))
Staines, Michael 89
Stewart, Jon 176
Stockdale, Grant 56
Stockman, David 93, 94
Sunak, Rishi 85
Sunningdale Agreement, The 79, 80
Synge, John Millington xvi–xviii, 4, 159n2
    The Aran Islands xvi, xvii, 4
    The Playboy of the Western World xvii

Tanglewood (Bolger) 77–78
Taylor, Miles 44
Taylor, Tess 136
Thatcher, Margaret 21, 40, 42, 44, 57,
    58, 94–99, 103, 105, 107, 108, 111,
    166, 171
    friendship with Ronald Reagan 3, 23,
        25, 58, 94–95, 107, 156, 158
    inflexibility toward hunger strikers
        96–97, 100–102, 105–106
Thatcherism 40, 43, 98
    and authoritarian populism 31, 41
    economic strategies of 44, 93
    and Victorianism 42, 43
Thompson, Neal 4, 5, 8, 30n6, 30n9
Toíbín, Colm 4, 176
Tonkin, Tom 117
total war (*see* Saint-Amour, Paul K.)
TransAtlantic (McCann) 52, 114, 162
traumatic memory 147
Treble, Patricia 166
Trespasses (Kennedy), 35, 78
Trevithick, Joseph 87
Trimble, David 35, 113, 115, 162, 168
Trump, Donald xiv, 3, 31, 33, 34, 45, 48,
    69, 81n1, 83, 85, 86, 92, 128, 134,
    137, 157, 159n8, 163, 164, 166, 175,
    177, 179–81, 183, 186, 188, 189
    and Brexit xv, 84, 88, 153, 155–58
    comparisons to Goldwater 48–51
    and COVID-19 xii, 129, 130, 171

and Doonbeg 83, 86, 87, 89, 90
and ethnic slurs 6, 33, 69, 171
and evangelical Christians 31, 45
and fictional villains 166
in Ireland xv, 83–90, 170, 188
on the Irish border 66
low comic persona of 179
as Nelson Mandela 181
and reading 137, 150, 152
record on the environment 88
self-fashioning of 151, 152, 166
selling the "God Bless the U.S.A"
    bible 46
Trump, Donald, Jr. 86, 169
Trump, Eric 86
Trump, Ivanka 33
Trump, Lara 46, 170
Trump, Melania 86
Trump International Golf Club
    (Doonbeg) 83, 84–85, 89–90
Trump time and Troubles time 125–32,
    182, 188
Trumpism (MAGA) xii, xv, xvi, xviii, 31,
    33, 35, 36, 45, 46, 51, 88, 128, 131,
    136, 170, 171, 173–77, 180, 182, 183,
    186, 188
    and authoritarian populism 40–44, 94
    and Christian nationalism 28, 31, 33
    and the perversion of language 171–72
Tubridy, Ryan 16, 17, 54, 81n9, 136
Twain, Mark 136

Ulster Defence Association (UDA) 79,
    82n21, 115, 186
Ulster Freedom Fighters (UFF) 116
Ulster Unionist Party (UUP) 108, 115,
    119, 162
Ulster Volunteer Force (UVF) 70, 71, 79,
    82n21, 115, 169, 186
United Kingdom Unionist Party
    (UKUP) 115
Updegrove, Mark K. 23, 26–28

Varadkar, Leo 83, 85–88, 156
Vendler, Helen 144, 146, 160n16
Volcker, Paul 91, 92, 98

Wade, Peter 87
Wall, Martin 78

Watters, Jesse 178
"We Shall Overcome" (Seeger) 68
Webb, James 7, 155
Webb, Richard 13, 29n2
Wehner, Peter 178, 180
Weiner, Jennifer 136–38
Weinraub, Bernard 53, 54, 81n6, 81n8
welfare state 43, 94, 98
Welles, Orson 124n8
Wheatley, Leesa, and Florian Krobb 82n11
Whitaker, T.K. 59
Whitelaw, William 100
Widgery, Lord John 38
Wilmeth, Don B. 6
Wilson, Andrew J. 81n8, 100, 105, 110, 114

Wilson, Harold 79
Wilson, Robert McLiam 40, 58, 133, 182
  Eureka Street 40, 58, 182
Wise, Lindsay 163
Witcover, Jules 113, 124n6, 159n7
Woolf, Virginia 188
  Mrs. Dalloway 188
"Wounds" (Longley) 142, 143
Wray, Christopher 34
Wright, Billy 115
Wright, Richard 136

Yeats, William Butler 127, 136, 168, 184
Young, Andrew 27
Youngkin, Glenn 129